African Catholicism
Essays in Discovery

Adrian Hastings

AFRICAN CATHOLICISM

Essays in Discovery

SCM PRESS
London

TRINITY PRESS INTERNATIONAL
Philadelphia

First published 1989

SCM Press
26–30 Tottenham Road
London N1 4BZ

Trinity Press International
3725 Chestnut Street
Philadelphia, Pa. 19104

British Library Cataloguing in Publication Data

Hastings, Adrian
  African Catholicism
  1. Africa. Catholicism
  I. Title
  282'.6

  ISBN 0–334–00019–X

Library of Congress Cataloging-in-Publication Data

Hastings, Adrian.
    African Catholicism : essays in discovery / Adrian Hastings.
        p.   cm.
    Bibliography: p.
    Includes index.
    ISBN 0–334—00019–X
    1. Catholic Church—Africa, Sub-Saharan.   2. Africa,
Sub-Saharan—Church history.   I.Title.
BX1680.3.H37   1989   89–4506
282'.67—dc20

Photoset by Input Typesetting Ltd, London
and printed in Great Britain by
Richard Clay Ltd, Bungay, Suffolk

For
Richard Gray and Andrew Walls

Contents

	Acknowledgments	ix
	Preface	xi
1	African Catholicism: Revival or New Arrival?	1
2	The Gospel and African Culture	21
3	Were Women a Special Case?	36
4	Mediums, Martyrs and Morals	52
5	Ganda Catholic Spirituality	69
6	African Theology	82
7	The Choice of Words for Christian Meanings in Eastern Africa	98
8	The Post-Conciliar Catholic Church in Eastern Africa	122
9	Emmanuel Milingo as Christian Healer	138
10	Mission, Church and State in Southern Africa: The First 150 Years	156
11	Why the Church in South Africa Matters	170
12	Our Daily Bread	184
	Notes	192
	Index	205

Acknowledgments

Chapter 1 was given as a lecture at St Edmund's College, Cambridge, in May 1986. Chapter 2 was a lecture given to the British Conference of Missionary Societies' annual Africa study session in April 1986 and subsequently published as a pamphlet by the Catholic Missionary Education Centre in 1988. Chapter 3 was read to a conference on the Impact of Missions on Women in September 1987 sponsored by the Intercultural Centre for Women's Studies, Queen Elizabeth House, Oxford. Chapter 4 was my inaugural lecture as Professor of Religious Studies at the University of Zimbabwe, delivered in Harare on 16 June 1983 and published in *Zambesia*, vol 11, no 1, 1983. Chapter 5 derives from a paper presented at a seminar at the School of Oriental and African Studies, London, in 1974 and printed in the *Journal of Religion in Africa*, VIII, 2, 1976. Chapters 6 and 7 likewise began as seminar papers at the School of Oriental and African Studies; 6 was published in the *Scottish Journal of Theology*, 1984, while 7 was delivered as the hundredth Manson Lecture in Manchester in February 1988. Chapter 8 first appeared in *World Catholicism in Transition* edited by Thomas M. Gannon, SJ, Macmillan 1988. Chapter 9 was a paper presented to a conference on African Medicine in December 1986 sponsored by the African Studies Centre in the University of Edinburgh and subsequently published in its proceedings, *African Medicine in the Modern World*, 1987. Chapter 10 was a lecture delivered at the sixth International Association for Mission Studies in Harare, January 1985, and published in *Mission Studies* 2.1, 1985. Chapter 11 first appeared in *Catholics in Apartheid Society*, ed Andrew Prior, David Philip, Cape Town 1982. All have been revised to a greater or lesser extent prior to publication here.

Preface

The Roman Catholic Church has some seventy million members in Africa today. It is, unquestionably, the largest Christian body upon the continent, but around it are many other very considerable churches, particularly Anglican and Lutheran, whose beliefs, religious practice and problems are not dissimilar. Collectively they have in the last half century come to constitute the majority religion of Bantu Africa. The African Catholicism this book discusses as a major religious and social reality of the contemporary world includes them all. Young as it may be in comparison with the Christianity of other continents, it is already a religion of tradition – a genuinely African traditional religion.

Its ministry, sacraments and creeds are even in a Christian sense traditional enough. It pays much respect to the Bible – often almost the only large book to be published in the vernacular – but in what is still for the most part an effectively illiterate society, the Bible's high authority is mediated by the community and its ministers. By far the greater proportion of those ministers are people with quite limited training and financial support from the church. They are peasant catechists and preachers. The beliefs of African Catholicism share their place in the consciousness of most Christians with the concepts of African traditional religion in its pre-Christian form. As a living religious reality, African Catholicism includes a great deal of the latter, even if it also struggles to suppress it. Christian belief is interpreted across traditional ideas, while those ideas are themselves reinterpreted with Christian paradigms. The two are united by a common vocabulary. Yet in public and ritual terms they can also still come into conflict, and indeed in mental and moral terms too. The pattern of religious life that results from all this often differs little between Catholics, Protestants and members of many an 'independent' church.

There are now many hundreds of African bishops, yet the character of the Catholicism they represent is probably little understood and has seldom been described at any great length. These essays explore only some aspects of a vast reality. If they draw quite considerably upon my experience and study in and of Buganda between twenty and thirty years ago that is, I believe, legitimate. The church in Buganda was always in its way a pace-setter, from the martyrdoms of the 1880s, the mass conversion movement of the 1890s and the early development of a Catholic clergy. In consequence its character was formed at least a generation before most of its sister churches.

The shape of things I experienced there then is today spread far more widely. The issues these essays range across include theology and culture, spirituality and ministry, religious vocabulary, spirit possession, the politics of liberation. They all illustrate facets of the way of living of what appears today as one of the principal areas of the Christian world. They have mostly been written since I came as Professor of Theology to Leeds in September 1985 but they stand in some continuity with my writing across several decades and there seems some point in briefly reviewing that writing here.

Forty years ago, in early 1949, I capitulated to a perhaps Quixotic but apparently overwhelming sense of calling to serve the church in Africa. It was during my final year reading history at Oxford and it took me on a long chase, via the missionary society of the White Fathers, the College of *Propaganda Fide* in Rome, the diocese of Masaka in Uganda and then other places too, like Kipalapala in Tanzania and Mindolo Ecumenical Foundation in Zambia until in the early 1970s I returned to Britain rather battered, to become relatively distanced not only geographically but even in heart and mind from that early commitment. Yet it has never ceased to exercise its spell and three years as Professor of Religious Studies in the University of Zimbabwe from 1982 to 1985 refreshed my sense of Africa and gave me a close taste of Zimbabwe to set beside that of Uganda, Tanzania and Zambia. So from the 1950s to the 1980s I have been in and out of Africa and the present book draws in its way on all those years and work of many different sorts: curate at Villa Maria and Bigada, teacher in the junior seminary at Bukalasa,

Visiting Professor at Lovanium, Kinshasa, editor of *Post-Vatican II* at Kipalapala, ecumenical lecturer at Mindolo, external examiner at Makerere, Visiting Lecturer at Gaba Pastoral Institute, Winter School Lecturer in South Africa, Professor in Harare.

While my beliefs, concerns and commitments have changed greatly during these years yet, if one compared these essays with early efforts such as *White Domination or Racial Peace*, published by the Africa Bureau in 1954 or *The Church and the Nations* (Sheed and Ward 1959), what might seem striking is rather the degree of continuity between them. Both were written before I actually reached Africa (the introduction to the latter being scribbled in the evenings in my little room at the top of John Fisher School, Purley, in January 1958 when doing a term of teaching practice there). These were followed in 1967 by *Church and Mission in Modern Africa* (Burns Oates and Fordham University Press, New York) which represents the principal surviving fruit of seven years of work in Uganda and co-operation with the early years of *AFER (The African Ecclesiastical Review)*. It also represents me at my most ecclesiastical – yet already seeming too radical to be quite acceptable ecclesiastically. In the early 1970s, as I moved away both from residence in Africa and from incorporation within a formal structure of clerical ministry, came *Mission and Ministry* (Sheed and Ward 1971), *Christian Marriage in Africa* (SPCK 1973) and *Wiriyamu* (Search Press and Orbis, New York 1974). The latter was written at Selly Oak. A year there was followed by three years at the School of Oriental and African Studies in London, 1973–6, and these by a lectureship in Aberdeen. From the viewpoint of my African writing, those years are represented by *African Christianity* (Geoffrey Chapman and Seabury Press 1976) and *A History of African Christianity 1950–1975* (Cambridge University Press 1979).

After that I tried to turn my attention away from Africa and produced instead *A History of English Christianity 1920–1985* (Collins 1986). In consequence the present collection represents my only African book of the 1980s. It owes a good deal to my three years in Zimbabwe, but it is essentially a Leeds book. It will, I hope, be followed in due course by a further history of the churches of Africa beginning in the fifteenth century, a volume for the *Oxford History of the Christian Church*.

In the meantime I would like to think that the present work may be seen as a contribution not only to the critical understanding of African Christianity but even to its enhancement. It is offered by a friend, almost an exile, whose mind has changed on many things but who wishes still to remain loyal – so far as he may – to the commitments of youth. In writing it I owe a special debt to Fr John Waliggo whom, years ago, I taught and from whom, more recently, I have learnt immensely. I am most grateful for his comments upon Chapter 7 and for material in both Chapter 1 and Chapter 3 derived from his thesis on the Catholic Church in Buddu, a thesis which should have been published long ago. I am grateful too to Mrs Ingrid Lawrie who has typed many of the chapters while more than busy with other things. This book is dedicated to two scholars who, between them, salvaged my career and guided it into academic waters when – the years in Africa over – it seemed to have lost its way. Professor Richard Gray devised the project which gained me three years of research at the School of Oriental and African Studies. Professor Andrew Walls followed this by welcoming me to the Department of Religious Studies in the University of Aberdeen. To both I owe more than I can say – not only honest work but friendship, the sharing of an open fellowship of imaginative learning, Christian faith and African sympathy.

Leeds
July 1988

1

African Catholicism:
Revival or New Arrival?

One of the most perennially lively controversies surrounding ancient church history has been that concerning the true nature and foundations of Donatism. If for Wiseman and Newman Donatism proved Canterbury wrong and Rome right, for some mid-twentieth-century scholars it provided a splendid example of an oppressed rural proletariat pursuing revolution, a movement best analysable in Marxist terms, with the religious dimension reduced to not much more than convenient colouring.[1] At much the same time Balandier and others were interpreting African religious independency of fifteen hundred years later in comparable terms. The scholarly battle has gone to and fro and doubtless it is not over yet. Were the Circumcellions itinerant landless workers, driven to desperation by the economic depression, their famous clubs (known as 'Israels') originally intended to dislodge olives from trees at harvest time? Or were they militant bands of holy men and women, squatting around the tombs of the martyrs and journeying through the villages on pilgrimage (prior to the suicide which would make them martyrs too), their 'Israels' being then immediately functional for knocking on the head – or behind the neck – recalcitrant Catholics?

The picture of a rural African Donatism dominant in inland Numidia and among the poor, resisting an upper-class, urban and imperial-linked Catholicism would be an over-simplification, but it is hard to doubt that there is some truth in it. Roman North Africa – and Roman Egypt too for that matter – did consist of an interlocked but dual society: rural, native, vernacular-speaking, poor at one end of the spectrum; urban, Roman in sense of identity, Latin or Greek in language, educated, cosmopolitan, wealthy at the other end. Individuals moved easily enough along the spectrum: Augustine's mother and her relatives were clearly pretty near one end of it, he himself by the time he had become a successful professor in Milan – still however regularly in touch with other fully cosmopolitanized African friends and relatives – was nearing the other end. But the deep divide within society was there, relatively hidden in imperialism's more successful ages, glaringly obvious in times of economic stress and political disorder. Christianity, undoubtedly, was to be found all along the spectrum: it grew up first, it would seem, among the urban poor – 'African' at least as much as 'Roman': from their names the first North African Christians we know of, the martyrs of Scilli (AD 180), appear to have been 'purely native'.[2] In the third century it spread alike to the 'Roman' middle class of Carthage and the rural Berber masses of Numidia.

When Catholics and Donatists divided in the fourth century, both claimed fidelity to the tradition of Cyprian of Carthage; both used Latin; both had town congregations and middle-class adherents as well as country ones. The Donatists were not devoid of intellectuals and, initially, they had appealed to Rome as confidently as their opponents.

Nevertheless, the more firmly the wider, non-African church and imperial government came down on the anti-Donatist side, the more, in the decades after Constantine, an empire-embellishing type of Catholicism became a pervasive reality interacting on a regular basis with the imperial bureaucracy, the more Donatism naturally turned for support to, and came to reflect, all that was more consciously African, provincial and anti-establishment. Yet the sheer superiority of Catholic leadership in the age of Augustine greatly modified this picture of an increasingly socio-political and cultural line-up. The Catholics prevailed because they out-argued the Donatists and provided an altogether larger view of Christian truth, quite as much as because imperial law now denied the latter any right to existence. But it remained, it would seem, too often a bitter prevailing. Augustine's church was not loved in the villages with the unfeigned intensity it required to see it through Vandal and Arab conquest.

In Egypt an underlying social and cultural divide between Copt and Graeco-Roman was also present, if again the two fused almost into one particularly in the urban mix of Alexandria. Here Christianity had, fairly clearly, developed first on the Graeco-Roman, urban side and it was probably monasticism as much as anything else – a very down-to-earth populist form of religiosity, extremely different from the gentlemanly, élitist monasticism of Augustine – which ensured in due course the profound rooting of Catholic Christianity in the peasantry of Upper Egypt. For that no event was more significant than what happened one day about AD 312. A young pagan boy had been conscripted from Upper Egypt for service in the imperial army of Maximin, and being taken down the Nile, was shut up with the other conscripts one night in the prison at Luxor. Some local Christians came in with food and drink to comfort the lads. The boy, surprised at such unexpected, kindness in what was proving an otherwise fearful experience, asked the reason and was told that Christians are men who bear the name of Christ and do good to all men, hoping in him who made heaven and earth.[3] The boy was named Pachomius. Within a few months Maximin was dead, his army disbanded and Pachomius was back in Upper Egypt in the village of Chenoboscia. Pachomius' conversion is important for us because it is very clearly the conversion of an African rather than an Alexandrian Greek to Christianity, and in its circumstances almost archetypal for many an African conversion even sixteen hundred years later. But it is important also because it led directly to the development of the vast monasteries, the *koinonia*, of the Pachomian model, the first really cenobite form of Christian monasticism – and monasteries which were certainly Coptic in culture, language and alphabet. It is not fanciful to see monasticism, in its Pachomian form, as the first 'new religious movement' within African Christianity and one arising – like many of those of modern times – within the originating context of mass rural conversion.

Of course the basic Alexandrine tradition of Egyptian Christianity, the tradition of Athanasius, was Greek through and through, just as the North African tradition of Cyprian was Latin. Yet in both a reviving provincial nationalism could in the fourth and fifth centuries be taking over the clothes of a more imperial past to construct from them an anti-Constantinopolitan, anti-Roman, local orthodoxy. Egyptian Monophysitism is in some ways at least an expression of a commitment to African-ness, of a nationalist reaction to late imperialism, and as such it was disposed to find Arab-Islamic rule hardly more tedious than that of Byzantium.

The picture I am trying to present is one in which Mother Africa is partially colonized by Europe, and in which Christianity entered African life across the colonization. It was by no means restricted to that colonization. It penetrated quickly enough and well enough in its Catholic universality into the urban proletariat, Numidian villages and Upper Nile Pachomian monasteries, but there remained a tension between Catholicity and particularity which in principle worked well enough but which could also come badly into trouble once Catholicity seemed too tied to imperial power, or was challenged by a separatist church claiming legitimation in local terms – fidelity to the theology of Cyprian or Athanasius – as well as appealing, maybe only covertly, to what the modern ecumenist calls 'non-theological factors'. The Berber and the Copt, Frend claims, were always natural dissenters.[4]

Great as the differences in nineteenth- and twentieth-century Africa must be, I am going to suggest that it is not too fanciful to apply to the modern church a comparable model.[5]

Where shall we start? Not, I think, in the towns of modern Africa. Here at once there is a difference. The old Christianity was in origin an urban phenomenon and only later spread from town to countryside, while modern African Catholicism has never yet found itself fully at home in an urban setting;[6] perhaps, you may say, modern Africans do not either. If in places they have done so – in Ibadan or Soweto for example – they can still hardly be regarded as prototypes of Catholicism. The first great modern Catholic breakthrough into an African society was in Buganda in the 1880s and 1890s, so we may begin there as well as anywhere, and there are indeed two additional reasons for doing so. The first is that the principal attack on the infant church in Buganda by the *Kabaka* Mwanga in May 1886 illustrates one or two of our central themes rather well. The second is that I can, for the Catholicism of Buganda, make use of John Waliggo's splendid Cambridge Ph. D. thesis, *The Catholic Church in the Buddu Province of Buganda, 1879–1925*.[7] John Waliggo is perhaps the most distinguished African Catholic to have been a member of St Edmund's so it is appropriate – as he cannot be here to give this lecture himself – that we make use of his lively reconstruction of the early history of what is surely the most authentic heartland of modern African Catholicism, the *saza* of Buddu, the diocese of Masaka.

There has been a lengthy debate in recent years, initiated by Robin Horton, especially in the periodical *Africa*, on the nature of conversion.[8] It has been Horton's thesis that conversion to Christianity or Islam in modern Africa can only be rendered intelligible or plausible in terms of the inherent existing tendencies of African religion in the context of a changing society. Conversion is to be explained in terms of continuity, not discontinuity. Enlargement of social scale naturally leads in religious terms to greater emphasis upon the 'High God' of the macrocosm while the ancestral and village spirits of the microcosm decline in importance. Quite apart, then, from the invasion of a world religion, one would expect – Horton claims – the late nineteenth-century African world to be turning towards monotheism. While being a rationally plausible hypothesis, this is not only a little too neat, it does not really fit enough of the evidence. Certainly in Buganda the impression one has is that the enlargement of the state and of the wider horizon had gone with an obscuring of *Katonda*, the old creator god, and an aggrandizement of the cult of the divinities, the *Balubaale*, like *Mukasa*, the god of the lake, *Kibuka*, the god of war, and *Kiwanuka*, the god whose temples, priests and rituals could be more effectively controlled by the monarchy.

The challenge of monotheism arose less from any inherent belief pattern and sense of direction in Ganda society than from the Arab traders who had been present in the country for half a century before the Christian missionaries. The monarchy patronized the new beliefs as an expression of modernization, but feared them as a source of rival authority. Many Ganda became Moslems and some died for it. Not continuity but challenge, the appeal of otherness, an uncontrollable new loyalty was here the primary characteristic of conversion, first to Islam then to Christianity. Modern African Christian theologians – John Mbiti, Bolaji Idowu, Gabriel Setiloane[9] – have tended to stress the degree of continuity existing between African traditional religion and Christianity and to berate the missionaries for an emphasis upon discontinuity. In a process of large-scale conversion, there must, undoubtedly, be both. In fact in African conversion there certainly have been both from the beginning, but – psychologically – the note of discontinuity, a discontinuity indeed worth dying for, had first to appear paramount. A Vatican II-style theologian (Walbert Bühlmann) may ecumenically affirm that 'a convert from paganism should not suddenly condemn what up till then was his legitimate religion',[10] but it just does not seem like that at the time. If the new did not in some way quite decisively challenge the old, why go to all the trouble of embracing it? Even so, it did not often do so quite as provocatively as when in May 1886 the newly baptized Princess Nalumansi, a sister of the king of Buganda, not only married – a thing princesses of the blood were forbidden to do – but, on being appointed guardian of the tomb of *Kabaka* Jjunju, and finding the custodian's house full of charms, made a bonfire of the lot. Moreover, when, on 22 May, her mother presented her with her umbilical cord which she was supposed to keep with the greatest reverence, as a symbol of the womb, the ancestral religion, from which she came, she cut it into pieces and threw it into a hole.[11] What more outrageous behaviour, what more unmitigated and manifest repudiation of traditional mores, could one imagine? Is it surprising, one might add, that ten days later, on 3 June, not pagan charms but the bodies of Christian converts were burning at Namugongo? Yet the Princess knew her book of traditions perfectly well. That indeed was the point. Six months earlier it had actually been she who, when Bishop Hannington was murdered on Mwanga's order on the road to Buganda, sent to advise the CMS missionaries, Mackay and Ashe, to propitiate the king by sending him a costly present – for such was correct Ganda behaviour in the circumstances.

The Ganda were trained to be brave, stoical in the face of death, and sudden death was always on the cards for anyone connected with the *Kabaka*'s court. It is hard to say whether the Christian faith altered the attitude to death as such, but it is clear enough that it did interpret it afresh; it provided the early converts with an extraordinarily positive and hopeful response to dying. It made some of them almost over-eager martyrs. Athanasius Bazzekuketta's complaint, 'The *Kabaka* ordered you to put us to death. Where are you taking us? Why don't you kill us here?' is typical – though, of course, there were plenty of other Christians who did avoid martyrdom if they could.[12] 'You are burning me,' said Charles Lwanga from the firewood, 'but it is as if you were pouring water over my body. I am dying for God's religion. Be warned in time or God whom you insult will one day plunge you into real fire.'[13]

'*Weraba, munnange.* Goodbye my friend, we shall meet again in heaven,' said Mathias Kalemba to Luke Bannabikintu, just before he was killed with exceptional cruelty. 'Yes, with God,' Luke replied. '*Katonda*' ('God'), Lwanga cried out a moment before death and this again was typical. They were consciously martyrs of *Katonda*, of the *dini ya Katonda*, God's religion, and *Katonda* was a name they had known long before missionaries had reached Buganda. Their practice of his religion was now reshaped by missionary teaching to give an integral blending of old and new. The name of *Katonda* is old, as is the warrior's heroism, though not, perhaps, the almost insolent refusal to flee which characterized many of the martyrs and which did surprise non-Christian friends. The rejection of the *Lubaale* and of the *Kabaka's* authority in matters religious is new, as is the vision of life with God after death – very different from the traditional view of the survival of ancestral spirits hanging round the banana grove. But what was established in those days a hundred years ago – as has been established by martyrdom in many other places and times of Christian history – was an ongoing local tradition of faith and commitment of such strength as to take it through a good many wars from that day to this. When Fr Clementi Mukasa, the former Rector of Bukalasa, was dragged from the altar and murdered a few years ago by Amin's soldiers, his martyrdom simply watered afresh an ongoing tradition of Ganda Christianity, already emphatically rooted – just as Numidian Donatist Christianity was rooted – in the blood and the cult of martyrs. It must be said that African Christianity in most parts of the continent has lacked, at least until recently, any comparable foundation charter.

It is, I think, important to note what a very small role the missionaries – White Fathers or CMS – played in these events. They watched awkwardly from the wings. Joseph Mukasa Balikuddembe had led the Catholic community with authority for two years, while there was no missionary in the country, and was killed very shortly after the White Fathers' return. It was only his death, in November 1885, that prompted the Fathers to baptize most of the future martyrs – Lwanga and Bazzekuketta among them – while Lwanga himself baptized some of the younger ones only just before the end.

The majority of the Christians were not killed; they multiplied rapidly in the following years and they were soon armed and fighting the king, the Moslems and one another for control of their country. Missionaries looking at the strange behaviour of the ragged Christian armies in 1889 might see all this as hardly more than 'a sort of twilight Christianity'.[14] It was certainly not what they had expected to achieve and in due course they would work very hard establishing the sort of churches they had known in Europe, but here – and in many other places – they never could quite get rid of that troublesome element of populist particularity: the otherness of a Christian commitment across the culture bar – and, at times, across the political bar too.

When in 1897 the *Kabaka* Mwanga revolted against the British rule which was now being firmly established in the country, the more politic Christian leaders obeyed their missionaries and stuck to the Union Jack. But Mwanga was not left with only pagan support. Catholics in fact divided down the middle and if Alikisi Sebbowa, the tough county chief of Buddu, their stronghold, held firmly to the Protectorate, his deputy Lui Kibanyi, an equally devout Christian, became Mwanga's chief minister. Gabrieli Kintu, the most brilliant of the Catholic war leaders, moreover, became once more Mwanga's commander-in-chief just as he had been when the Moslems were driven from the capital seven years before. Kintu and Kibanyi did not falter in their Catholicism when they fought for their king against the British and were excommunicated by the bishop for doing so, Gabrieli's excommunication being solemnly read out in the churches on 10 October. 'Judge for yourselves,' declared Kibanyi, at his trial, to his former colleagues Kaggwa and Mugwanya, 'if those who obeyed their king were the rebels and not you who obeyed the Europeans.'[15] He was hanged, crucifix and rosary in hand, two days later. Gabrieli's later letters to the White Fathers from exile in Tanganyika are truly moving in their insistence that his 'rebellion' had not been a repudiation of his Catholicism. They are more. They are evidence of religion's quick crossing of the frontier, from a European and imperial world to an independently African one: what missionaries claimed to want time and again but could hardly stomach when they saw it bravely happening.

Nevertheless the quite special significance of Buganda and Buddu for our subject did not terminate in the 1890s.[16] Bishop Streicher might solemnly excommunicate Gabrieli Kintu, but it was he more than anyone else who ensured that Buddu would remain the very vanguard of Catholicism by pressing ahead, when most other missionaries were more than tepid, with the formation of an African clergy – and a clergy as little Europeanized as possible. The first two priests were ordained, after many years of training, in 1913. By the early 1930s all the churches in Buddu had been handed over to local priests and in 1939 it was established as an independent vicariate with the first Catholic African bishop of modern times – Joseph Kiwanuka. There would not be another for fifteen years and then only in a small neighbouring area of Tanganyika. Bishop Kiwanuka – a man of exceptional strength, both of character and of pastoral sense – became, through all the middle years of this century, at home and internationally, the principal living symbol of the renewed existence of an African Catholic Church. By the 1950s there were nearly a hundred local priests in his diocese of Masaka and the Catholic priesthood had become deeply rooted in the consciousness of the people in a way that was also the case for Ufipa or Ukerewe Island or parts of Igboland but which has only later become widely so elsewhere. It was a very localized clergy with undeniably limited horizons. (Fr Kabuye, the parish priest whose curate I became in 1958, spoke no English. We had to converse in Latin or Luganda from the word go!) They lived on the produce from their vegetable gardens, they read their Catholic Luganda newspaper, *Munno*, they occasionally re-read their Latin seminary textbooks. They were already at least as much part of a traditional Africa as of an innovating élite but they were – it must be stressed – quite atypical of African dioceses of the 1950s; churches almost everywhere were still overwhelmingly dominated by missionaries whose evening conversation was of Irish, American or Quebec politics, while smoking Dutch cigars and surviving with the help of tinned food. The Masaka pattern might have seemed at the time a survival from the past in contrast with a certain cosmopolitan modernity cultivated elsewhere. And yet, looking at Africa from the vantage point of the 1980s, we can see that it was, at least as much, the pattern of a larger future.

For the most part the high era of Catholic missionary action and achievement in Africa in the first half of the twentieth century was not a time in which African-ness was cultivated.[17] The Catholic

Church seldom grew as it did in Buganda, from a fiercely fought-over foundation charter. More often it grew from the half-choice of school children, from political and cultural pressures not easily resisted but, equally, not easily resulting in a sense of absolute belonging. In fact, despite occasional lip-service to the contrary, it was an era of as consistent a European control and Roman model as was possible. This only really noticeably began to change at the close of the 1950s. Numbers were going ever up – the number of the baptized, the number of village churches, the number too of the effectively excommunicate. And then, suddenly, almost out of the blue, the Second Vatican Council appeared to encourage a very different pattern of ecclesiastical existence – a pluralist diversity in place of the ultramontanism which had been held in a particularly simplistic manner by most missionaries.[18] By the end of the 1960s the politics of independence, the international economic order and the demography of the population explosion had begun to produce, in place of the apparent order of late colonial society, a new and vast confusion: a confusion of coup and civil war and famine, the breakdown of structures (government and administration still more than the ecclesiastical), the survival and revival of small units: a bit like the Africa of Augustine's later years. As all this happens the Christian state of Buganda in the 1880s and 90s, or even the pastoral situation of Buddu in the 1940s and 50s, start to return as a model of what is going on in thousands of uncharted places as half a continent exgurgitates a Christian, if at times seemingly twilight Christian, culture and sense of self-identity merging the message it had heard from Bible, church and missionaries with its own intuition of what still matters in non-Christian tradition as well as in contemporary need. Historians, sociologists and educationalists writing about the churches in Africa have tended to see them as élitist, progressive, sub-imperialist agencies. What is more important now is to recognize them on the contrary as populist, conservative and at least implicitly rather nationalist bodies.

It will be a long time before anyone can see clearly what is to come out from the dark tunnel that the African continent seems at present to be traversing. Within the tunnel, one hopes at least, the Catholic Church like other churches, is shedding its imposed character of obedient outreach to a European institution and becoming instead something permanently viable on the other side of the cultural frontier. One cannot be too sure. Until the 1960s, while indigenization was culturally easier in Catholicism than in Protestantism, it was as a matter of policy far more a characteristic of other churches than of the Catholic. Again today – after a brief interlude of post-Vatican II adaptation – Rome is not encouraging, except with the thinnest of occasional rhetoric, any such revolution. Moreover in many places the established hierarchy, black or white, and its resident nuncio are so clearly frightened of any alternative to the canonical model, and still so firmly in institutional control of the ministry, that the thrust of Christian vitality in Africa which, in the conciliar sixties, was so considerably harnessed by the Catholic Church, is today increasingly diverted into other more accommodating bodies. Yet it is also true that for Africa today all institutional authority, secular or religious, is pretty impotent. Nyerere, Mobutu or Mugabe may have their plans, good or bad, imaginative or bombastic, but they can seldom actually realize them. They can, of course, build a Conference Centre in the capital with Yugoslav assistance, or a grandiose new Party Headquarters. Village Africa simply goes its own way, with a long-suffering, slightly cynical indifference. And this is largely true ecclesiastically as well. The observer can, I think, do little more than suggest that if a wide African Catholicism other than a colonialist outreach is in due course to mature and thrive – not only in immediate numerical terms, but as something which will weather the storms as well as Buganda's Catholicism has managed to do these last hundred years – then it must have its own well-rooted and characteristic institutions. Perhaps the cult of the martyrs did provide that for the rural churches of Numidia in the fourth century, but the wretched division between Donatism and Catholicism schismatized and exaggerated a basically Catholic institution, leaving the Catholic Church unprovided with a genuinely local base. Probably the monasteries of Egypt and Ethiopia remain the principal key to the survival of Christianity through isolation and the manifold strains of a difficult history in both countries.

Are there comparable institutions developing within contemporary African Christianity? Clearly it is early days yet. In very many parts of Africa a Catholic community hardly existed until well after the First World War, if not still later. It is little more than fifty years since, in most places, the mass Christian conversion of rural

Africa really got under way. If, for a moment, we equate the martyrs of Scilli (AD 180) with the martyrs of Buganda (1886) and remember that the mass conversion of the north African countryside was only taking place nearly a hundred years after the former, and that one has still fifty years to wait for Donatism and more than a hundred for Augustine, Bishop of Hippo, then – even with the contractions of a modern timescale – it is fair to recognize that modern African Catholicism needs time. One cannot assess it quite as one might that of Brazil, South India or the Philippines. The shape has not yet set.

In some places, as I have argued already for Buganda, the clergy are themselves such an institution, but not yet in many. The body of Joseph Kiwanuka lying embalmed in Rubaga Cathedral may be in its way as potent a local symbol as was that of Jeremy Bentham in University College, London, a century earlier: each would ensure, if in a rather macabre way, the continuing presence of the master and his vision for society among the clerisy of the future. The first cathedral at Rubaga was burnt down in January 1891 in the Battle of Mengo after the Catholic army led by Gabrieli Kintu and Stanislaus Mugwanya had fled before the bullets of Captain Lugard's maxim gun. Kiwanuka died early in 1966 in a still peaceful Uganda and amid the early after-glow of the Second Vatican Council. The atmosphere of 1891 seemed very far away. To many foreign Catholics in that still self-confidently modernizing age the embalming of his body appeared a slightly queer thing to do. Yet only a month or two later battle would be renewed at Mengo as Milton Obote's soldiers stormed the palace of the *Kabaka* Mutesa II. In the next twenty years of continually renewed disturbance, oppression and civil war, under Obote, Amin and their successors, Ganda Catholics – people and priests – have often taken refuge in and around Rubaga Cathedral, close to the residence of Kiwanuka's successor, Cardinal Nsubuga. It was indeed on the hill only just below the cathedral that their principal lay leader, Benedicto Kiwanuka, the country's first Prime Minister and later Chief Justice, had made his home – as if to be close to sanctuary. Not that this saved him from being hacked to death by soldiers when he incurred Amin's wrath in 1973. As the people have gathered time and again in the cathedral, the presence of Bishop Kiwanuka's body has remained undoubtedly a symbol of identity and endurance; a memorial of the dead, like the shrine of the martyrs at Namugongo, to fortify the living.

Again it has to be said that the role of the priesthood, living or dead, is not generally so potent. The African priesthood remains not just too few in number, but by and large too shaped according to a pattern of clerical existence not organically related to the reality of the African church. Its self-confidence is embarrassed by contradiction. While tied by the law of celibacy and expected actually to expatiate upon the value of that law, it is common knowledge in some dioceses that hardly a priest is without children of his own. The great seminaries such as Katigondo, Kipalapala, Enugu and Mayidi have indeed been key institutions for the church in Africa, citadels of a certain sort of Catholicism, but it could not be said as yet for the African Catholic Church in general that its clergy is a principal pillar of its strength. In too many places it is plainly not so, being either absent or ineffective and still far outnumbered by foreign missionary clergy.

Still more is there an absence of influential monastic life among men. On no point does the contrast appear greater between modern African Christianity and that of the first millenium. Indeed, even to make contemporary comparisons, there is no other continent in which male religious life – of the traditional kind – is so weak. And yet when we start to talk of religious community we are indeed entering an era of still unexplored vitality – the area, for instance, of that mysterious movement of the married, *Jamaa*,[19] with its intense spiritualization of sexual relationships, of the communal religious life of many independent churches, but also of the extremely numerous and committed world of sisterhoods.

Noe Mwaggali, a potter in Ssingo, was sought out as a Christian, speared and fed to dogs on 31 May 1886 at Mityana. The day before, only too aware of what was likely to happen, he had said to his sister, Munaku, aged about twenty, 'For myself, I am convinced that there is a life after death, and I am not afraid of losing this one; but what about you? Are you determined to remain true to the Faith?' She was not, after all, as yet baptized. 'Certainly I am,' she replied. When Noe was killed, Munaku gave herself up to his executioners and asked them to kill her too. 'My brother has died for his religion. I wish to die also. Plunge your spears into me.' 'You are mad,' they replied, but took her prisoner and their leader decided to add her to his wives. This she utterly refused despite being put in his stocks for a month. Finally he sold her to the White Fathers for a gun and some ammunition. Munaku was baptized in August 1886 and confided the same day that she had promised never to marry anyone but Christ. In October she was allowed to make a vow for one year. 'We now have a black sister,' the missionaries could write and Munaku was soon looking after their orphanage, teaching catechism for two hours a day as well as attending daily mass and meditation. In due course she became leader of the women who looked after the seminarians and was always exemplary up to her death in 1938 at Bukalasa seminary.[20]

Perhaps all this sounds rather too like the hagiography of improbable *acta martyrum* set in the persecution of Diocletian. It may look like a myth, only it happens to be true, and it was out of the tradition of Munaku, of Princess Nalumansi and of other women as brave that the feminine commitment and religious life in modern African Catholicism really sprang forth. The congregation of the Bannabikira in Buganda, founded in 1910, was to be followed by numerous others all across Africa. The number of African sisters has long been five times or more that of priests or brothers. Despite much poor guidance and ill-use from the clergy – as well as the chauvinistic prescriptions of canon law – there is among them a sense of confidence of belonging, but also of being significantly radical in African social terms. In all the churches, not only Catholic, it is the role of women that has often been both the most sure-footed and the most discontinuous in relationship to the pattern of African society. And that is something which Professor Horton might ponder.

The other great African Catholic institution is that of the catechist.[21] Here is something which has developed in a thoroughly local form, something simply non-existent in the church from which missionaries came. Fortunately, as a result, it does not feature in canon law and has therefore never been tied canonically as has the priesthood and religious life. 'I have fourteen catechists,' I remember a White Father in eastern Buganda saying to me many years ago, 'and the whole work of the parish depends upon them, but not one can come to communion!' Ruminate over that if you want to understand the odd reality of the church we are considering. The catechist, married, poorly trained and still more poorly paid, if at but often only semi-literate, and often technically well on the wrong side of canon law, has yet been for a century the Trojan of the African church – criticized, maligned, mocked, theoretically phased out of existence but in fact the abiding ministerial reality of the village. He is the father of the church, of priest, sisters and bishops and he remains when they depart for the town, the seminary, for Europe, for Rome, for Cambridge. He remains in civil war, in famine, and in the long breakdown of rural communications brought on by the shortage alike of petrol and of spare parts for car and motor cycle. He remains teaching, baptizing, preaching and re-preaching eloquently enough the sermons he heard years ago from some historic missionary long returned to retirement in Dublin, Verona or Mill Hill. And yet when maybe a priest returns, albeit briefly though triumphalistically to the village, the catechist can still not receive communion for that troublesome matter of his marriage has never quite been rectified. That is the sort of institution which may keep a church going on the other side of the frontier.

In religious conversion there are bound to be numerous elements both of continuity and of separation. The latter are required to make the point of conversion emphatically clear, the former to make the transition in commitment intellectually possible and to undergird the new world-view by reinforcing it with props from the past. While some discontinuities are absolutely needed, it is a mistake to enlarge their secular ambit excessively. Beer drinking could be near to the heart of African social life. It was a good thing that the Catholic could go on drinking his beer and the Catholic missionary might even employ his own beer brewer, and it was an unnecessary burden that the Protestant was often forbidden so to do. But lines of continuity and discontinuity are most necessary and most painful the nearer one gets to the heart of the religion itself. Take again the name of God. God is nameless and yet we cannot but name him.

The major traditional names, at least in Bantu Africa, are widely diffused – *Nzambi, Leza, Mulungu, Mwari, Iluva, Katonda*. Almost everywhere missionaries accepted an African word at this crucial point, thus establishing a bridge of fundamental continuity where so much of the secondary conceptualization would be discontinuous – and the religious would be symbolized by an importation of all sorts of Latin words to cope with this or that element of post-Tridentine Catholic faith. Of course, a verbal continuity is no proof of total continuity of meaning; indeed it is very clear that the meaning of god-words changed considerably as has, of course, happened everywhere. There was not anyway a full identity of meaning between, say, *Mwari* and *Katonda*. Nevertheless there was sufficient between both and Yahweh to help enormously the transition in religious consciousness. Conversion seemed as a consequence not entirely a matter of changing faiths but also of a growth in understanding, a shared experiential reshaping of the meaning of words and concepts already basically there.

But move down from Horton's macrocosm to the microcosmic level and consider the ancestral spirits, Mbiti's 'Living Dead', and Catholic experience was here very different. They had simply to be rejected; of this the nineteenth-century missionary had no doubt. Yet they were a constituent part of daily life, of popular rituals of every sort – of passage, sickness, harvest – much more obviously involved, indeed, than *Nzambi* or *Leza*. Here lies the inner struggle of African Christianity, the battle not yet won, the issues not yet even quite clearly demarcated. Are they, or are they not, the same issues as those of the perennial Asian question of 'the Chinese Rites'?

Our Ganda martyrs with their undoubtedly very fresh sense of the meaning of death and of life after death could have had, I am sure, no truck with ancestor cults. Yet still today, as is very widely recognized, Catholics 'are puzzled, bewildered and confused by the conflict they experience between the loyalty to their ancestors and their loyalty to Christ.'[22]

Attempts are now being made in some places to purify and Christianize rites in which ancestor spirits are approached. Some theologians like the Tanzanian priest Charles Nyamiti are endeavouring even to develop a theology of 'African Christian Ancestorship'.[23] Take the case of the Shona *Kurova Guva* ceremony, a year or so after burial in which, it is believed, 'the spirit is brought home' – home both to other ancestral spirits and to its living descendants. Until then it is thought to be 'black' and wandering in the wild. Joseph Kumbirai, a Shona Catholic priest and learned in these matters, has written: 'To ignore the *Kurova Guva* ceremony is to make it impossible for the new spirit to join the ancestral spirits. This is to leave the spirit to wander about the forest as a lost sheep, as a friendless, dejected and marooned individual, entirely out of contact with both the living and the dead.'[24] What would Noe Mwaggali have had to say to that? Kumbirai argued that as vast numbers of Christians do in fact still perform the *Kurova Guva* ceremony, it ought to be 'adapted to the Christian Faith'. And this in fact the Catholic Church in Zimbabwe has tried to do with its *Kuchenura Munhu* ceremony. But is there really any theological foundation on which to base such an adaptation?[25] The mere persistence of rites and beliefs in a profoundly syncretistic situation can hardly provide grounds for their Christian acceptance. Replacement by vigorous substitution rather than a modified adaptationism may make more sense, especially as African ancestor cults are mostly unworkable without spirit possession, than which nothing seems more alien to the Christian ritual tradition.[26]

The purpose here, however, is not to assess the viability of a Christian *Kurova Guva* or of the theology, learned as it surely is, of a Nyamiti. What matters to us in both is the evidence of a prolonged struggle over continuity and discontinuity in regard to a proper relationship between the living and the dead. Another name for *Kurova Guva* is *Kutamba Guva*, 'to dance at the grave'. That was an ancient North African custom too. All night dancing, even at the grave of Cyprian, was a practice Augustine had occasion to deplore.[27] It was one to which the Circumcellians, apparently, were particularly addicted. Was Augustine being merely puritanical in his objection to it, or was he resisting a basically foreign intrusion within the world of Christian belief? Catholicism with its long preoccupation over saints and martyrs should at least be well equipped for understanding and coping with such things, and equipped, perhaps, to provide a rather more nuanced response than the *Christus solus* of the conservative evangelical.

'I visit pagan shrines, I consult witch-doctors and diviners, but I do not forsake the Church of God. I am a Catholic.' Such a remark might well be made by someone in almost any congregation in modern Africa. In point of fact it was made by one of Augustine's congregation in Hippo![28] What do you do? Turn a blind eye. Discipline the back-slider. Synthesize the traditions after 'dialogue'. Each has been tried. A fascinating recent study of the observance of All Souls' Day in the Guinea-Bissau region asks whether it is to be understood as 'A Christian Holy Day, An African Harvest Festival, An African New Year's Celebration, or all of the above(?)'[29] Frei Pedro da Trindade was one of the most influential and long-lived Dominican mission priests on the middle Zambezi in the eighteenth century. He lived at Zumbo, location of a much-used fair. He was a holy man but also canny and rich, with his own gold mine worked by his slaves. He was an asset to Zumbo but eventually, in 1751, he died and had no missionary successor. However when about a hundred years later – in 1861 to be exact – a Portuguese, Albino Manuel Pacheco led an expedition to Zumbo to reopen the fair, he found Frei Pedro still actively at work. His spirit now spoke through a medium. The missionary had been finally, and usefully, converted to the religion of his slaves.[30] In this case at least a too small dose of Christianity was wholly absorbed into a non-Christian thought world and, characteristically, into a case of mediumship by possession. Christianity in Africa may never find it easy to get beyond a simplistic model of ecclesiastical ultramontanism or evangelical fundamentalism without arriving finally at the plight of this good Dominican, but it will have to go on trying. We have seen ways in which a relationship with dead spiritual ancestors, the establishers and continuers of the community's foundation charter, can be crucial to African Catholicism – as it is crucial to Catholicism everywhere: a community, after all made visibly one by sharing in a sacramental *memoriale*. Yet a refusal to incorporate within the church's own formalization of this relationship the mechanics of spirit possession may, I suspect, remain the crucial test in regard to this culture of Christianity's essential otherness.

When the early church advanced from Carthage or Alexandria into the African countryside, it had behind it in each case a localized yet orthodox tradition of theology which its converts could and did make their own. Cyprian was the authority to whom Donatists appealed, Anthony and Pachomius enjoyed the friendship of Athanasius. Ganda Catholicism in its foundation charter did at least inherit the sense of a duality of founding authority – Mapera and Stensera, much loved foreign missionaries upon the one hand but, no less important in the story, Lwanga and Mukasa, Ganda Christians, upon the other. But in general the modern African church has lacked much sense of indigenous foundation or a theological tradition to perceive as its own. Catholic roots were laid in the high era of post-Vatican I Romanism and watered by men whose commitment to ultramontanism was for the most not only absolute but singularly unthinking. The clergy of Buddu were in practice Cisalpine enough, but the theology they had unquestioningly imbibed from their Latin text books at Katigondo was the driest of ultramontanism and no one could have been less prepared for the teachings of the Second Vatican Council. Such bishops as have subsequently appeared to deviate from the Roman straight and narrow, demonstrating a mind of their own, like Patrick Kalilombe or Emmanuel Milingo,[31] have been artfully removed from the continent to Europe where they will do less harm.

The African Catholicism of the twentieth century has indeed taken up the task and something of the predicament and the preoccupation of the ancient Catholicism of North Africa, upper Egypt and Nubia. It, like them, is near or over the frontier. It requires, as much as they did, to escape the bonds of Europeanism if it is truly to be sufficiently at home not only to advance but to sustain its advance in the heartlands of Africa: not ashamed to remain fully within the Catholic communion, yet at the same time so authentically indigenous that it can withstand the appeals of separatism or of Islam. It has to be African without being quite swallowed up by African-ness. In the manifold troubles of today's Africa, the tutelage of Rome, the immediate safeguards of the ultramontane model, are attractive enough, and most bishops still find them so. Like Jim's friends in Belloc's *Cautionary Verse* they must see point in the advice to

always keep a-hold of Nurse,
For fear of finding something worse.

It is not unreasonable, though it may be over-timorous, to fear that, while one may start with a Dominican bravely preaching the blessings of liberation theology and a people's church, one will end – like poor Frei da Trindade – swallowed whole in the warm embrace of Africa's perennial populist religion, more spirit-possessed than possessed by the Spirit.

Yet perhaps the African church of today, in search of a *persona* and a theology, might consider more seriously than hitherto the possibility of an Augustinian *via media*. Augustine stood, in point of fact, despite his thoroughly Roman education, baptism by Ambrose in Milan and tendency to fall back rather too easily on imperial authority, for a finally creative integration of the Catholic, the local and the personal.[32] He was certainly a Catholic first and foremost, continually conscious of the privilege and obligation of membership of the *universus orbis Christianus*, but he was also self-consciously an 'African writing to Africans' (*Afer scribens Afris*), struggling with the aftermath of the breakdown of empire, heir to the ecclesiology of Cyprian and no believer in a monarchical or – to return to the terminology of so much later a period – ultramontane church. He was, too, a man for all seasons, who learnt from experience – and a long experience too. Ecclesiologically, I would suggest, Augustine remains all in all the African church's safest indigenous guide.

There are undoubtedly worse things than the dictates of Rome lurking in the shadows. Nevertheless the flowering of an African Catholicism, baulked so many times in the past by a variety of circumstances, could indeed fail again if the message of Pope Paul VI at Kampala in 1968, 'You may and you must have an African Christianity' is not applied in ways well beyond anything permitted at present by the regulations of canon law.

2

The Gospel and African Culture

The attempt to consider, in a rather general way, the historic interaction within Africa over the last hundred years or so of the two realities of gospel and culture is not at all the same thing as to decide what has been right or wrong at any given point in so immense a process. On the contrary, it seems necessary – at least initially – to try to relativize that question as something not indeed wholly inappropriate to ask, yet as one which can only be misleadingly answered if divorced from context – a context not of two static realities but rather of the dynamics of interaction, the dialectic of an on-moving historical relationship. The most appropriate answer here and now to any seemingly theoretical question relating to human behaviour and morality depends enormously upon the circumstances, cultural, political, psychological, within which the question is asked. To understand better the circumstances relevant to the interaction of gospel and culture it may be helpful to start by attempting roughly to 'periodize' that interaction, and while not, like Shakespeare, applying a model of Seven Ages, I would suggest five. In each of them the answers given to formally unchanging questions (such as, what judgment the Christian should come to in regard to the practice of polygamy, the cult of ancestors, forms of spirit possession) have been profoundly and inevitably affected by the ethos, the dynamics, the practicabilities, the implicit agenda of that particular period.

The first period was in most places a very limited one, if it existed at all: it might indeed almost be thought of as a hypothetical rather than a real period. It is that of the meeting of African culture and Christian gospel in a genuinely pre-colonial situation, one in which African political, economic and cultural structures were, in that place and time, the dominant ones. On the coast it probably never existed anywhere – a secular colonial presence was always too much in evidence – but in the interior one can think of the early encounter in Ashanti or Benin, Gubulawayo or Buganda. If the missionary message included or called for social change and the rejection of significant elements of the traditional order, then that message could only be preached and implemented in the face of traditional authority, either acquiescing or resisting. There was no higher local authority to sanction or uphold the messengers of change and their converts. When the king of Buganda ordered leading Christians to be killed there was no secular appeal from that command, and the missionaries themselves did not contemplate any.

In our second period African custom still existed very nearly as a whole in any particular place but in more and more places it was now being vociferously challenged by a gospel coming culturally from without. The decisive difference was that it was being proclaimed by people conscious that, at the end of the day, they enjoyed the protection of the political kingdom. African custom was thereby maimed because it was deprived of its inherent political edge. Strange as the socio-religious message of these foreign teachers might be, it was beginning to be recognized as leading no longer to probable political ostracism but rather as an *open-sesame* to the possession of sources of power far greater than any contained within tradition – keys to the new order which had dawned so mysteriously, but also so irrevocably.

Our third period was one of settled white dominance – Africa's classical colonial era, stretching in most parts of the continent from not later than 1910 to not much later than 1950. Christianity was already in some sense an intrinsic element within many an African society: the catechist was now the accepted local leader, the mission station the accepted source of the new mores – accepted not by all, but by many, at least publicly and in many places at least as almost normative for the young. The missionary appeared to himself and to the observer to be sitting self-confidently enough, authoritatively, almost brazenly, astride the broken if still pulsating wreckage of tradition.

Move on to our fourth age (quintessentially the early sixties), that of decolonization, political, organizational, mental. Admittedly, more of a matter of personalities and rhetoric than of a structural or educational revolution. But it was far from being pure rhetoric. The direction of advance had altered and with it the logic of persuasion. Black leadership had taken over the reins in state, church and scholarship. Religion was a prime area for the implementation of a programme for cultural authenticity. The reassertion of African selfhood was done against a backdrop of colonial experience, and its critique in fairly simplistic Marxist or other anti-imperialist terms. And the application of such a critique to the missionary field seemed particularly easy. People of my age were brought up in our third period but many at least responded happily to the fourth. It may for us be particularly necessary to note that in the late 1980s that period too has now gone, except in Zimbabwe. We are today in a fifth age. Colonialism was really a very brief experience in most of Africa and Africans are not, I think, very historically-minded people – they are not at all, one might say, like Irishmen. The past fades quickly into the mists of time: that is, perhaps, one reason why they can be so forgiving. The Africa of the later 1980s is a continent in which we are, in some ways, getting surprisingly close to our very first period: colonial domination has come and gone, yet Christianity is now as indigenous as maize meal or banana beer.

It is especially important for us to become aware of the difference between our fourth and fifth ages, but before spelling that out I would like to say a little more about the first period. Crucial at the start of the encounter was an overwhelming missionary ignorance of African religion and culture. There is nothing very surprising about this missionary ignorance, for there was really no way in which missionaries could have been other than ignorant – in the case of religions without any written scripture and of societies about which no one in the West knew much. It would take a great deal of experience, thought and re-education before even the greatest among them could begin to overcome it. Missionary ignorance was very much part of a vaster European insensibility to a world as different as that of Africa, particularly at the time of Europe's greatest sense of its own cultural superiority.

But we have to add to that a note of intolerance characteristic particularly of the missionaries. They were seldom people of wide reading – even of wide theological reading. Moreover, they came on the whole from the more severely intransigent sections of their home churches, rather than from the more accommodating. There was, in point of fact, a good deal of accommodation at home, for instance within the Church of England, with all sorts of unchristian aspects of Victorian society: in a state church that had to be the case. Missionaries were not, however, temperamentally establishmentarians, at least not accommodating establishmentarians. Rather they had a vision of a perfect Christian society which they hoped to establish among their new converts: almost a Calvin's Geneva. A refusal to tolerate imperfection, a rather puritan approach to the whole relationship between religion and culture, as well as ignorance or condemnation of the diversities within the Christian tradition itself – all this seems widely characteristic of most missionaries, Catholic as well as Protestant. If it had been otherwise most of them would not, perhaps, have volunteered to become missionaries.

Upon the other side, in Africa itself there was an absolutely integral relationship between religion and culture. African tradition was inherently holistic. Here less than anywhere could you mark off the secular from the sacred. The religious permeated pretty well everything or – one might well say – the secular permeated everything. Thus you can analyse ancestor veneration in almost entirely secular terms, and many good social scientists have done so, or you can analyse it in almost entirely religious terms. But you certainly can not separate it into two. There was an integrality of social relationships, ritual practice and belief in the powers of the unseen which made it almost impossible to apply sensibly the classical missionary principles devised, for instance, by the Roman Congregation of *Propaganda Fide* about being careful not to change the culture but only to reject the religiously erroneous. Such a distinction could make little sense and, in point of fact, missionaries realized this quickly enough. Every custom had its religious dimension, so – logically – every custom would have to be rejected. Some missionaries applied that logic with very little mitigation and some early converts embraced its conclusions unreservedly.

At an early stage in the process of personal conversion (and particularly when personal conversion comes at an early stage in a wide social movement of conversion) there is in fact likely to be an overwhelming need for a very sharp break. Whether or not this is theoretically or intellectually required, or might seem altogether appropriate on later mature reflection, it is psychologically required at the time. If you are going to give up a system of belief and practice which has wholly dominated your life, your perceptions as well as your public conventions and adopt another, you may have to do so with a ruthlessness which the bystander is likely to find excessive. I remember years ago, in the 1950s, a seminarian at *Propaganda Fide* in Rome, discussing this very issue. A young man from Tanzania, the child of Christian parents, who had received his education in a minor seminary and had therefore never personally experienced the strains of conversion, declared (like many an African theologian since) that traditional religious practices should be retained and simply given new meaning in the process of conversion. Another, older seminarian, a Japanese graduate, who had been converted to Christianity as an adult, remarked to me afterwards how in reality for the convert himself or herself, that is simply impossible. Conversion is only made tolerable at all by some sharp distancing from the symbols and sacraments of one's former convictions.

If we turn now to our third period, that of an apparently settled white dominance (roughly speaking, the first half of the twentieth century), we may notice first of all a certain decline in missionary intransigence – by no means a revolution in attitude, but a certain growth in tolerance, even in sympathy. It was the age of Edwin Smith. There were anthropologists around who were able to explain things, reinforcing and extending the discoveries of many a missionary scholar like Smith himself. There was the awkward reality, which could nevertheless not be ignored, of the amount of traditional belief and practice carried on by many quite committed church people. There was, perhaps, most potently of all, an unformulated feeling that Christianity was little by little getting on top of tradition, but that it was going to be a long haul and that a fair amount of tolerance might not in the meantime come amiss. The nineteenth-century missionary may have perceived himself in somewhat first-century terms. The twentieth century turned more naturally to a medieval paradigm. Doubtless such a measure of tolerance as I am hinting at was neither unqualified nor universal, but the more the mission churches came to be rooted in Africa, the less strong was the sense of immediate confrontation with its past. As African Christian society itself developed, its attitude to tradition tended to splinter. Formally it adopted the more conservative and anti-adaptionist approach of the early missionaries, looking nearly always a little askance at the more liberal, constructive wing of a missionary avant-garde. In practice, however, lay African Christianity lived with a degree of fusion, syncretism, or dual-mindedness such as almost no missionary could appreciate or tolerate.

The position can be seen most evidently in the extensive presence of polygamists in nearly all the larger churches, at least by the 1920s. You may find the issue being argued out in, say, the Anglican synod in Uganda: what to do about leading polygamist chiefs? Discipline them and you may lose the influence and support of people upon whom so much of the conversion of Uganda has hitherto depended. Turn a blind eye and you are in fact accepting a double standard. Doubtless there was in fact little alternative and the double standard has become a quite important part of the shape of the modern African church, just as it has been in other circumstances and centuries where Christianity has come through a process of mass conversion. Theoretically, admission to communion held the line, but in a church where priests were so few and communion so rare, non-admission to communion was a relatively insignificant barrier. In practice synodical decisions could make little difference one way or another: polygamist Christians, ancestor-venerating Christians, witch-fearing Christians were here to stay. That was not a matter of cultural adaptation but of double identity. For a description of it John Taylor's 1950s account *The Growth of the Church in Buganda* has never been bettered.

Our third period was the golden age of the prophet movements and independent churches which – to put it rather too simplistically – represent people determined to cling to a very much larger amount of culture and custom than the missionary church was prepared to allow. The African case even then was often defended vigorously in terms of a biblical interpretation, which seemed fair enough to African eyes but which the western mentor disallowed. The polygamy argument, with its straightforward Old Testament appeal, was a good example of this but by no means unique. All in all this period was not, however, a very theological one. it was rather one in which the internal contradictions, present in the initial confrontation between Christianity and African culture, began to work themselves out in a number of rather different directions within the context of a very rapidly growing church undergirded with a quite inadequately critical sense of either the gospel or African tradition. The formal image of this period remains one of the primacy of the European mind.

The mood of period four, beginning in the mid-1950s, was very different. It is our shortest age, lasting in most places hardly more than twenty years. It was, outside southern Africa, almost over by the end of the 1970s. It represents the cultural and intellectual counterpart to the coming of political independence, beginning with that of Ghana in 1957 and ending with that of Zimbabwe in 1980. In each country it predates its political independence by five or ten years and continues after it by some fifteen. Naturally, however, as countries are not isolated, the later the political independence the more the intellectual development has predated its arrival. Obviously this period sees a sharp reversal, mentally as much as politically, of the age of white domination. The theology of the Christianity/African culture relationship is no exception to this. What stands out is the fierce attack by people like Bolaji Idowu upon missionary incomprehension. The primary task was now seen as the construction of an 'African Theology' able to vindicate within a Christian horizon the religion of tradition. It was easy enough for African writers of this period to berate the missionary inadequacies of the past – and it was, indeed, in a way necessary that they should do so, even if they were in fact themselves dependent more than might appear on missionary 'liberals' like Smith, Geoffrey Parrinder or John Taylor. The new stress was upon the value of African religion, tradition and culture and the continuity between all that and Christianity. The impression given was that the pre-colonial condition was almost a golden age of humanity in which the concept of God and the basic norms of morality were strangely close to those of late nineteenth-century Protestantism. An African agnostic like Okot p'Bitek might challenge the whole approach but in the African Christian response of the 1960s and 70s one finds a confident, optimistic, almost cocky spirit, culture-preoccupied but rather ahistorical. The African theology of John Mbiti, Bolaji Idowu, Burgess Carr or Gabriel Setiloane – to name but a few – should be seen as part of the wider African cultural renaissance, literary and historical, of the post-Independence years.

It was for the continent a great and exciting time when it seemed feasible to relate a Christianity shorn of all unnecessary Europeanism to what was really integral in African culture. This was helped greatly by three things. Upon the one hand, the prophet movements and independent churches of Africa, hitherto largely ignored as nationalistic syncretisms, were now suddenly hailed – just about as simplistically – as almost a model for what a truly African Christian church ought to be. The late 1960s witnessed a flood of books and articles seeking to find a message, some formula for Africanization, in independency.

Secondly, the early 1960s witnessed outside Africa a far wider movement of intense renewal in religion and culture, exemplified most obviously by the Second Vatican Council and such books as John Robinson's *Honest to God*. The general mood was liberal, optimistic, critical of the European past, ecumenical, open to a special enthusiasm at any mention of pluralism. None of that really happened because of Africa but it helped the African post-Independence ecclesiastical and theological renaissance greatly by providing for it a highly sympathetic world church. At that point liberal western theologians were prepared to accept and go along with almost any criticism which African theologians cared to make of the eurocentric model of the past. The writings of people like Hans Küng could be seen, correctly enough, as making the same sort of point in Europe as the new wave of theologians were making in regard to Africa. If African political independence had come ten years earlier, there would have been simply no comparable responding voice within the Roman Catholic tradition and not nearly as much elsewhere as there was in the 1960s and early 70s.

Modern critical theology and biblical scholarship were really getting through to the gospel-culture relationship in Africa for the first time. Hitherto the missionary had been by and large, both Protestant and Catholic, a great fundamentalist and the African Christian was no less. It was one thing to recognize now and again that there were around the edges of the gospel areas open to compromise and diversity. It was another to have to admit that even if you were able to disentangle the message of the gospel from medieval and Victorian superstructures, you still had a culture-bound gospel from the word go. The African response to this was often enough: well, that culture is so close to ours anyway that we find it (unlike the post-Enlightenment European) no problem. But again the missionary scholar might feel less sure that this was really so or that – in so far as harmony between the two could be found –

it resolved the issue of how to go forward in the post-traditional Africa of the late twentieth century. One way or another, modern biblical scholarship made it harder than ever before to declare with confidence any given course unquestionably right or wrong.

Thirdly and finally, there was at that time money for conferences, collaborative enterprises, research, new journals, the All Africa Conference of Churches and its many projects. The enterprise of cultural renewal was well oiled financially by international foundations and funding agencies, ecclesiastical and secular, which temporarily overcame the natural isolation of small institutions divided by many frontiers. The political multiplicity of Africa does not make for cultural co-operation any more than does its basic poverty. However, for a short while in the hopeful atmosphere of the post-Independence years and with much foreign help, these factors seemed, culturally and academically at least, surpassable.

Important as all that has been, and impossible as it certainly is to go back – either in Europe or in Africa – upon the 1960s, we have all the same to recognize that we are now in a fifth, very different and more sombre age: one notably difficult to characterize. Despite Zimbabwe's continued success story, economic and cultural, the wider mood in Africa in the late 1980s is vastly different from what it was twenty-five years ago, just as it is in the West. The neo-conservative, anti-socialist, hard-nosed mood of the western world today, in which the voice of students and trade unions – for instance – has been reduced so drastically from what was taken for granted in the 1960s, no longer includes any large sympathy for the aspirations of the third world. Yet in point of fact Africa stands in greater need of understanding than ever. But within Africa too both circumstances and their interpretation have altered, and not altogether differently from the way the West has altered: although the one has been within a further growth in prosperity, the other – in most places – within a severe economic retrogression.

Scholarship and research have not developed within Africa to the degree that would have been expected twenty years ago. On the contrary African universities are, many of them, shorn of funds, gravely short of books, losing their more distinguished figures in exile abroad: this is true of almost every discipline. At the same time in Britain and elsewhere African studies have declined considerably. Posts are lost. There is little money for research trips to Africa.

There are far fewer interested students. The government appears to see very little point in African studies and even young British people not so much, while African students cannot afford our fees. Almost every Africanist discipline in Britain, built up in the 1950s, peaking in the late 60s, is now in deep decline. Yet, even internationally, African scholars are not themselves very noticeably taking over the leadership in their own fields. The stagnation within the African academic world at home inhibits any wider international impact.[1]

When we look back today we can see well enough that the optimism of the Africa of the 1960s was far from justified. Nevertheless, in those years things did get better in all sorts of ways. As Julius Nyerere has admitted for Tanzania, they improved in the 1960s, but deteriorated in the 1970s. The pattern of ups and downs has not been the same everywhere – Nigerian oil, for example, made a very great difference indeed to that country in the later 1970s. But, roughly speaking, for almost every country north of Zimbabwe prospects by the 1980s were grim indeed in relation to what had been anticipated twenty years earlier. The reasons are many and the balance between them can be argued over. There is, first, the internal political cause: inefficiency, corruption on a massive scale, coups, dictators, the sheer megalomania of an Amin or a Mobutu. Almost more debilitating than the crimes has been a pettifogging bureaucratic inefficiency quite unable to cope with the real problems. For a large part governments have just not maintained a credible administration across the countryside. But that is only the beginning of the story. Add to it the international economic crisis, not only in the price of oil but in the steady alteration of terms of trade almost always to the disadvantage of African primary producers. Even Nigeria, Africa's principal oil producer was back in economic depression by the late 1980s. Add to this massive droughts and consequent famine. Add too a population growth unparalleled in past human history and the effect of that, in areas of marginal rainfall, on land depreciation. Add a whole series of civil wars – in the Sudan, Chad, Ethiopia, Eritrea, Mozambique, Angola, Uganda. Add, finally, the impact of AIDS, still quite inadequately appreciated.

A realistic picture of today's Africa is bound to be a very sombre, even in some senses a pessimistic one. Such a context will certainly affect the theology written, in so far as theology is written at all. In fact the major figures of the 1960s were academics, professors and lecturers in the new departments of Religious Studies developing in the universities of East and West Africa. Without those departments we would hardly have had the works of African theology of men like Harry Sawyerr and John Mbiti. Departments of Religious Studies and Theology, like those at Makerere, Nsukka and Kinshasa, have suffered as much as any other disciplines from the wider economic and political malaise of these years; still more, perhaps, from a sense of lost direction. All this may help to explain why there is in truth almost no academic theologian with any wide reputation working in Africa today. It is not quite without significance that John Pobee and Lamin Sanneh, the best-known of the younger generation, have now for years been based in Geneva and Harvard. There may well be a feeling of dissatisfaction with the scholars of the last generation and their particular orientation, but their books have not been replaced.

This altogether sombre state of black Africa today has, I think, contributed to a more restrained scholarship, even a certain lack of confident direction in regard to the way forward. The agenda of the 1960s has not been rejected. Departments and journals of religious studies continue to tick over more or less. Mbiti's *African Religions and Philosophy* or Idowu's *Olódùmarè* are appealed to again and again, yet criticized again and again too. Certainly some of the reformist ideas in regard to the church and culture, proposed by the theologians and more liberal missionaries of the 1960s, have in part been put into practice: thus the Zairean liturgy is often pointed to as proof of sucessful inculturation. The Catholic Church in Africa could, indeed, hardly have survived without the wave of pastoral and liturgical renewal stimulated by Vatican II. But in subtler aspects of the relationship of religion to culture than the use of drums or a fly-whisk much less has been achieved than those active at the time anticipated or hoped for. Too many of the theological leadership have either removed themselves or been removed: not only Sanneh and Pobee, but John Mbiti, Burgess Carr, Patrick Kalilombe, Emmanuel Milingo. Those six have this in common: they have all for years not lived in Africa.

In South Africa it is, paradoxically, very different. There at least is to be found a lively world of theology, both black and white, plenty of journals, conferences, publications of every sort. South Africa was a natural cultural leader of Christian Africa for several generations until the middle of this century. It lost its place as the rest of the Africa became independent while the South succumbed to apartheid. Thirty years later the relationship is altering again. The very strain of battling with apartheid has revivified the Christian leadership of the South. Today Desmond Tutu, Manas Buthelezi, Frank Chikane, Albert Nolan, Allan Boesak provide, unquestionably, Christian Africa's most impressive leadership and the theology they propound is 'black theology' rather than 'African theology'. The difference is not inconsiderable,[2] particularly in regard to the theme of culture. African theology was culture-orientated and, on the whole, rather uncritical in its approach to traditional culture. The less attractive aspects of the latter, as typified by witchcraft, were largely left unmentioned. Black theology is, on the contrary, a critical and abrasive theology, more concerned with present politics than past culture. Its proponents do not deny that culture is part of liberation and that the blacks of South Africa need more than the vote and better pay. But they are now an urban rather than a rural community and, as a whole, the pursuit of a rapprochement between Christian faith and the imagined cultural tradition of pre-colonial Africa is a relatively small part of their agenda.

But the effective replacement of African by black theology at the growing edge of Christian intellectual activity is only part of the altered attitude to culture characteristic of our final period. Another is an alteration in significance as regards both the weight and the character of religious independency. In a sense, in the 1980s, it has become almost a misnomer even to talk of African independent churches as a group to be distinguished from another labelled roughly the mission churches. The latter have now for so long been under black leadership; the presence of foreign missionaries in many of them is so few; the control of or even regular contact with churches abroad is now so slight, that they can hardly be regarded as less 'African' or less 'independent' than the so-called 'independent' ones. But the more this has gone on, the more the contemporary significance in wider cultural or ecclesiastical terms of the latter has been reduced. They are not unimportant but in most countries the vitality of independent churches of the old sort, particularly if their character is of a noticeably Africanizing type, would seem to have diminished. The new independency of the 1980s has been for the most part, curiously enough, almost anti-Africanizing. While I was at the University of Zimbabwe, my students made some small surveys of independent African churches in their home areas. We classified them according to certain issues particularly in regard to custom and tradition. The results were somewhat as follows: the churches which dated from fifteen or more years previously were mostly very concerned with and accepting of customary elements such as food taboos and polygamy. But besides these older churches there were also many small, very new and lively ones, almost nameless, which without exception took quite a different line to tradition. They did not seem at all interested in being, in Sithole's phrase, '*mudzimu* Christians'. Their character was, on the contrary, intensely evangelical of a rather New Testament sort. Much the same seems to be happening in Nigeria and elsewhere.[3] This is to say, what one might call the main thrust of contemporary religious 'independency' in Africa is looking more and more like evangelical, charismatic and house churches in other parts of the Christian world. Twenty or thirty years ago the thrust of religious independency seemed a key positive indicator of the things which mattered in the gospel/culture relationship. No more. At least, the concerns it now registers are rather a reversal of those of that time. It can instead be seen as an easy prey to the most stridently fundamentalistic wing of the contemporary American Protestant missionary movement,[4] while it is in fact the main churches that are now clearly enough the principal locus for most of what is going on of positive value on the gospel/culture front.

Yet something not entirely dissimilar has been happening within the mission churches too. In Zimbabwe, for instance, after the Second Vatican Council and especially in the 1970s, the Catholic Church made a great effort to incorporate the *Kurova Guva* (the bringing home of the spirit of the dead person) ceremony within the liturgy. Today that attempt at adaptation is under severe attack. Is it really possible to 'authorize' or transform the *Kurova Guva* without effectively sanctioning spirit possession too and indeed an integrated view of death and its consequences basically alien to the Christian tradition? It is one thing to recognize tolerantly that many Christians live in two separated thought worlds. It is another to try to fuse those two worlds in a formal mish-mash which makes no real sense in either.

The 1960s were an optimistic age. People rather easily assumed that, with good will, there was a solution to every problem. Today it is different. This is true of the West and the world in general but most true of Africa. It has lived with fifteen or more bad years. If there is a loss of confidence in political or economic solutions, so is there in cultural ones. In practice the churches and Christianity survive and grow largely by re-assimilating the strengths of their own past without too much formal re-analysis. The foreign scholars of an earlier day, urging a new look at this or that, the Geoffrey Parrinders, Noel Kings, John V. Taylors, have few successors. Bishops have multiplied but are often suspicious of such local scholars as do exist. Certainly, the problems have not gone away. Many African Christians continue to be polygamists; many continue to join in ancestor rituals of various sorts; many continue to believe in witchcraft and arm themselves against it. It is true that the 1988 Lambeth Conference recommended the recognition of polygamous marriage in some circumstances, thus reversing the Lambeth resolution of 1888. Significant as this might be, it was more the delayed conclusion to a lengthy process begun in the 1960s than anything characteristic of the 1980s. In general, especially for the Catholic Church, it remains true that there is now less concern shown to resolve the problems of cultural interaction institutionally. Such attempts are seen as involving too much effort, as never actually getting accepted or implemented anyway, and as having dubious foundations.

Perhaps such a critique of the programmes and high hopes of the 1960s and 70s is not too misdirected or theologically misplaced. Every culture falls utterly short of the demands of the gospel. There can really be no question of establishing a Christian culture anywhere. There was not one in Europe and the traditional culture of Africa cannot be – bar a point or two changed here or there – declared implicitly Christian either. Some human practices are more awful than others. Some, often the most ephemeral, more divine. Some are more open to reform in this predicament or that. Culture is never unchanging and there can be no question of achieving a realized harmony between gospel and world, only a provisionality of appropriate challenge.

The Gospel and African Culture

The institutional churches are, anyway, pretty impotent – much as the secular authorities are – when it comes to actually getting anything done when faced with the vastness, poverty, self-renewing vitality of rural Africa. Even war, famine and AIDS won't end that. It survives, comes to its own myriad pragmatic solutions but cannot be controlled. Africa and its churches are going in poverty and faith through a long dark tunnel and they are not likely to come out at the other end for another twenty or thirty years. Perhaps in the 1960s it was right to raise the issue of culture and see it as central to the current enterprise. At present, I would judge, it is no longer so. The crucial issue today is that of gospel and justice rather than that of gospel and culture. Of course we are relating, and re-relating, gospel and culture all the time, if we believe in a living gospel at all, because it is by culture that we are the sort of human beings and social clusters of human beings that we are. We just cannot be cultureless and if the gospel has any significance, mental and behavioural, for humankind, then it must be a cultural significance too. But perhaps it is a sign of an unhealthy culture and an unhealthy church to be too culture-conscious. It's like being too clothes-conscious – and clothes are, of course, a quintessential expression of culture. Our concern should not be so much with culture as with love, truth, justice. You don't create a healthy culture by being preoccupied with culture. A healthy culture today, I would suggest, is a justice-conscious culture; an unhealthy culture is a culture-conscious culture. The gospel will serve a healthy culture by turning mind and heart away from a certain inward-looking characteristic of cultural preoccupations, outward to the service of justice and love. Such service will all the same not do away with culture but renew it almost unperceived.

3

Were Women a Special Case?

Were women a special case in the impact which the Christian missionary made upon nineteenth and twentieth-century Africa? I think that a first answer to that could rightly be 'No'. They were an integral part of a society challenged as a whole by the gospel and a vastly different way of life connected with it. Women and men shared the same beliefs, the same fears, the same sense of right and wrong. Custom, taboo, marriage and kinship obligations, all this and much else was accepted by all in an essentially unreflective way. It was moreover one vast web in which the religious could not be separated from the secular, the personal from the public. Female duties were, evidently, largely different from male duties but they were correlative and integrated within a unitary whole which provided support, meaning and some degree of happiness for all participants.

Missionary Christianity in its western garb and never entirely hidden colonial connections challenged that unitary whole from top to bottom. But it challenged some societies a good deal more sharply than others, and it challenged some aspects of that unitary whole more obviously and immediately than others. African societies were anyway mostly anything but static in the late nineteenth-century. They were already subject to tension, if not caught within large-scale conflict; they were changing; they had their own internal contradictions. It was natural and inevitable that missionary Christianity found a way into them very largely through cracks already produced by tension, change and internal contradiction. In all societies there was a range of personal roles and in the more complex societies there was a structural classification such that while some people must benefit from the maintenance of the status quo, others could benefit by its dissolution.

Men and women, old and young, chiefs, commoners and slaves, polygamists and non-polygamists, priests, diviners, traders: they were all in a way special cases when it came to the impact of the Christian mission. Buganda, for instance, proved as a whole to be very much a special case, but to some extent every other society was too. There was no absolutely standard response or reaction. This becomes still more obvious when one adds in the variables of Christianity itself (Moravians or Holy Ghost Fathers?) and of the degree of linkage with European conquest and trade.

As I look at the literature I notice how little consideration there has been of the feminine case. African society was apparently so male-dominated that the impact of Christianity upon it has been treated overwhelmingly in male terms. But the nature of nineteenth-century western Christianity is also a factor. It allowed almost no public role to women in the main churches. Except for organizations like the Salvation Army this was definitely not the century of women's ordination. A largely male-dominated missionary church encountered a largely male-dominated traditional Africa. Two forms of patriarchy appeared to fit together well enough. Where African custom was matrilineal, missionaries could be bewildered and attack this (like so many other aspects of custom) as being opposed to the law of God. For the most part in the history of the wider encounter women have had the briefest of mentions. This remains the case when one turns to thoughtful and critical re-examinations by modern African historians (like Jacob Ajayi and Emmanuel Ayandele) of nineteenth-century missionary history – studies with such subtitles as 'The making of a new élite' or 'A political and social analysis' – where one still finds no extended consideration at all of what all this meant for women: the social analysis has stopped well short of a gender analysis. Even the routine discussion of the issue of polygamy is conducted overwhelmingly in male-orientated terms.

Nevertheless, things were not as simple as that. African tradition did not entirely subordinate woman to man any more than European tradition did, while the missions would appear to have provided scope for female initiative to a degree rarely possible in the sending society. By the later nineteenth-century there were many women,

37

married and unmarried, engaged in missionary work. They would soon be a majority of all mission workers. Doubtless they were mostly in rather subordinate positions in terms of the missionary hierarchy and few indeed stand out clearly with the strength of a Mary Slessor. Nevertheless, the missionary church saw itself as champion of the dignity and education of women and in terms of a local African environment the impact of a woman missionary must often have been very considerable: the impact on education, midwifery, dress and deportment, the washing of plates, the airing of blankets, but still more upon the psychology of individual expectations. The ministry of all the churches had to be a great deal more flexible in the missionary and frontier situation than it was at home, and such flexibility could only redound to the advantage of those who at home were deprived of much opportunity to express or assert themselves. Despite obvious rigidities the missionary situation should be seen as one of comparative freedom in which things could be done, sometimes well, sometimes disastrously, which would have been almost unthinkable elsewhere.

That sense of freedom, of a co-operative effort in which men and women were both strenuously engaged, was quite often, I believe, communicated to African converts, women particularly. So that a first reason why women were affected in a different way was due to the character of some missions themselves – the impression they communicated in life as well as by formal message that women were equal, free and capable of independent responsibility. This led on naturally enough to the experiencing of this freedom by African women, especially in the early, less structured, phases of the missionary enterprise. It is noticeable that the first converts were often women. This may in part have been due to a feeling that they did not matter: the adherence of some women to the missionaries was seen at first as permissible, simply because it was socially and politically so insignificant. The same could be true of male slaves. But their presence within the young – or indeed hitherto non-existent – church could not in fact be socially insignificant. And, of course, biblically-conscious missionaries would be glad enough at that point to lay stress on the Christian equality of men and women, following Galatians 3.28: 'There is neither male nor female.' In a fair amount of early African mission history one has the impression of a degree of what may reasonably be called female exuberance and self-assertion, not wholly unlike that communicated in the New Testament itself. In the early days this attitude occasionally led to the marriage of white missionaries and black women. The black wives of Johannes Van der Kemp and James Read, for instance, must have made a very considerable impact upon the early Christian church in South Africa. The white missionary was so much the leader and if he was married to a black woman, this could not but affect the overall status of African women. Later on, of course, missionary societies opposed the inter-racial marriage of missionaries very emphatically. Indeed missionaries so doing were almost invariably disconnected.

The next reason for the particular impact of Christianity on African women was that missionary Christian morality tended to impinge particularly upon various specific aspects of female existence, and in such a way as a few at least would regard as liberating. In some cases the liberation may be more a matter of the missionary's perspective, even a missionary misunderstanding, but there can be no doubt that in terms of what the modern feminist position would see as the rights of woman, the missionary was by and large standing clearly enough on the liberationist side against the bondage of tradition. We could instance polygamy, the payment of bridewealth, clitoridectomy, the killing of twins, the pursuit of alleged witches. The missionary onslaught on these areas – even if at some points, as in the matter of bridewealth, it was much mistaken – was certainly, as we shall see, one capable of reverberating in the feminine heart.

Another, not unconnected, reason is that converts were often drop-outs – people who in one way or another no longer belonged to a society either because that society was actually disintegrating or because it had driven them out or wished to kill them and they had fled. Such drop-outs were by no means, of course, all women but quite a number were. They might be escaping cruel husbands, a marriage they did not want, confinement to a chief's harem, punishment for some offence, or even being sacrificed at the death of a king.

If Samuel Ajayi Crowther, the Yoruba slave boy liberated by the British navy, educated at Freetown by the CMS and in due course sent back to Nigeria to evangelize it, is the primal figure of nineteenth-century West African Christianity, his most symbolic action was surely his return to Abeokuta to find his mother and there baptize her.

Again and again in a mission history the early significant baptisms were mostly of women. Bethelsdorp was the first black Christian community in southern Africa. By the end of 1806 its total baptized consisted of forty-three women, eighteen men and sixty-two children.[1] That may provide something of a guideline – with women rather more than twice the number of men – though the Hottentot and coloured people of the western Cape were clearly not typical of Africa as a whole. Yet Dr Akama remarks of the very different society of Isokoland, Nigeria, in the early twentieth-century, 'It is a noticeable phenomenon that with the growth of Christianity in the area, the number of women converts in all the congregations became decisively larger than those of men.'[2] Again and again one notes how the first Christian in a place is a woman like Fiambarema, the Moravians' 'first fruit' in 1897 in Rungwe, or Kapuleya-Ndondolilwe, in 1909 at Mkoma's.[3]

In the very early period of a mission too, while boys would see no point in coming to school, girls might begin to do so. That was true of Mrs Smith's knitting school of Bethelsdorp from 1805, or the sewing school of Mrs Wrigley and then Elizabeth Waldron at Cape Coast from 1836. Again it was true of early times at Onitsha where the first primary school, opened in November 1858, consisted of 14 girls. Occasionally there, we read, a group of boys 'would rush into the house, proudly gaze at the alphabet board and with an air of disdain mimick the names of the letters pronounced by the schoolmaster and repeated by the girls, as if it were a thing only fit for females'.[4] Even in Buganda the first boarding school opened by the CMS was one for girls – at Gayaza in 1902. The boys' boarding school at Budo followed two years later. Attending a mission school involved wearing clothes of some more or less European sort. Dress seemed essential to Christianity and in many parts of Africa the missionary invented forms of female dress for the first schools which became in due course extremely popular – the 'Bordingi' in Uganda, the 'Cabasroto' in Ghana – but to begin with such dress must have enhanced the strange liminal character of females-out-of-line: out of line yet at the same time obtaining thereby a sort of motherly power in the still shadowy new dispensation. At Rungwe, Fiambarema's position as senior Christian was institutionalized by the convention that subsequent applicants for baptism would approach her to intercede on their behalf.

A little to the south in modern Zambia two early headmen appointed by Bishop Dupont at the great White Father mission of Chilubula were in fact head women, Nandola and Chipasha. Each was subsequently murdered by her husband and each of the murderers committed suicide.[5] To the possible significance of that tragic sequence of events we will return. But I have cited enough evidence here to suggest the special position of women in the earliest Christian phase in many though not all places. In Buganda, it has certainly to be admitted, women played a relatively small role even in the earliest phase, but in this as in many other things Buganda may have been the exception rather more than the rule,[6] though even here the exception might be more apparent than real.

Women attached themselves to the missions for a multitude of reasons: they might be escaping brutal husbands or unwelcome marriages, particularly as additional wives to some rich polygamist. They might be objecting to having to let their baby die because it had not cried at birth or because it was a twin. In some African societies twins, if feared, were also much honoured, but in many others – both in the east and in the west – their birth was so feared that they were left to die. The brief ministry of Bernard Mizeki in Mashonaland[7] or the earlier years of Mary Slessor in Calabar were punctuated by battles to save the lives of twin babies but, quite often, this could mean a battle to save the mother too. At no point did deep maternal feminine instinct cry out so emphatically against custom and in favour of the Christian view, just as at no other point did the Christian missionary feel so required to challenge immediately and absolutely the practice of custom.

Let us consider the story of the conversion of southern Isokoland, an area near the Niger Delta where at the beginning of this century Christianity had still not penetrated. There was an Ijo woman named Berebolo Bribrina who became a Christian in 1905 when near the CMS mission at Patani. She later gave birth to twins and according to Ijo tradition was required to put one of them to death by abandoning it in the bush. As a Christian she refused to do so and was banished from her community. Fellow Christians ferried her and her twin babies across the Patani river and left them alone on an island where a certain Mr Ebiegbe, an Igbide trader returning from a trip to Patani market, met and took pity on her. He took her to Igbide and later married her. At Igbide, Bribrina began to evangelize the people and to organize a church so that it became the pioneer Christian centre within Isokoland. However the growth of the church resulted in persecution until in 1911 Bribrina, her husband and other faithful Christians fled away to found Obhodokpokpo, meaning 'New Town', a Christian community. To it people were soon coming from all parts, so that in 1912 the CMS missionary Aitken visited it to help organize the new church. Such is the myth, perhaps the history too, of the origin of Christianity in Isoko South and its founder, Bribrina – an extraordinarily rich symbolic account of the start of the conversion of the Isoko – the emergence of the 'New Town', the church, out of the decision of one woman not to allow her twin child to die.[8]

In the area of marriage itself the issues are more complex. One might start perhaps, a little provocatively, by remembering the very widespread traditional African preoccupation with female fatness as a sign of beauty. The girl being fattened up for marriage, even caned when she fails to keep drinking from the milk bottle, is a recurring motif in nineteenth-century literature from East, West and South Africa. It was not, for the missionary, a pleasing practice. And so in 1879 Mrs Price, daughter of Robert Moffat, sister-in-law of David Livingstone and wife of the missionary Robert Price, wrote to her Kwena friend Bantsan (daughter of the chief Sechele) in the following way. 'In civilized and especially Christian countries, she declared, 'a slender figure is admired', unlike the fat African model, because it is thought a dishonour to eat too much. 'The more civilized and more Christ-like' the Bakwena became, continued Mrs Price, the more they would admire slenderness and not fatness.[9]

The African woman had then, on becoming a Christian, to be reshaped as well as reclothed. She had, quite possibly, also to be remarried or at least married in a very different way from that of tradition. The battle with twin-killing was a relatively short one in which missionaries had behind them the weight of colonial authority. The battle with polygamy was to be a long-drawn one, never really won, in which colonial authority resolutely refused to be involved. Consider a fairly early incident in Mary Slessor's life in Calabar. She was visiting a village called Ibaka on the Cross estuary in 1882. One morning there was a row. Two girl wives of one of the chiefs had been caught in the hut of a young man. The village council promptly ordered each to receive a hundred lashes, quite likely a sentence of death. Mary had the council reconvened, harangued all and sundry, and finally got the sentence reduced to ten lashes. The girls were then brought to her, bleeding profusely. She bandaged them, dosed them with laudanum and kept them lying on their stomachs on the floor of her hut for the rest of her stay.[10] That sort of thing reinforced the missionary conviction that African women were, through polygamy especially, in a sort of slavery. And, of course, in some cases they were. Missionaries in the early period had most to do with chiefs and chiefs had large numbers of wives. This kind of polygamy could – for junior wives – be very enslaving. It was, moreover, unlikely to have been entered into with much consideration of the woman's wishes. But polygamy could be very different from that and it is not fanciful to think that small-scale polygamy was often desired as much by the women as by the men: it provided companionship, economic co-operation, and enhanced status for the senior wife. When this kind of marriage was terminated by Christian conversion, it was the women who suffered most.

There were missionaries, and not only John Colenso, who thought polygamy temporarily tolerable, but by and large they set their faces against it so firmly that an official monogamy became almost the principal mark of the mission church and later on in some – though by no means all – cases, the acceptance of polygamy became in turn a mark of the independent church. There can be little doubt that the large effect for good and ill of the Christian mission upon African women centred upon this. If Christian missions had been weaker, as they easily could have been, the movement towards Islam of black Africa, already well under way in both West and East, would, almost inevitably, have been much quickened by the arrival of colonialism. And Islam could only have reinforced the traditional judgment that the marriage of one man to as many women as he could afford was an excellent thing. The advance of Christianity did not banish so well-established a custom, but it did remarkably alter the public sense of the marital ideal, particularly among women. However much the successful African male may still incline to polygamy, the norm of official monogamy is not seriously challenged.[11] The mission impact upon marriage was, however, a more complicated matter than the disfavouring of polygamy. First and foremost it stressed the necessity for the woman of freedom of choice – something formerly present in many African marriages but by no means in all. Probably missionaries underestimated the proportion of marriages in which it had existed; nevertheless the new Christian stress on freedom and its welcoming acceptance by women are undeniable.

In the areas of bridewealth and divorce the value of the missionary input is less easily gauged. Initially missionaries, especially in southern Africa, were emphatically opposed to bridewealth which they regarded as tantamount to the buying and selling of women. Yet they were, of course, strong on indissolubility. It took them some time to realize that within African custom the payment of bridewealth was a guarantee of the bride's recognized value and the most notable force for the permanence of marriage. Some at least did see this as time passed – indeed so much so that in some cases they even tried to introduce the payment of bridewealth among matrilineal peoples where it was not customary. Yet they mostly believed that both insistence upon indissolubility and the restraint (if not abolition) of bridewealth must enhance the status of down-trodden women. In point of fact neither of them did so. In tradition the ill-treated wife would run away to her parents. If a husband wanted her back he would have to convince the parents, offer presents, perhaps abase himself. If he failed to do so he would lose his wife. The very missionary stress upon absolute indissolubility undermined the wife's main post-marital source of protection, just as the early attack on bridewealth undermined the wider family commitment to ensuring that a marriage worked. If the missionary assault upon traditional marriage (and, of course, both varied immensely across the continent) certainly gave something of a new sense of freedom to women, it hardly produced the controlled and ordered freedom missionaries were hoping for.[12] 'A wife of the ring' might all in all be less protected in her dignity than her pagan mother had been. She was probably more conscious of her rights and of a feeling of freedom than of the positive advantages her ring marriage in fact brought her. By the 1930s the Nyakyusa were blaming Christians for the practice of wooing in secret before a man had consulted the father. 'The Christians say "It is good to woo in secret first" but pagan fathers object, saying "We will not eat the cattle properly".'[13] The dislocation of traditional custom in a heavily

44

Christianized country like Buganda had already brought with it a permissiveness on both male and female sides and a dissatisfaction with the new marital order which alarmed missionaries of the second generation. Thus in 1918 the Provincial Commissioner in Buganda wrote to the Chief Secretary that 'local missionaries of both denominations consider that the women should be punishable (in cases of adultery etc.) equally with the men, as in many cases they are the chief offenders. They also suggest whipping as the most suitable penalty. The chiefs whom I consulted concurred, and myself I consider these recommendations sound.' Accordingly a law was passed for the flogging of women and continued until 1927 when it was abolished on account of abuse (Law of 16 November 1927). A popular women's song of the period ran thus:

> I pity very much the man I shall marry
> That man will die of constant quarrelling
> The only advice I offer him
> is to prepare his beating stick beforehand.[14]

'I am fed up with this Christian marriage' ran another Ganda song of that period, '*Ssammanyirirwa*'. A researcher into Igbo women at much the same time observed that for many 'Christian marriage' was seen as a 'prison', polygamous marriage as a more open and socially satisfying institution.[15] 'Our main grievance is that we are not so happy as we were before' declared women rioters comprehensively, if vaguely, at Owerrinta, Nigeria, in 1929.[16]

By this time – the 1920s and 30s – African women had been far overtaken by men on the educational front. We noticed how initially women were often ahead of men in elementary schooling. This did not last long, and it was, surely, an expression of the low esteem in which western education was held. Once society saw the point in schooling, it was the boys who got it. The magisterial Phelps-Stokes Report on *Education in Africa* (A Study of West, South and Equatorial Africa by the African Education Committee) of 1920 declared, 'It is rather surprising that missions and schools have not made more serious efforts to bring the girls into the schools and to provide suitable training for them. The chief reason for this apparent neglect is probably the indifference and sometimes the opposition of the native people themselves to the education of their girls. Schools here followed the line of least resistance, accepting the boys who have applied . . .'(p.24). Compare that with our picture of the little Onitsha school in 1858! The education of girls only really started to improve again on a large scale after the Second World War.

I remember how at the All Africa Conference of Churches in Lusaka in 1974 a distinguished African theologian made an attack on the western imperialist imposition by missionaries of monogamy upon Africa and called on the African church to reject it in favour of the indigenous tradition of polygamy. He was immediately followed by two ladies of striking stature and forcefulness, one from Sierra Leone, the other from South Africa, who insisted that monogamy was the greatest gift the missionary church had brought to African womanhood and that there could not be the slightest question of going back upon it. No more was heard about that. In the nineteenth-century Christian insistence upon monogamy could be more destructive of the lives of women than of men – women prevented, like the Xhosa Princess Emma, from marrying into their class at all,[17] women lower down the social scale rejected by their husbands and separated from their children. In retrospect, however, women had here been the gainers and it is hard to deny that the repeated calls of African theologians in the 1960s and 70s for the church to accept polygamy have been in part at least an expression of male chauvinism. As a matter of fact in due course men had won most of the more spectacular prizes, educational and otherwise, to be obtained by membership of the Christian churches from archbishoprics downwards. In Christian Buganda women were expected to kneel before men as much as ever – and they did so! The acquisition by women of the publicly approved model of monogamous marriage and free marital choice (including the freedom not to marry) is, all the same, not – despite any inconveniences – to be derided or reversed.

But this discussion has taken me rather a long way from the main theme and I would like to return to the earlier phase, of conversion and the first generation, rather than that of establishment and the second generation. In Barotseland when the Paris Mission Society, led by Francois Coillard, arrived in the 1870s they found King Lewanika installed in the capital of Lealui but his sister, Mokwae, as a sort of viceroy in the second city of the realm, Nalolo. Both were much attracted by the missionaries, both were frequently expected to convert but for many years neither did so. Lewanika, like many another African king, said at times that it was just a matter of polygamy – 'without that we should soon be Christians' declared Moshesh of the Basuto. Yet Mokwae was not a polygamist. What really held her and her brother back was principally a much deeper sense of the coherence of their authority, tribal identity and independence with their beliefs and practices. When one considers a great African lady like Mokwae, women cease to be a special case, even if after thirty-five years of hesitation, Mokwae, unlike her brother, did actually become a Christian in 1921.[18] Her husband had preceded her.

Mokwae approached things, I feel, not so much as a woman but rather as did her brother the king, with the caution appropriate to people of power. We have much the same impression of the young women of nineteenth-century Buganda when we manage to get a glimpse of them: they could be as headily radical as their brothers. There were indeed no women among the martyrs of 1885–6 but that was not because there were no female Christian converts willing to be martyred but rather that the customs of Buganda were averse to the killing of women. It is true that one woman, Sara Nakima,[19] had been taken to execution with the very first victims but she was reprieved. When Noe Mwaggali was martyred at Mityana (as we have seen) his sister Munaku actually pleaded with his executioners that they should kill her as well but they refused to do so, simply taking her prisoner. Women were presumably not regarded as being sufficiently responsible to be executed for their behaviour. This may seem the more odd in that it was the Princess Clara Nalumansi who triggered off the persecution in the first place by behaviour which in traditional terms was no less than outrageous. She had cast away her umbilical cord. The martyrs may have died in consequence but Nalumansi remained at the time untouched. The early Ganda female converts appear, then, to have adopted Christianity much as did their brothers and husbands, with the same heady enthusiasm. Missionary insistence upon monogamy did, of course, affect them differently. They were not polygamists: unlike many of the men they did not have to set aside their additional husbands. On the other hand a number of them *were* additional wives – divorced by their husbands at the moment of baptism. In some cases they remarried, in others they adopted the role of pious widowhood in the neighbourhood of a mission. That was the easier in that among some women the call to celibacy was immediately heard. Munaku was the first of these. The commitment she entered into immediately after conversion in 1886 she kept until her death in 1938, spending her life teaching catechism and, later, running the gardens and kitchens of Bukalasa seminary.

This proved not only an option open to drop-outs. The call of female virginity could be heard in the greatest houses in the land. The leader of the Catholics over many years was Stanislaus Mugwanya, the second *Katikiro* (or Prime Minister) and in due course a Knight of St Gregory. His sister, Isabella Birabwa, was married to the county chief of Buddu, the formidable Alikisi Sebbowa. Through long years Sebbowa adhered to monogamy despite the childlessness of Isabella – a considerable moral achievement in missionary eyes. And she was all that a great chief's wife should be, leading the sixty or so women of her household to morning prayers in their chapel, and on Sunday to mass at the mission.[20] Her brother's household was run on similar lines. Yet when in 1897 Mugwanya's daughter, Angela Nabbogo, confided to him that she intended never to marry but 'to work all my life for the Fathers' he was far from pleased: he had already arranged a suitable marriage for her. 'Let both of us pray to Our Lady and whatever she will inspire we shall do,' Angela piously replied. Her will proved the stronger and in due course she did indeed become a nun and remained so for seventy years. Naturally if the great Mugwanya had had to leave his daughter free to do this, lesser fathers could hardly refuse, and this may help to explain the scale of growth of the sisterhood of the Bannabikira. Elsewhere it could be much more of a battle, as in Eastern Zimbabwe (then Rhodesia) where, for instance, in 1937 the Native Commissioner sentenced an aspirant nun named Clara to fourteen days hard labour for refusing to return home. Around Triashill this had been a running battle for decades between the Mariannhill Fathers and an alliance of parents and colonial authorities. 'Freedom of conscience,' wrote Fr Fleischer back in 1911, 'cannot be taken away by parents or guardians. We think a human soul is of greater value than the *lobola*.'[21]

As the church grew more central to African society, it came – as we have seen – to reflect, even reinforce, in most of its central concerns the traditions of male primacy. The training of the clergy and the development of the school system were predominantly to the advantage of men. When the church itself was marginal to society, in an initial liminal period, the women had been more central to it, dangerously central indeed at times as the murder of the Chilubula head women might suggest. At such a moment the church might seem to be reversing society in some sort of ongoing *communitas* experience. But as the church became more socially central, women's roles within it appeared to grow far more marginal: the basic requirements of patriarchy were reasserted. The dominant impression of African Christian life in the great missionary age of the first half of the twentieth century remains not one of the liberation of women but, on the contrary, of a lack of freedom. The new rules of marriage and schooling imposed by the missionary could all in all be more, not less, restrictive than the old. Catholic girls were not free to marry other than Catholics. The immediate experience of Christian conversion was one of freedom from taboo and discrimination; the lasting experience was too often the imposition of a load of burdens enforced as much as ever upon the young by corporal punishment. 'Mother was very strict and did not like to spare the rod,' wrote one woman of her Christian upbringing in the 1930s. 'The Reverend Fathers had taught that it was very wrong to spare the rod, no matter how trivial the offence committed by the child.'[22]

Yet the Catholic sisterhoods, the Protestant female societies like the *Manyano* of South Africa and *Rukwadzano* of Zimbabwe[23] and the striking numerical dominance of women within most Zionist and Aladura churches all suggest that this was only part of the truth. At least from the 1950s one senses a great female comeback in African Christianity, both in the mission churches and in independent churches. The nuns multiply far more than the priests; the organized *Manyano* becomes, despite much male clerical suspicion, the clear centre of religious vitality; the prophetesses multiply – Ma Nku and Ma Mbele, Alice Lenshina and Mai Chaza, Mariam Ragot and Mrs Paul. As communities the churches in Africa returned to being (if in reality they had ever ceased to be) what they were in most places at the start, predominantly feminine entities – perhaps, indeed feminine alternative societies to the male-dominated secular world. At the start and then again from the 1950s the gospel seemed to appeal to women with a special intensity which we may reasonably relate in a broad way to the issue of specifically female freedoms – freedom not to have to abandon your twin children, freedom not to be married off to a rich old polygamist, freedom to be valued sufficiently to be taught in school, freedom to choose your husband, freedom to woo in secret before your father knows, freedom to choose not to marry at all and be a nun, freedom to live an independent existence as a woman, made manifest to the male world by the habit of your order or the red blouse of your *Rukwadzano* membership. It symbolized a female fellowship, at once communal and freely-chosen.

To make the point that women are more religious than men seems so generally true that it hardly helps us here. The question for us is precisely how female religiosity has related to the phenomenal growth of Christianity in Africa over the last 150 years: a process of rapid change. It may, after all, equally be remarked that women are more conservative than men and in point of fact it is a widely observable phenomenon in Africa – particularly in areas of Islamic penetration – that the new religion has come with the men while the custodians of traditional beliefs across several generations of transition have been the women. On this model female religiosity in Africa would not contribute to its Christianizing but on the contrary provide the strongest bulwark of resistance. And that, undoubtedly, was at times the case. The people we have been considering were after all the tiniest minority among women and most of them were socially, politically and even ecclesiastically insignificant. Yet it is equally true that they proved in the long run far from insignificant in religious, social, cultural and even ecclesiastical terms. They were the new women embracing Christian faith because in particular and exciting ways it liberated and elevated. Cross the river with your twins, cast away the umbilical cord, refuse to marry though it deprive your father of *lobola* and outrage even the District Commissioner.

Early Christianity could be socially revolutionary. It was, of course, intended by the missionaries to be so in some ways and not ways entirely different from those perceived by their early female converts – and yet very different too. If the experience of liberation was succeeded in many cases only too quickly by that of a new subjugation, this was hardly alien to the missionary plan but it was for the second generation of Christian women a profound disappointment. Patriarchal Christianity wrapped up in a highly legalistic and authoritarian form, whether Catholic or Protestant, seemed none too liberating. Take the third generation, however, and the women are breaking through regardless, reshaping the realities of African church life according to their intrinsic expectations. It was perfectly possible that missionary Christianity would spread in Africa almost entirely through men, offering gifts of education and status to the male, while generally resisted by the religiosity of women adhering to the cults of tradition. But it was not so and Christianity would have been infinitely weaker if it had been so. There was just enough in the Christian package to ensure that women would put their weight behind the new as well as the old, and then the new much more than the old, until in due course they would in their own way assume the lead and in the second half of the twentieth century ensure the consolidation of Christianity as the religion, not just of the élite or of the institutions of western provenance, but of the countryside and of the *povo*. Their men might take to politics and ensure the triumph of nationalism. The women, while not averse to that cause, would combine it with an at least equal attachment to Christianity. Look, for instance, at Robert Mugabe, the very model of the new African man, and his church-worker sisters or at Maurice Nyagumbo, ZANU's General Secretary, and his sister, a nun. The Christianity of African women with its quest for healing and community and the strength to carry on through poverty, riot and famine, is profoundly other-worldly but profoundly this-worldly too. It is anything but Utopian. It is very patient. It draws at every point upon the traditional religiosity of the pagan past but combines it with a sharper sense of female dignity, social purpose and personal piety culled from Bible and ecclesiastical practice. It is undoubtedly Christianity's principal asset in Africa today and it would probably not be there, at least not with anything like the vigour it has acquired, were it not for the element of feminist liberation which the nineteenth-century male missionary did proclaim – often almost *malgré soi* – and which the female missionary incarnated to very practical effect (though almost never in explicitly feminist terms) not only in such exceptionally memorable figures as Mary Slessor, Mother Kevin or Patricia Chater,[24] but in countless others too. Yes, women were and remain a special case.

4

Mediums, Martyrs and Morals

Every university department and every academic discipline needs its justification. For its own devotees a discipline may well justify itself simply in terms of the pursuit of truth, but for those outside any particular magic circle and especially for the university administrators and government piper-payers dividing up a limited cake among many bidders, the justification will have to be couched in some sort of social form. Even the richest university is not likely to maintain indefinitely a discipline whose only point is the esoteric interest of its experts. This is as true of Religious Studies as of anything else and an inaugural lecture seems as suitable a moment as any for mapping out the rough lines of an appropriate *apologia*. Of course, the *apologia* that I offer will not be quite the same as that which my colleagues might provide. Nevertheless, I would hope that my own way of justifying the discipline and the Department of Religious Studies is not merely subjective, but at least a fair appraisal from the viewpoint of today's Zimbabwe of some of the commanding heights of what is, by any standards, a vast and intriguing territory.

I am not the first to attempt this exercise within this university. My predecessor, the first Professor of Theology, Robert Craig, gave his inaugural lecture here on 20 April 1964. In one way he was, to be precise, not my predecessor because he was Professor of Theology, I of Religious Studies. Our department was renamed three years ago. Yet it is noticeable that his lecture was entitled *Religion, Its Reality and Its Relevance*. We were, then, we may claim, in reality a Department of Religious Studies from the start, as we are explicitly today. Equally, when we changed our name, we did not abandon a concern for theology. We remain committed to the view that the University of Zimbabwe needs the study of

Christian theology, but that Christian theology here, or anywhere, is almost bound to miss its own target if it avoids its proper context, the study of religions.

Where we part company with Professor Craig and also with his successor, Professor T. A. Burkill, is not a recognition of religion beyond the biblical and Christian tradition, but rather in the localization of that wider recognition. Reading their inaugural lectures, the one delivered in 1964, the other in May 1971, I was struck by the total absence from both of the slightest reference to the traditional religions of Africa. The Department had been located very clearly within a tradition of Anglo-Saxon theological thought. It was not located mentally in any significant way within the continent wherein it was placed physically. That was a weakness. The religious experience of Africa is not to be so easily dismissed. It is in fact a highly rewarding subject of study and research, on any grounds; especially for someone at work in the context of today's Zimbabwe, endeavouring as it is to reappropriate in a living way its innate cultural tradition, while not rejecting – needless to say – the vast positive acquisitions drawn from abroad over the last hundred years. At the heart of Zimbabwe's traditional culture lay the religious understanding of its people. Equally, among the acquisitions of the last century nothing has been more taken to the heart of many Zimbabweans than Christian faith. Our department has to stand upon the knife edge where those two traditions meet.

While theoretically the task of a Department of Religious Studies embraces all religions, there has in practice to be a recognition of priorities; ours is to focus attention upon what is most significant for the society of Zimbabwe and its African neighbours: the three great streams of traditional religion, Christianity and Islam.

These religions, their adherents, their beliefs, their interaction with society, actual or potential, are things of great public significance, for the unbeliever as well as for the believer. The social task of a university department is to concentrate its powers of scholarship, interpretation and pedagogy upon that which manifestly bears upon human beings, here and now. It is our claim that today as much as ever religion is immensely important for the understanding and enhancement of human experience. It is not something primarily 'primitive', 'medieval', or of antiquarian interest. It is essentially a modern reality, as it has always been, something culturally continuous with the contemporary world, and to be found present in both the latter's conservative and its radical dimensions. The study of religion is an extremely complex, multi-faceted, exercise – a process which cannot be short-circuited, and which is no more safely dispensable than that of any other major aspect of human living. That is the basic ground of our *apologia* – a ground as sound for the believer in any religion or in none. We do not base our existence as a department in a modern university on the ground of the existence of God or the objectivity of the object of religious belief, but on the objectivity and influence of religion itself as an ongoing human reality.

One way in which the social importance of religion is demonstrated is the number of its full-time practitioners and their wider influence. It is one task of a university to service the major public professions and to enable their members to maintain and improve their specific expertise. A Department of Religious Studies has the responsibility not only of helping society understand religion, but also of helping religion and its leaders understand themselves. Where this does not happen, not only may the churches themselves be gravely hampered in their work, not only will they be diminished in their self-understanding and intellectual flexibility, but society as a whole is left with churches which may be no less influential for being less critically self-aware, less enlightened in their approach to the relationship between religion and society. It is, then, greatly in the interests of society to have a well educated clergy rather than a poorly educated one. A university Department of Religious Studies is one way in which society not only recognizes religion but also influences it, thus to some extent ensuring against the dominance of reactionary religion – a danger to which the modern world remains very much exposed as we may observe, for example, in the Ayatollah Khomeini's Iran.

A department such as ours should, then, be the point not only at which different religious traditions meet but also where a constant dialogue is in progress between religion and society. Such a dialogue is to be conducted without reductionism. Religion is not here to be explained away in terms of psychology, sociology, politics or economics by any full surrender to the dogmas of Freud, Marx or Durkheim. It is accepted as a reality in its own terms, though its understanding does require the constant intervention of psychology, sociology, politics and economics, as abrasive tools of analysis, for religion does not constitute a segregated area of reality but one aspect of the human being's finally single experience.

Much of our subject can, doubtless, be studied in other departments and, of course, it is. We have no complaint that Sociology or History prey upon a great deal of religious material. They have the right to take as much as is of use for their own discipline. It is, indeed, a homage to the importance of our subject that they take a great deal. Here, as throughout the academic world, there is bound to be some overlapping, especially at the more humdrum and quantitative level. Yet for the study of religion in itself the quantitative must, I believe, remain of rather secondary significance. We are certainly interested in Christians and Buddhists, but we are basically a great deal more interested in the Christ and the Buddha. If we wish to grasp the specificity of religion and its peculiar power, we need to focus our attention above all upon its high and formative points, upon the people, moments, ways of behaviour which through some sort of special spiritual intensity escape the regular, more predictable patterns of human living (including more conventional religious behaviour) to forge anew a compelling communicable vision. It is this that millions of less intense people subsequently accept as normative in the understanding of themselves and the world.

It is in an attempt to find some sort of structure for the commanding heights of religious experience that I wish now to turn your attention to mediums, martyrs, morals and also memories, and I intend to illustrate this synthesis above all in African terms.

The unpredictable Christ is certainly not to be dissociated from the predictable Christian. One of our primary concerns, indeed, is just how to link them. The sociology of religion suggests a link in the routinization of charisma. However charismatic the prophet, the charisma, to survive, must needs be routinized through the establishment of predictable structure including, very especially, ritual structure. Ritual, while not necessarily or specifically a religious phenomenon, is the great common carrier and communicator of religious reality. It is, nevertheless, not self-justifying. Doubtless in established churches ritual can and does, to some extent, become an end in itself (though even then one would probably always be able to find a further hidden agenda, aesthetic or social) but healthy ritual always points, and pretty clearly points, to things outside itself: there is a foundation charter behind it and there is a message of moral and social purpose before it.

Take the foundation charter. It is in the nature of ritual to be performed on account of some past authority which it recalls more or less explicitly. At its most explicit this becomes a formal *memoriale*: do this in memory of me. It recalls some unforgettable moment in history, a theophany, the death of a martyr, and the authoritative message of a medium or prophet interpreting that moment. This is, of course, particularly clear in that ritual which, I would suggest, is the most symbolically comprehensive of all – the Christian mass, an explicit memorial meal of the death of Jesus of Nazareth, performed at his own command. But good ritual looks forward still more than it looks back: it renews in fact the essentially non-ritual concerns of the originating moment, concerns of moral and social order, of claiming the future, of symbolically asserting the primacy of the spiritual within the material, of weaving an image of healing and the salvation of human beings. Ritual, then, while being the common language and tool of religion, is in no way its source or its *raison d'être*. It points to non-ritual. It is striking that the most religiously decisive figures are seldom themselves ritual specialists. Here again the Christian example is enlightening: if the mass is ritual, *par excellence*, it recalls Jesus who was in no way whatsoever, so far as is recorded, a ritualist. Religion is carried on and applied by ritual, it is not begun by it. It is begun, just as it is revitalized, by the medium or prophet, and the martyr.

Raymond Firth, in his magnificent sociological study *Rank and Religion in Tikopia*[1] establishes a contrast between the medium and the prophet: the medium does not need to be personally identified with the supernatural message received through him as does the prophet. He is, indeed, more or less unconscious and in a trance, while the spirit speaks directly, not to him but through him, *oratio recta*. The medium has not, as a consequence, to bear personal responsiblity for its interpretation as had Elijah, Isaiah or Jeremiah. Once the message is given, the state of spirit possession terminated, the medium's role is over. The prophet, on the contrary, passes on the message he has received through his own deliberate words and actions, *oratio obliqua*. He remains morally one with the word that he proclaims and, if that word is unpopular, he will have to suffer for it. In formal terms Firth's distinction is a genuine one, and it is certainly possible in practice to separate the two phenomena to a considerable extent. Nevertheless, it would be mistaken to argue for a systematic separation of the two. A prophet must obtain his message and mission from some sort of very special personal experience, and that experience is often mediumistic. In a society where mediums are an important part of the culture, a prophet is most likely to be a medium, just as in very priest-ridden churches a prophet is very likely to be a priest.

To illustrate this one cannot do better than to refer to Shona mediums and, very particularly, the part they played in the first *Chimurenga* of 1896–7. Mediums are crucial to Shona culture and they cannot well be restricted, like Tikopian mediums, within Firth's rather narrow typology. Indeed it is widely true in Africa that the strictly mediumistic activities of the *n'anga* are a fairly small part of a wider pastoral or priestly ministry though not, normally, a particularly prophetic ministry. Through them the ancestral spirits regulate the morals of family and clan. But the mediums of the great *Mhondoro* have frequently had a wider role. That of Chaminuka in the wars against the Ndebele, that of Nehanda and Kagubi in the first *Chimurenga* became far more that of a prophet than – in Firth's typology – that of a mere medium.[2]

In 1967 Professor Terence Ranger in his classic *Revolt in Southern Rhodesia 1896–7* went so far as to claim – in this representing much earlier opinion – that the religious personalities of the revolt, like Mkwati, Kagubi and Nehanda, were in fact its true political leaders, combining prophetic fervour with an amazingly wide-ranging political skill. Kagubi, in particular, he maintained, played 'a very important role in co-ordinating the rising at a supra-tribal level'.[3] More recently other historians, especially Julian Cobbing and David Beach,[4] have sharply challenged this thesis and demonstrated, on the whole fairly convincingly, that the leadership of the rising, both among the Ndebele and among the Shona, was far more firmly in lay and chiefly hands than Ranger had argued. In terms of power, of the effective initiation and co-ordination of the movements of rebellion, this is doubtless the case.[5] Our conclusion, nevertheless, should not be that Kagubi and Nehanda did not matter, that the popular mythology which has remembered them so emphatically is somehow groundless. It means rather that their truly religious and prophetic function should not, in interpretation, be over-politicized. Theirs was not so much one of straight political leadership. It is in fact unlikely to be a prophetic stance for a priest to become Prime Minister even in a state of emergency. His influence is not thereby enhanced. The prophetic role is rather one of the instilling of enthusiasm and a more than rational conviction, of moral interpretation, of the construction and enhancement of an ongoing tradition of meaning, of the symbolization of a cause in a single person.

The achievement of Kagubi and Nehanda should, I suspect, be seen on such lines. It had, furthermore, not a little to do with their dying, executed in a colonial prison in 1898, though it is true that Kagubi's Christian baptism immediately before execution adds a further touch of ambiguity – yet a very authentic one – to his message. He had proclaimed national salvation through the killing of the White invaders. It had not worked. Now by becoming one of the first of his people to be baptized a Catholic Christian, while surely not ceasing to be a Shona nationalist, he did in fact point prophetically enough to the future. Nor should the deaths of Nehanda and Kagubi be entirely separated in our view from that of the Anglican catechist, Bernard Mizeki, upon the other side. The scope of prophetic martyrdom at that point can encompass both. When in April 1977, in the second *Chimurenga*, Basil Nyabadza, priest of the little church of St Francis, Makoni, was shot at night by security forces beside his church, these two martyr traditions – that of Nehanda upon the one side, Mizeki upon the other – somehow coalesced. Each prophet, each martyr-witness, has his limitation; yet each from a brief localized set of events generates a myth, an ongoing *memoriale*, a story with its own in-built moral imperative for people to come.

Eighty years earlier than Kagubi and Nehanda there lived two, perhaps still more remarkable, African prophets – Nxele and Ntsikana. These two Xhosa mediums, one of whom died in 1820, the other in 1821, present in an extaordinary way the intellectual and moral alternatives that Africans had then, and have had many times since, to face. As a recent writer, J. B. Peires, has remarked, 'The contrast between the two would surely be taken for a myth if it were not known to be a reality.'[6] At the time when they lived, British colonialism was pressing upon the Xhosa and driving them eastward from their homes with a ruthlessness that they had previously never experienced. Both Nxele and Ntsikana were mediums who had come into contact with Christianity. Nxele reacted to become the prophet of violent resistance, a true predecessor to Kagubi. He died attempting to escape from Robben Island. Ntsikana was the pacifist, the preacher of submission, but of much more than submission. He was the author of some of the most powerful oral literature of southern Africa – his Great Hymn above all.[7] Like Jeremiah he taught by symbols. As he lay dying, he asked his family to bury him in the ground in the Christian way. When they appeared to hesitate he grasped a wooden spade and turned the first sods. Ten thousand men marched behind Nxele in his attack upon Grahamstown; hardly a handful of people were convinced by Ntsikana, yet many millions have since sung his hymns. If prophecy is largely concerned with evil and the proper response to it, it is likely to oscillate between the two poles of militant resistance and pacifism. This has seldom been better shown than in the contrast between Nxele and Ntsikana.

Twenty-five years after Kagubi, in 1921, Simon Kimbangu began one of the most striking of prophetic movements in modern Africa in the country of the Bakongo. He had many of the characteristics of a traditional medium, an *ngunza*; he had also a Christian, Baptist, background and the conviction that God had called him personally to a mission of preaching and healing. His attitude to authority appears consistently pacifist, his teaching both theistic and moralistic. Crowds flocked to hear him. Simon was quickly judged a threat to colonial order; he was arrested, flogged during his trial, and sentenced to death on the flimsiest of charges. The sentence was commuted by the King of the Belgians to one of life imprisonment and for thirty years Kimbangu remained in prison, never once permitted a visit by either a member of his family or a Protestant pastor. He died on a Friday afternoon in October 1951. Out of that long silence grew the Kimbanguist *Eglise*.

Twentieth-century Africa has been replete with prophets and a vast literature has arisen concerning them since Bengt Sundkler wrote in 1948 his seminal *Bantu Prophets in South Africa*.[8] Between them and mediums there are obvious links of similarity or – at times – near identity. Their individual significance varies. Only a few are truly prophetic. As a whole they represent a wrestling between the tradition of the medium and the tradition of the Bible as rural society as a whole passes through the pangs of altering its prime religious identity. If I have selected Kimbangu from among them, it is because he seems to me to express what this is all about at its most decisive but also most enigmatic. There is an apparently unbridgeable gap in causality between those few months of almost incoherent mission in 1921 and the great Kimbanguist church of today. Despite the many books and scores of articles devoted to him, he remains a figure of mystery which we can hardly dissect in cool secular terms. Perhaps more than anyone else in modern African history he is a Christ-figure – medium and prophet, suffering servant, the giver of a foundation charter for what is today a large and thriving community.

The controversy over the role of mediums in the *Chimurenga* is not entirely unlike that provoked at much the same time concerning the political character of Jesus of Nazareth. What sort of a prophet was he? Just one year after Ranger's *Revolt* Professor S. G. F. Brandon published his remarkable study, *The Trial of Jesus of Nazareth*, in which he claimed that Jesus had been a far more political figure than the gospels suggest and that it was precisely as a dangerous rebel leader that he was executed by the Romans. The gospels depict Jesus in frequent conflict with the 'collaborationist' Sadducees and Pharisees, they are quite silent about his opinion of the Jewish nationalist resistance movement, the Zealots. They do, however, consistently portray him as someone who had rejected a pursuit of 'the kingdoms of the world' (Matt. 4.8) as his greatest temptation, who taught his followers in the Sermon on the Mount to shun violent resistance and who, when directly challenged over the morality of paying the imperial taxes, replied, 'Give to Caesar what is Caesar's.' Yet Brandon, and he was by no means the first scholar so to argue, maintained that this sort of picture of Jesus was a highly misleading one. It was a picture influenced more by the preoccupations of second generation Roman Christians than by the historical facts. For him Jesus' plan during his last free days in Jerusalem had been no less than a 'Messianic *coup d'état*' against the existing order. It was 'dynamic political action of a revolutionary kind', 'a direct challenge to the Roman government of Judaea'. Jesus' action in the Temple was, Brandon even suggests, part of a wider 'concerted attack' in which the main force of the Zealots led by Barabbas assaulted the Romans themselves in the fortress of the Antonia.[9]

Jesus, the Freedom Fighter, the Kagubi, the Nxele, organizer of a messianic *coup d'état*, is a beguiling figure, especially in an age of liberation theology. Alas, while we cannot here explore the ins and outs of this exceedingly learned controversy, we have, I think, to accept that Brandon's arguments have been refuted.[10] Jesus was far too consistently un-Zealotlike. While he was not by any means an 'other-worldly' prophet uninterested in the things of here and now, justice and oppression, he did quite deliberately transcend the exceedingly narrow, nationalist and essentially reactionary outlook of his Zealot contemporaries. Far from sharing with Barabbas a seat on the revolutionary central committee, he was a good deal nearer to Jeremiah, Ntsikana, and Kimbangu.

Brandon dealt with Jesus a little too much in the way in which Ranger dealt with Kagubi: both tried to force their religious heroes into overly political categories. It is worth noting in passing how well these two books of 1967–8 reflect the religious mood of those years with its rather optimistic rechannelling of religious fervour in political directions – the age of the conference of the Latin American bishops at Medellín, of the World Council at Uppsala. Of course some prophets are, and need to be, a good deal more overtly political than others. On the whole, however, their *raison d'être* is not to organize the coming kingdom on the model of some immediate revolutionary programme. The prophet's task is rather to insinuate and symbolize his vision in a more immediately impractical, a more ultimately undefeatable way.

As we see again and again, he or she may well do this most decisively by martyrdom, as Socrates did. 'Unless the seed going into the earth die . . .' There is a strange, almost perverse, consistency in this odd world of ours between prophecy and martyrdom. It is, first of all, a biblical and Christian theme as Professor Geoffrey Lampe has recently stressed in a beautiful little posthumous study 'Martyrdom and Inspiration'.[11] Jesus' own scathing denunciation of Scribes and Pharisees as 'sons of those who murdered the prophets . . . Jerusalem, Jerusalem, still killing the prophets' (Matt. 23.31) doubtless helped to ensure that he himself went the same way. When Stephen, the Christian protomartyr, is stoned to death he is depicted by the author of Acts as continuing the tradition. But this is not just a biblical and Christian motif; it is rather a central pattern of religion itself.

In the letter to the Romans Paul commented on the meaning of Jesus' death in oft-quoted words: 'While we were yet helpless, at the right time Christ died for the ungodly. Why, one will hardly die for a righteous man – though, perhaps, for a good man one will dare even to die. But God shows his love for us in that while we are yet sinners Christ died for us' (Rom. 6.6–8). If Christians have used these verses to suggest the unique moral character of what Jesus did, they could perhaps still better be taken as referring to a peak of creative self-sacrifice which is to be found on rare occasions in many of man's noblest traditions. When Maximilian Kolbe in the Nazi concentration camp of Auschwitz volunteered to replace another prisoner in the starvation chamber, and died there encouraging his fellow victims to the last, he became, perhaps, the most perfect such figure of our age: in that very hell he incarnated a morality of love against one of hate. His memory lives on. But his very achievement of being in the mid-twentieth century a priest-prophet turned martyr authenticates the possibility of many such a person in the more easily myth-derided past. You cannot very easily demythologize Maximilian Kolbe, any more than you can really very successfully demythologize Nxele and Ntsikana or Basil Nyabadza. Nor, for that matter, Nelson Mandela, enduring twenty years of imprisonment on Robben Island for the freedom of his people. These people really do exist. They do accept suffering and death for the sake of the message that they proclaim, and their combination of witness and suffering really does forge an ongoing moral tradition, the living memorial of a committed community.

Let us turn now to a seemingly far more mythical figure – the 'priest-king' destined never to die in his bed of old age, who dominated the vast tapestry of Sir James Frazer's stupendous survey of religious phenomena, *The Golden Bough*.[12] For Frazer the key for the interprctation of religion was the King-Priest in the grove of Diana at Nemi in classical times, awaiting night by night the murderer who would inherit his crown and continue his function. The king must so die as not to die. The king never dies. Long live the king. Upon his death and life depends the life of nature and society. Frazer seemed to imagine that if some such mystical formula can be found at the heart of all religion, Christianity included, then they must all be equally invalid.

Frazer did stand in need of some hard contemporary evidence that such things were not just part of the classical imagination, and he found his best evidence in reports which anthropologists like the Seligmans brought back to Europe early this century from the Sudan about the customs of the Shilluk and Dinka. They indeed, it seemed, really did possess divine kings who, generation after generation, were never allowed to die naturally but either arranged their own deaths or were deliberately killed by their subjects, on the principle of Caiaphas that 'one man should die for the people so that the whole nation should not perish' (John 11.50). As the author of the Fourth Gospel commented, 'He, being high priest that year, prophesied.' Here among Shilluk and Dinka the myth at the heart of all religion was, apparently, still being factually realized.

Sir Edward Evans-Pritchard disagreed. Probably the most distinguished social anthropologist of this century, he had ceased to share Frazer's agnosticism and perhaps in some unformulated way he felt that, if the Shilluk king's ritual murder really never took place, this somehow weakened the ground beneath Frazer's vast debunking of religion. Anyway, when in 1948 he delivered the Frazer lecture, Evans-Pritchard devoted himself to demythologizing Shilluk regicide. He greatly doubted whether Shilluk kings had ever really been killed in the traditional way when they became sick or old. The myth of regicide, he argued, was really simply a cloak for a socio-political order in which the royal power was weak and rebellions frequently occured.[13]

I greatly admire Evans-Pritchard, but here I have to disagree. It really will not do. The Shilluk evidence in recent times may be inconclusive but that for their closely related Dinka neighbours is not. No one, I think, can read Godfrey Lienhardt's *Divinity and Experience* and be left with any doubt that, well into the twentieth century, aged Masters of the Fishing Spear really have died at the hands of their friends and followers. If this is true for the Dinka Spear Master, it seems unlikely that mystical regicide never had a factual basis in the case of the Shilluk *Reth*. For the British colonial authority murdering an aged chief, with or without his consent, was – quite understandably – a disgraceful and primitive custom, to be stamped out. I would suggest that, from both the Dinka perspective and that of world religions, it could also be seen as providing a peak of spiritual and moral experience, to be put beside creative martyr deaths in so many other traditions. The identification, world-wide, of hints of Frazer's central myth, far from destroying its inner objective credibility witnesses rather to a sort of trans-cultural spiritual need. The heroic meeting of such need seems to me already a kind of truth, rather than a kind of falsehood.

The Masters of the Fishing Spear, we are told, 'carry the life' of their people, they are 'the lamps of the Dinka'.[14] Mediums, they and they alone are possessed by the divinity *Ring* (flesh) which, Lienhardt explains, is 'the principal inspiration of masters of the fishing-spear, the grounds of their ability ideally to "light the way", to pronounce and define truth, to prevail in prayers, and to reconcile conflicting groups and interests'.[15]

In much of this the Spear Master is not very different from many other sacred chiefly figures. What is special to him, as to the Shilluk *Reth* and the divine queen of the Lovedu, is that he is also *ex professo* a martyr-to-be. He does not kill himself. In some cases he may indeed be killed by his people against his will, but typically and also in many cases in historical fact, an aged Master has invited his people to bury him alive – not for his sake but for theirs. Lying in his grave, he will give his people his last advice. When he ceases to speak, they will cover him with dung and out of death, freely accepted, life will be renewed. In a typical Dinka text we read: 'He will not be afraid of death; he will be put ino the earth while singing his songs. Nobody among his people will wail or cry because their man is dead. They will be joyful because their master of the fishing spear will give them life.'[16]

Strange and horrifying as such a rite may seem to the outsider, is it so much more strange than the sacrificial willingness of many a soldier to die for his country, or, again, the confidence of Jesus when going to his death: 'He began to teach them that the Son of Man must . . . be killed, and after three days rise again' (Mark 8.31)? In the Spear Master, as in Jesus, we have a bonding together of the bearer of absolute truth, sacrificial death and the ordered ethical life of man, the new covenant – medium, martyr, morality.

The death of a Master of the Fishing Spear is not merely exemplary, indeed it is hardly exemplary at all; it is, rather, vicarious and expiatory. It is in fact redemptive. It seems silly for Christian theologians to want to whittle down the sense of Christ's death into a matter of mere exemplarity, when the martyr deaths of historic figures across the world are clearly so much more. Martyrdom is the sealing through suffering and death of commitment to a cause held absolutely with love of the martyr's fellow human beings, in a way so powerfully to commend the martyr's message as to require its remembrance: its handing on, its *traditio*. It originates a memorial ritual and around it a moral community. The further martyrdom of disciples reinforces the strength of both. Each dying Spear Master renews the meaning of the rituals. The death of each freedom fighter, we may well remember on 16 June, Soweto Day, enhances the sacred significance of their cause. The early Christians triumphed especially through their uncompromising commitment to the acceptance of martyrdom: *Sanguis martyrum*. It is through the constancy of the martyr and the near-martyr confessor in prison – whether it be the prisons of ancient Rome, of Auschwitz, of Robben Island, of the Gulag Archipelago, that prophecy is proved, that certain principles of living are witnessed to, compellingly, as having an absolutely absolute claim, come fair weather, come foul weather, upon human beings.

Within the material order it seems impossible to find an absolute morality. It is neither morally good nor bad that a volcano erupts to destroy the towns and kill the people in the vicinity. It is not wicked for a lion to devour a lamb, nor for a crocodile to snatch to her death the woman washing clothes in the river. If human beings are but the development of the lion or the ape with an enlarged cranial capacity, they may grow more shrewd in their lifestyle, more calculating in their treatment of others, but a principle of material utility cannot turn itself into a quite different one of moral obligation. In material terms there is no evident reason why we should not wipe out a backward tribe and give their land to the more technically advanced. The survival of the fittest is a sensible enough norm in terms of the overall advantage of the race.

If humans are perennially conscious that the order of power, of efficiency, even of the greatest benefit of the greatest number, is not an adequately exacting norm for the conduct of human affairs, it is because we cannot escape the sense of there being an absolute morality. Human beings are not, obviously enough, compelled to be good, but – unlike the crocodile – they consciously belong to an ethical world in which action is always judgable in ultimately moral terms. Like Kant I find it hard to make sense of such a predicament except by positing an ultimate, objective and divine principle of ethical value which, as Thomas Aquinas would say, is what we call God. Nothing less can leap the hurdle from the pragmatic and the utilitarian to the absolute.

The moral sense exists, I am suggesting, in a way that is, at least implicitly, theistic, but its objective referent and its power to command are never well secured by reason alone. In practice it needs to be channelled and goaded on by the authority of specific revelation. That is where the medium, the prophet, the martyr is so decisively important – together with his memorial, even the centenary celebration of his death and burial in Highgate Cemetery.

At the first of this university's new series of public lectures the Prime Minister, Robert Mugabe, while outlining the sort of university he wanted, appealed for both socialist philosophers and socialist theologians. We were, of course, in our department pleased at this explicit recognition of the need for both its sections, but there was at that point some laughter and the Prime Minister twice repeated 'socialist theologians'.[17] I wonder why exactly people laughed. It is not a particularly new idea. Professor Craig may not himself have been a socialist, but undoubtedly the subject which was most his own and on which he wrote his principal book was *Social Concern in the Thought of William Temple*.[18] Temple was, of course, the most influential figure in English church life in the first half of this century. He began as a philosopher don at Oxford, and he died as Archbishop of Canterbury. Now it was Temple who declared as long ago as 1908: 'The alternatives stand before us – Socialism or Heresy; we are involved in one or the other.'[19]

That was surely a word of prophecy, even if it could also be judged the seemingly simplistic words of an enthusiastic young man. He himself might have wished to qualify it later but he would not, I think, ever have repudiated it. Temple was not a medium – the socio-cultural pattern of twentieth-century Britain takes other forms – but he was in the eyes of many a great prophet. So, if Craig was the disciple of Temple but also the founder of our department and one of the most influential figures in the development of this university, of which he was vice-chancellor for many years, we are entitled to claim that our own foundation charter includes within it a commitment to theological socialism. We do not need to invent this prophet's mantle today but only to wear it appropriately for our time.

I do not want to explore here the issues of what socialism should really mean for us except to say that it does, I believe, consist less in a particular system of economics or politics or even a theory of history, and very much more in a passionate ethical commitment to seeking, through the adjustment of social structures, the good of all, the poor and the weak first of all. Probably Temple never really worked out what he meant by it; in that he would not be unusual. To understand its relationship to religion today, I would turn rather to martyrs like Camilo Torres and Oscar Romero, or even to that present labourer in the shipyard at Gdansk, Lech Walesa. What all these people would agree about is that religion, especially the religion of prophets and martyrs, and Christianity very much in particular, is all about morality – a relevant, liberating, contemporary morality, personal and social. Christianity has often been exceedingly spiritualized but, like most African religions, it does basically relate morality very deeply to the material and the communal – to bread and wine, to flesh and blood, to bodies. Temple, to quote him once more, was not mistaken when he called Christianity the most materialist of religions. It is, indeed, all about 'flesh'. Certainly religion cannot escape from morality. It may be confirmatory or it may be challenging to existing society, to the mores of our world. It may, of course, like the Spear Master's death, be both at once. I would hold that the contemporary moral challenge of prophetic religion should be at once socialistic and personalistic in a ceaseless urging of justice for all, and by all I mean all.

To what conclusion have we come? I have sought to provide, in a somewhat rambling manner, a basic model for religion as a working primary reality, recognizable world-wide across human experience but illustrated here by a Christian-African dialogue. Is it true? The religion of the Dinka can hardly be valid for the non-Dinka, but it worked pretty well for the Dinka. Is the spiritual achievement of the dying Spear Master invalidated, or is it not rather enhanced by that other figure of the young carpenter, all bloodied with beating and a crown of thorns, going yet eagerly to his death 'for many' on the hill of Golgotha? Are both just myths? As Peires has said of Nxele and Ntsikana, each must 'surely be taken for a myth if it were not known to be a reality'. Where does the one begin, the other end?

The study of religion remains rooted in the study of history. The people we have spoken of are real people; their deaths, real deaths. Are their dreams, their convictions, their inner willingness to suffer and die for truth and goodness and the freedom of their brethren, as they see them, just myths, or reality too? That the religious leaders and systems of the past were limited enough and in part self-deceiving is not hard to believe. But if they were wholly deceived, then our world is surely a drearier place, the arena only of material pressures, of the survival of the fittest, of sophisticated up-graded crocodiles, of some accidental concourse of atoms. Mediums, martyrs, morality, these things stand together to assert absolute ultimacy of meaning over non-meaning, and it is to the human sense that ultimate meaning is perennially worth searching for that both Philosophy and Religious Studies are committed. That is our *apologia*. I believe it to be a sufficient one.

5

Ganda Catholic Spirituality[1]

The church of Villa Maria is very old, the oldest building in all its countryside. It stands amid the green hills and the banana plantations and above the papyrus swamps of the *ssaza* or 'county' of Buddu in Uganda. It is a dark place – dark at least in comparison with the bright equatorial sun outside – but vast and well able to accommodate beneath its interlacing roof beams some thousands of the Banna-buddu. It stands unchanging in its great cross form with twenty massive white pillars, its little round-headed windows and the smell of countless bats inhabiting the inaccessible rafters.

Besides its age and size, this church possesses a great holiness, for it goes back almost to the age of the martyrs and it was here that so many had to come from afar, before the modern parishes were set up, for baptism and catechism and confirmation. It is here that the priests have been made year after year since 1913, hallowed, respected men who mastered Latin when learning was still something rare and wonderful. They were trained for years in the seminary of Katigondo on the hill above, and then they knelt here in the great sanctuary by the bishop's throne, and here they were anointed and priested – in more recent years by the African bishop of Masaka, but formerly by Munsenyere Stensera himself,[2] the apostle of Buddu, their grandfather in the faith. It was he who founded the mission back in the last century, at the very time of the civil war, he who began the baptism register whose opening entry is dated 1891; it was he who built this present church in the last years of the old century after its predecessor had been burnt down in 1897 in *Kabaka* Mwanga's final revolt when Gabrieli Kintu, the *Mujasi*, general of the army, earlier the Catholic's own champion and war leader, had re-embraced the ancient political loyalties (while retaining his

69

Christian faith) in the last organized struggle of the kingdom against the power of the white men. Yes, it was Munsenyere Stensera who founded the mission and built the church and ordained the first priests.[3] It was he, with simple faith, iron determination and effective planning, who made of all this land a Catholic countryside and impressed on it his own ideals and enthusiasm, the strength and the narrowness of the Catholicism of his own homeland far away in Alsace. And his residence, the *Tabarca*, is there just above Villa Maria church, cool and thick-walled and attractive, a farm-house of Alsace, still housing faded photographs and the simple furniture of a missionary bishop. But most important of all he himself is here, buried close below the main altar, awe-inspiring still in his presence, a shrine where the people come to pray.

A hundred years later the church of Villa Maria stands, as do a number of other late nineteenth-century African churches, as the historic symbol of a quite decisive religious and spiritual conversion which has taken place within African life across the continent and across the coming and going of colonialism: a mixed and muddled conversion it certainly has been, yet no less decisive for that, and nowhere more decisive than in the county of Buddu which became, in due course, the principal part of the modern diocese of Masaka.

Bishop Stensera died in 1952 after years of quiet retirement in the *Tabarca*. Six years later, in October 1958, I arrived as a young man, the only white priest incardinated in this proto-black diocese, and was given a room in the now unoccupied *Tabarca*. I was to be a curate of the parish of Villa Maria. From then until 1966 I lived as a member of the diocesan clergy. I was most warmly welcomed and made to feel very much at home. For most of the time I was teaching in the minor seminary of Bukalasa, under its rector (and later martyr), Father Clementi Mukasa. However, for fifteen months at the beginning and three months at the end I worked as a parish curate and it is this experience which I mostly draw on here. I did not go to Masaka to investigate its working or the behaviour of its members but to serve, to learn from my elders, to give what I could. Now many years later a few personal reflections can only take a rather impressionistic form – an attempt to express something of a way of life and a pattern of spirituality which appear to me undeniably both African and Catholic, expressive of a quiet symbiosis which had occurred, quite unconnected with appeals for authenticity or any systematic search for Africanization.

Masaka diocese was established with an African bishop, Mgr Joseph Kiwanuka, in 1939; all its parishes had already been manned by African priests for some six years before that. White Fathers remained in the diocese on the staff of the major seminary at Katigondo, the minor at Bukalasa, and as chaplains to the generalates of the African sisters and brothers (Bannabikira at Bwanda, Bannakaroli at Kiteredde), though subsequent to my arrival they returned to take over two new parishes (Kalungu and Katimba) at the repeated request of the bishop; however by then they had withdrawn from Bwanda and Kiteredde, as they have done now also from Bukalasa, the minor seminary. In 1961 Mgr Kiwanuka became Archbishop of Rubaga and was succeeded as Bishop of Masaka by Mgr Adrian Ddungu.

So when I arrived at Villa Maria in 1958 I came to a diocese which had been in African hands for twenty years and to a parish which, founded in 1891, had been under African direction for over twenty-five years. Bigada, my second parish, had been founded in 1938 and there had never been any European priest resident there before me, though occasionally people had gone there for a few weeks to learn the language.

I say this to show why Masaka can be taken as a good example for discussing African Christian spirituality. It was, at the time, untypical from the Catholic point of view. Nowhere else in the whole continent has there been for so long such a relative absence of external missionary influence. Although, of course, that influence was not completely absent here. The diocese was small in size (100 miles north-south, 60 miles east-west, roughly) and the remaining White Fathers would undoubtedly have heard about all that was going on and their influence remained very strong with the bishop (himself, though Muganda, a member of their society). The old missionary bishop, Mgr Streicher who first arrived in 1891 and retired in 1933, returned to Villa Maria and remained there until his death and burial in 1952. While very careful not to interfere in the running of the diocese, he undoubtedly remained influential in private.

The Catholicism and spirituality of Masaka diocese grew over the decades out of the interaction of two primary influences, each very positive and each very sympathetic to the other: Baganda society and the White Fathers. They had in some sense been welded together across a decade of persecution, civil war and social upheaval during the 1880s and 1890s. Upon the one side there was Buganda in all its pride, a very authoritarian society in which king and county chiefs could act with impunity in a highly arbitrary manner and continued to do so after Christian conversion. Alikisi Sebbowa, county chief for many decades, was not a man to be trifled with. This was a society with a long history, intense national consciousness, great quickness off the mark in embracing new things but always so as to incorporate them within the traditional system; in many ways it was profoundly conservative, but also comfortably wealthy by African standards; it is the class of the solid small farmer which has been most closely identified with the church. Upon the other side were the early White Fathers, mostly French, many of them remarkable linguists, nearly all of them deeply in love with the country, its people and language (the quite special love affair lasting across several generations between missionaries and Buganda is an interesting phenomenon), ultramontane in their church loyalties, intensely Marian in their personal piety, tending to Jansenism in their moral attitudes, equally authoritarian, utterly uncompromising when they judged an issue of principle to be at stake. Their words and commandments, mediated across the minds of several generations of Catholic Baganda, took on something of the character of a foundation charter from which it is not safe to deviate, a charter guaranteed both by their real moral grandeur and by an almost mythical status which the greatest of them acquired with the years – Mapera and Stensera, Lourdel and Streicher.

While Buganda was dominated by Protestants in court and capital, in Masaka it was the other way round. The greater part of the diocese consisted of Buddu county, the most important single county in Buganda and the main Catholic stronghold. Its county chief and almost all its *gombolola* chiefs were and had to be Catholics. Bishop and county chief were the twin heads of society and for a long time they both lived near Villa Maria. There were pockets of Muslims and Protestants, and some 'pagans' among the old, the poor and (especially) immigrants, but the majority of the population by 1958 considered itself Catholic.

In Masaka diocese as elsewhere there have been various changes in recent years as a consequence of the Second Vatican Council and the convictions of a new generation of priests. These changes, however, have probably been less and slower in coming in Masaka than in most places – or almost anywhere else in Africa. For the most part they are not quickly welcomed by the people, the majority of the clergy, or the bishop. The strongest pressure group in favour of them would be the few foreign priests still connected with the diocese. My observations, anyway, relate chiefly to 1958–9 and not at all to anything after May 1966 when I ceased to live in the diocese (six months after the close of the Vatican Council), and certainly very little change indeed had taken place by then.

I remember early in my time at Villa an elderly man sympathizing with my language difficulties and then remarking enthusiastically, 'Soon you will be able to preach splendidly *Katonda, Katonda, Katonda.'* *Katonda* is the name of God the creator. I once asked my fellow curate, Fr Yohana Ssewajje, a man in his sixties, what he had been teaching about – he taught people with unimpeded fluency and at great length but with little or no preparation. *'Ebigambo bya Katonda'* he replied emphatically, hurrying away to work in his beloved garden, 'the words of God'. The basic Luganda catechism is entitled *Eddini ya Katonda* – the religion of God, and very little is said about Jesus Christ for many pages. I feel that this is a profound characteristic of traditional Ganda spirituality: it is emphatically the worship of *Katonda*, whose name was well known before the missionaries ever came. Indeed the success of much of their work and the way it could be received in depth came precisely from this, that it was a revelation about the *Katonda* they already knew. This was reinforced by Cardinal Lavigerie's instructions to his missionaries that in the first years of the catechumenate, very probably the most impressionable years, they were not to go beyond natural theology.

There has never been a complete Catholic Luganda edition of the Bible; even the publication of the full text of the four gospels came relatively late in the day. The decisive literature was the catechism, hymn books, certain standard Catholic prayers, the salvation history (an extensive summary of biblical history) and a church history. There was no attempt whatsoever to Africanize hymns, prayers or ritual; everything was imported, translated and accepted as it stood. In the early years of the century, when Masaka's model was firmly

laid down, no other way of doing things would have been considered.
Certainly there have been linguistic changes over the years (at least
in the earlier years) but it is easily forgotten that these have taken
place and that the founder, Mapera (Fr Lourdel), did not really
speak in Luganda quite as we do now. The *kibina*, body of Christians,
received the legacy as a whole and is faithful to it. Probably in no
part of Africa was there less desire to introduce drums, dancing or
African hymn tunes into church. On the contrary, much of that
could appear extremely shocking except to the young. Nevertheless
what was inherited has been in a real way assimilated and Africanized. It was clear to my ears that their way of singing hymns of
European origin was not all in all a European way. Seventy years
of hymn singing produced their own pattern, very different from
what one would find in Europe.

The importance of the sacramental-ritual dimension in Ganda
religious life is unquestionable. Masses were well attended on
Sundays and the major feast days, people still walking miles to get
to the parish church rather than make do with the catechist's service
in the village chapel (though, of course, the majority of people
went to the latter; almost everyone in the more distant villages).
Confession was much in demand, often (as in Europe) from devout
people with little to confess, but it was also an important way of
coping with serious sin and with ambiguous situations: an effective
method of making peace with a person's Christian half after serious
relapse into non-Christian practices.

The pattern of liturgy seemed from the clerical end strongly
objective and hierarchical, rather than flexible, intelligible and
participatory; in all this it would, of course, be conforming with
standard conservative Catholic practice elsewhere. And yet it had
a genuinely participatory quality as well. While the priest prayed in
Latin the people, led by a catechist, repeated loudly together in
Luganda prayers which carefully corresponded with those of the
celebrant. This was a strikingly different practice from anything one
was likely to experience in western Europe at that time – and indeed
visiting Europeans often commented upon it with irritation.

Special rituals were often rather drearily performed, with
considerable care to get them formally right but little to make them
intelligible or impressive to the people. The lengthy sermons on
such occasions would relate less to the meaning of this specific ritual

than to general moral exhortation – to avoid drunkenness and Communism, to pay church tax and send your children to school. At sung mass communion could not be given in the mass at all, but only afterwards (this was changed not long after). Sanctuaries were wide; there were many little boys dressed up in red cassocks and white cottas around the altar but the people were a long way off and down a number of steps. At the school mass on a weekday for the Junior Secondary boys, I tried to remedy this and encourage participation by bringing the boys (aged roughly twelve to twenty) up into the sanctuary, in and around the benches reserved to the clergy, but I was forbidden to do this as it was said to be improper for such boys to occupy the places of senior people (*abakulu*).

Vast crowds attended at Easter and Christmas, if it was not raining; other very popular days were Ash Wednesday, Palm Sunday and Corpus Christi. The special rituals of the imposition of ashes, the blessing and bearing of palms in procession, the outside eucharistic procession all the way from Bwanda, were greatly loved. So was holy water used daily for sprinkling in the home. A large amount of water was blessed each Sunday by a priest in the sacristy before mass, and many people placed their bottles outside the door which the sacristan then filled up with the blessed water. On the other hand, baptism seemed to be performed in an almost perfunctory manner. Fathers or other relatives very seldom attended the baptism of their children. The regular time for baptism was a fixed one (say Wednesday 10 a.m.) and there was often a long row of mothers with their babies, each with one godparent. Many parents certainly did not delay the baptism of their children, which might take place within two or three weeks of birth. The mothers and babies sat quiet, cheerful, relaxed; the ritual was carried out almost casually and without much explanation. I was surprised to find one large and well established parish church where no one had ever bothered to provide a font, and I believe there were others. For baptism a common basin and pepsi-cola bottle might be used. The relaxed, casual manner did not signify that baptism was not thought important. On the contrary. It was rather an expression of its complete acceptance as a ritual of life, though in many cases of people living far from church it was long delayed.

Beside the major feasts the whole round of saints' days was undoubtedly something appreciated. Popular calendars were printed each year, including a name or two names for every day of the year, and some people were named according to the saint of the day of their birth. Every now and then someone turned up with his whole family for mass because it was his feast day. The angels were, undoubtedly, particularly popular. The early catechism has a considerable section about angels, including the names of Michael, Raphael and Gabriel; and these three names were certainly frequently chosen by Baganda Catholics.

I became very conscious of the special character of Villa Maria as a holy place, a sort of religious city in which a few priests, nuns and other specially devoted church people lived but to which vast numbers came for the great festivals, for an ordination or the celebration of a jubilee, or when they were sick. The tomb of Munsenyere Stensera, in the middle of the great church, a little to one side of the high altar, was a particular place of veneration and prayer. Around the church were a multitude of schools and below them the large old hospital, itself centred around the hospital chapel in which prayers were said publicly night and morning. When I arrived the hospital was run by a most able White Sister with long experience, but there was no qualified doctor. The patients were placed in many little houses and their relatives stayed round about, cooking in the communal kitchen and bringing their food to the patients. From time to time a priest came down to celebrate mass in the chapel, sprinkle the patients with holy water and give holy communion to those who desired it. It is often claimed that missionary medicine separated the spiritual from the scientific. Here at least it did not do so. Above the parish was a little chapel of the Blessed Virgin upon a hill, and up we toiled every Saturday morning to say mass on the hill top. Almost every aspect of the 'holy city' of some independent churches up and down Africa could be paralleled in the Villa Maria of the 1950s.

Buddu may be a largely Catholic county, it is also thick with spirits, diviners and tenaciously held ritual practices, relating to various situations (such as the birth of twins), which were seen as incompatible with Christian belief. On many occasions in life there is a strong sense of rival pulls and needs, the influence of unseen forces. As I have suggested, the possibility of personal confession and sacramental absolution appeared to be a real help in such conflicts, as in the more general business of repairing the fences of a person's moral life; so, in their different ways, were holy water, the rosaries hanging on the walls of houses, the medals worn by almost everyone.

The moral and spiritual life of the the Catholic clergy inevitably follows a rather different pattern. Masaka had about 100 African priests in my time and with those who had died over the years and the few who had left there were in all some 130 men who had belonged as priests to the diocese. They remained amicably linked with a far larger number of laymen who had been educated in part in the seminary but had failed to make it to ordination. Some were now leading figures in other fields and the wider influence of the church owed a very great deal to these links and to the continued loyalty of former seminarians. Bukalasa and Katigondo remained the oldest and most prestigious institutions of education in the district.

The priests of Masaka all had at least twelve years' training in minor and major seminary which stand side by side on a hill, one on each side of the road, just above the original parish of Villa Maria. The clergy share a strong *esprit de corps* from the oldest (Victor Mukasa ordained in 1913 and still active in the 1960s) down. Elsewhere in Africa it is often said with a good deal of truth that Africans have no appreciation of celibacy and strongly oppose their children becoming celibate priests. In Buganda this never seems to have been true. There was eagerness rather than reluctance in most Catholic families to let a son go to the seminary. They are often indignant if a boy is later sent away or leaves of his own accord. Nor can it be said that when ordained they lack status in society. On the contrary, their position is as respected as that of Catholic priests in most other rural, rather strongly Catholic parts of the world. The general picture is that of a group of men who have become an absolutely integral part of local society, clearly differentiated, extremely influential in every sphere of life, entering into the traditional authority pattern of Buganda. I was often worried to see a young woman or teenage girl kneeling before a priest, even during a quite long conversation. Cassocks were always worn, clearly distinguishable from but not so very unlike the long white *kanzus* worn by many Baganda, chiefly the older men.

While celibacy was highly respected and there would be consider-able opposition from laity and older clergy alike to a change of rule, some lapses in its observance were now treated with relative indulgence: though in earlier years they had been dealt with very severely indeed by the bishop. In general it was clearly maintained and the laity would have been offended if ecclesiastical authority simply closed its eyes to regular breaches of the rule.

The gospel which the old missionaries had taught was a strongly otherworldly one. As regards the things of this world, 'Blessed are the poor.' There can be little doubt that many of the early diocesan priests took this message and applied it to themselves very seriously indeed. Money, none the less, was clearly needed and it was certainly part of a priest's duty to plant coffee trees and encourage the catechists to do so as well. Poverty was still more a fact than a virtue. One or two priests were regarded as being personally well off, either because of family property or because of private foreign connections, but for most life was a continuous struggle with lack of cash. The priests lived in large well-built parish houses of the type established by missionaries – much better than those of most, but not quite all, of their parishioners in appearance. Most of the younger priests acquired a motor cycle or car, though some of the older men had never had more than a bicycle with which to carry out parochial visiting to the further villages; all the mission houses had a fair amount of land – the older ones, really considerable areas. The appearance then was one of moderate affluence, but the reality was rather different. The mission land was given over to many uses – school buildings, a convent for the African sisters, another for the brothers, gardens for each, and so on. The priests received very little money from outside the parish or diocese, financial support from the faithful was seldom very generous and it was a constant battle to keep going. What personal money they had went mostly either in contributing to the school fees of numerous young relatives or in keeping a car or motor cycle on the road – it was a tool of work but also, in part, a personal status symbol; but the models they had were mostly old and very often out of order. Even if the mission house was well built, the furniture inside was limited. Very little food was bought – sugar, tea, salt, an occasional hunk of meat or loaf of bread. They lived largely on the produce of their own gardens, but the problem here was regular labour. They had mostly too much else to do to work on them adequately themselves and tended to recruit catechumens, school children, a nephew or niece, anyone available to work for them, paid or unpaid. A good deal of a priest's time was in fact occupied in supervising the work of his garden, or doing it himself.

As both baptisms and weddings were normally performed for a group at a set weekly time, and as many Catholics were prevented from coming to confession by some permanent matrimonial irregularity, the sacramental ministry was rather less onerous than might be expected for a parish of many thousand Christians, though a single visit to take the sacraments to the dying might use up many hours. A parish priest's role was, in its own way, primarily a managerial one. His round of work, besides mass and other prayers mostly said in church at more or less fixed times (the bishop had ordered the White Father routine to be carried on by his African diocesan priests), consisted largely in material concerns and in hours of discussion over human problems of one sort or another relating to the parish organization or brought to him by one of his flock. There were long meetings with catechists and other senior men and not much time for anything else: religious instruction given in the many primary schools of the parish or visiting the villages away from the parish church itself appeared as occasional rather than regular occupations, though a great effort was always made in Lent to get round the village churches to preach and hear confessions – probably two days were spent at each place. Lent and the days before Christmas were the times for confession.

Theoretically the pattern was a strongly hierarchical one – the first African bishop, true pastor as he was, had been very autocratic in manner, as were many of the missionaries, and some African parish priests were also, especially perhaps the younger ones. But the necessity of obtaining the co-operation of others – catechists and senior laity, men and women – if anything was ever really to be done, greatly modified this in practice, and the final impression was rather one of almost endless discussion than of authoritarianism.

Two portraits may help illustrate the more general picture:

Father Rafaele Kabuye was the parish priest of Villa Maria when I arrived. He was a man of sixty and had been ordained in 1928 just thirty years before. He was generally considered to be one of the most reliable men in the diocese and had been a parish priest for very many years; he was also dean and on the bishop's council. He was short and thick, every inch a shrewd, unimaginative peasant.

He had never had more than a bicycle and when he needed to go to town he arranged for one of his parishioners to take him by car. Doubtless in earlier years he would have gone far and regularly on his bicycle, but now he seldom cycled beyond the nearest villages with a boy accompanying him to push the bicycle up the hills. He was very careful with the money of the parish and his own – the diocese had been in serious financial trouble more than once, but Fr Kabuye's parish could be relied on not to cause difficulties. He had, of course, a large and relatively wealthy congregation, but his system was really to have no expenses at all. Money remained in the bank; before getting there it was kept under his bed with the sugar. It was rumoured that he was personally very rich having saved money all his life; it was also rumoured that he gave much away, wholly unobtrusively, to needy old widows.

Fr Kabuye knew no English either to speak or to read; from the first day our conversation had to be either in Luganda or in Latin, and no foreign visitor did he ever greet in English. He was always polite and kindly to me and worried if I was not eating, but he could not make much sense of this young white priest with his many enthusiasms and foreign ideas. He was tolerant but did his best to keep me from doing more harm than I need. I was sent off to hear confessions in the church if there was to be a parochial meeting of importance, even though there was next to no one in the church at the time. He was extremely regular in his visits to the church for prayer in the morning, before lunch and supper and at night. He had no external interests; his family links seemed few. He was greatly respected but – I suspect – not widely loved.

Father Yohana Ssewajje, the senior curate, was about the same age; he had been ordained in 1929. He was tall and very thin, full of a quiet humour, of interests and absurd stories, a minor aristocrat. He had been brought up in the household of Apolo Kaggwa, the Protestant Prime Minister, of whom he had a rather poor opinion. He knew a fair amount of English and a few words of French, of which he was very proud, and was extremely fluent in Latin. He had been a parish priest in various places but seldom for long; he was extremely disorganized, always engaged in special errands, and fascinated by farming. He had planted trees wherever he lived and (in 1959) owned two barely functioning tractors, which when working passed between Villa Maria and his family estate in a remote and arid area of Mubende. Much of his time he spent dressed in an old khaki cassock, working on the mission land with such boys or girls as he could pay or persuade to work there too. His agricultural plans were always of a most ambitious kind, but little was ever actually produced from his fields (Fr Kabuye supervised a far, far smaller but more productive plot.) He was a fine shot and enjoyed nothing more than a couple of days away hunting. His interests were immensely varied and his bedroom contained a collection of old junk – bits of motorcar, a host of broken watches, anything that might some time be mended or come in useful somewhere. He had at one time taught Luganda and Latin in the minor seminary and had a passionate love for Luganda grammar.

Father Ssewajje was certainly a man of deep prayer but he was far less regular in church and one never quite knew where he might be at any given moment; he was famed as a splendidly moving preacher and in demand for special occasions. He was one of the gentlest, most sincere, most loving people I have ever met – and very courageous too, perhaps the only priest in the diocese who dared to stand up to Bishop Kiwanuka. (They were ordained the same year.) If people were in real trouble they went to Fr Ssewajje and he never let them down, wherever it meant going or however many other sheep had to be left unattended in the meantime.

In the general life of the diocesan clergy prayer, the tackling of material needs and pastoral care were all closely fused together in a cheerful struggle to keep going somehow in overall fidelity to the instructions laid down in the past and any new rule that might come through from the bishop. Adultery and 'pagan' practices and drunkenness were to be condemned, church going and all the virtues encouraged, those in distress comforted, jubilees celebrated with feast and song, while dealing at the same time in a probably provisional manner with a leaky church roof, finding a man to wash the clothes, getting the motor cycle repaired, or slowly debating the human problems raised by a quarrelsome catechist, a drunken teacher or a Catholic girl living with a Muslim butcher. It was, all of it, 'the work of God'.

6

African Theology

Edward Schillebeeckx in *The Understanding of Faith* (Sheed and Ward 1974, p. 154) defined or described theology as 'the critical self-consciousness of Christian praxis in the world and the church'. Others may prefer another definition, but it can be agreed that Christian theology is not revelation and it is not church doctrine; both of these while inevitably formulated within time yet aspire to, and may acquire, certain qualities of timelessness which are neither possible nor desirable for 'theology'. Theology rather requires a continuous contemporaneity if it is not to cease to be theology and become doctrine. It is a 'critical self consciousness' – an extended intelligent response of people of faith both to the word of God and to their own world. At times it may appear to concentrate more upon that word, as found in the scriptures, while interpreting and applying it aptly and acutely in the light of contemporary culture; at other times theology will appear to concentrate more upon the contemporary world, or upon some part of it decisively significant for this theologian or the group of Christians of which he or she forms part, interpreting it and judging it in the light of scripture. Behind appearances theology, to be true to itself, has always to do both.

It is, of course, true that scripture itself is already both 'word' and 'world'. There never was pure revelation, a word of God only. It was always a human word too: a word in the world, a word to the world, a word about the world. Moreover the scriptural 'world' was both the world as it still is (our world) and the world as it then was but is now no more. Both word and world in scripture have a true universality – otherwise it could in no way be normative for us – but that universality is always troublesomely but necessarily embedded within a true particularity which, if normative at all, is only so by some sort of analogy of circumstance.

The enfleshed, particular character of the scriptures ensures that they already contain a whole series of theologies. Nevertheless the canonization of the scriptures and the fact that they become, from the second century or whenever, unalterable from age to age sets our subsequent theologies apart from the scriptural ones. Ours have to relate both to the entire scriptural complex (of word and world) and to the contemporary world. They have to be other than scripture yet analogically in line with it.

Again, if we are to believe in any way at all in a Spirit–guided church, then church tradition, theological history and the contemporary church all constitute at one and the same time a partially mediating, and even authoritative, guide to the understanding of scripture (at the very least a newly added but pregnant footnote to the written word of God) and a segment of that world which has now to be understood for its own sake in the light of scripture. Scripture is certainly for us inseparable from our ecclesiastical and exegetical interpretation of it; yet that interpretation is itself part of our contemporary consciousness, part in fact of 'the world'. Modern exegesis, in particular, would be unthinkable apart from modern culture as a whole. The church too is both the fellowship of believers endeavouring to live according to God's word – the extension of a scriptural reality, the community indeed which created 'the Bible' as a composite unity in the first place – and absolutely part of 'the world' of today. Word and world are in fact at no point closed off, distinct realities. Nevertheless for the Christian theologian two distinct points of reference always remain: on the one hand the scriptures as something given from the past and basically unchanging from age to age, on the other 'the world' as something essentially contemporary and never the same in two ages. You can never put your foot twice in the same world.

True theology, then, is not even ideally to be measured by the standard of a pure interpretation of *scriptura sola*. It is rather a wrestling between revelation and something else, some part of the contemporary praxis of humankind, and what is required is a double fidelity. However theology be defined, there has as a matter of fact in the complexity of Christian history been a ceaseless multiplicity of theologies, to a greater or lesser extent diverse or overlapping, but relating to and stemming from the multiplicity of cultural, ethical, economic, psychological situations out of which believers theologize, as well as from the intellectual and imaginative genius of the individual theologian. Quite certainly, such has always been the case. Wherever the church has existed theologies of a greater or lesser degree of sophistication have sprung up, influencing, and related to, each other, yet manifestly diverse. The question is not how to justify but how best to characterize and understand such theologies – whether, for instance, according to a personal, local, national, a confessional, methodological or conceptual basis.

That all this applies today in Africa – where there are now far more than a hundred million Christians and flourishing churches in many different countries[1] – is too obvious to need stressing. Just as in the classical theological era of the fourth and fifth centuries, the churches of Antioch, Alexandria and the Latin West had their own distinct and recognizable theologies so today it should be anything but surprising that the churches of Africa develop their own 'African theology'. The term, certainly, is now much used. How much does it signify? Is it a reality or rather an aspiration? Is there in fact a recognizable 'African theology' in existence?[2] Again, is it something for Africans consciously to pursue? If the term is in one way undoubtedly helpful, may it not also – at least if overemphasized – mislead both practitioner and observers?

'African theology' is obviously a proper denotative term for referring to theology as written or expressed by Africans or in Africa. Two basic questions which may be asked are first, how much more weight than that it can rightly bear at present as indicative of a recognizable school or tendency of theology and second, whether it is something deliberately to be cultivated. How far can it be consciously, even self-consciously, pursued? One can, for instance, clearly speak of 'German theology', 'Greek theology' or 'English theology', if one is speaking in second order terms (looking at a group of writers or a movement of thought somehow from outside it, historically or descriptively); but would it be acceptable for a German theologian to cultivate (or even to advert to) the 'Germanic' character of his theologizing while actually at work? We should remember here that in fact in any discipline one normally works inside a 'school' and according to its mental traditions and ethos, conscious of a certain difference of approach from that of other schools in the same discipline. And such schools can, and usually do, take on local, national or continental names. The comparison for theology here should be less with physics or mathematics than with history, sociology, or economics. Yet while immediately (and not only in historical retrospect) a scholar working in these fields will be conscious of a definite local, even national, cultural-scientific tradition, movement or grouping of writers to which he is proud to belong within a universal discipline, and which quite definitely affects his presuppositions and methodology, yet he would still be in danger of betraying both the universal discipline and his own school if he somehow purposefully pursued the enhancement of the latter's particularist character. The 'German Christians' of the 1930s and their nationalist and worthless theology provide the historical note of warning here. The vitality and noteworthy character of a particular school must derive not from the degree to which the particular is sought but rather from the degree to which the general is sought with outstanding vigour in these particular circumstances.

If as a general rule it has to be admitted – and indeed urged most emphatically – that the Greeks should not pursue a Greek theology consciously, Germans a German theology, nor Africans an African theology, we can nevertheless, I believe, rightly argue that as a matter of tactics, Africa provides temporarily something of a special case. In its short-term contemporary cultural situation, and as a short-term explicit reaction to, and escape from, the heavily European and white character not only of most missionary doctrine but of the whole mainstream of Christian theology in the recent past, it is appropriate as well as inevitable for Africans to pursue for a time an explicitly African or black theology. Further, while a judgmental condemnation of any harping on the phrase might seem scientifically defensible, such condemnation could very easily be understood at the more popular and pastoral level as yet another white trick, racism sheltering behind a pose of scientific superiority. European Christians have so often implicitly, or even explicitly, adopted a 'The Faith is Europe' approach; they have so largely treated 'western' 'European' 'white' and 'Christian' as near synony-mous terms, and so particularly have they done this within Africa, that they at least can hardly point the finger if others affirm some positive relationship between their own particularisms and Christianity, and assert the need for a deliberately black face for what is fast becoming as much an African as a European faith. One is not merely saying here that Europeans are not the ones to sit in judgment on a conscious pursuit of 'African' theology, but – far more importantly – that within the context of decolonization such a pursuit is not only forgivable but is actually evangelically and theologically necessary.

In practice, it has to be admitted, the analogy of other modern 'national' schools of theology will not really get us very far, though it may point us in the right direction. While one could make a few general remarks about German theology as a unity, they would probably – if valid – be little more than remarks about linguistic style, the use of footnotes, or (more significantly) the authorities thought worth a mention and the preponderantly academic ethos of the world in which and for which it is written. In terms of content, methodology, prior concern or overall doctrinal position, Bultmann, Barth, Moltmann, Rahner, Küng, Pannenberg differ so widely among themselves that a term such as 'German theology' must come quickly to seem a hindrance rather than a help in understanding. We have to proceed from the singular to the plural. As a matter of fact the same is becoming true in Africa. The very reasons why one demands the right for an African theology to exist against the claims of a single universal theology become quickly reasons why one cannot really allow an African theology as such to exist for long – the singular must again become the plural. To such an extent is this already so that the use of the singular may not only be of little explanatory value, but actually be positively misleading. It can belittle the dimensions of the theological task in today's Africa. If the nature of dogma or doctrine tends to the singular, the inner law of theology tends to plurality. The smaller, the more homogeneous a church, the more it is likely to remain satisfied with a substantially single theology; but ecclesial multiplicity and diversity require theological diversity. The sheer size and range of the Christian churches in Africa today, not to speak of their vitality, can hardly not require the emergence of a whole range of theologies, and equally of liturgies and of spiritualities. Africa has after all not for centuries been linguistically, culturally, politically or religiously homogeneous, though people – Africans as well as non-Africans – often carelessly speak as if it had been. A Christianity straddling so many traditions is hardly likely to produce a homogeneous theology.

If, north of the Limpopo, there is today something looking a little like a single African theology at the level of publication in a European language, this is essentially due both to the rather limited quantity of such published work hitherto and the relatively homogeneous character of the academic environment in the earlier years of the post-colonial era, though there does exist a fairly clear difference between English language and French language publications, as well as a Catholic/Protestant difference, and some others too If major variations at this academic level do exist, they do so still more at the wider, and really more important, level of popular theology.

If one accepts that what is beginning to appear is already a range of African theologies rather than an African theology, could it nevertheless not be claimed that the former still constitute such a network with varying emphases but so many common themes, that they maintain a sufficiently recognizable family unity, as to justify the over-arching umbrella of a singular name? Before attempting to answer that question, it is necessary to attempt some sort of typology of theology in Africa as it exists today. Such a typology might be developed from varying perspectives.

There is, obviously enough, the denominational or confessionnal viewpoint. No theologian can be unaffected by his own confessional tradition – Catholic, Protestant, Anglican, Lutheran, Orthodox. Mbiti comes out of one tradition (or perhaps two), Nyamiti and Tshibangu come from another, Buthelezi from a third. This inevitably influenced each one's prior concerns, methodology, the deep inner sense of the proper relationship between theology and Christian and ecclesial life. Is this going to remain a major divide within African theology as it still does, despite decades of ecumenism, within European theology? Certainly Idowu's Methodism, Nyamiti's Catholicism, Buthelezi's Lutheranism are by no means insignificant influences on their work. Nevertheless there does seem to be arising an issue-orientated approach to theology which sidesteps, or reduces to a relatively insignificant marginality, these confessional traditions.

If every living Christian theology derives from the interplay between Bible and some type of human experience, the dominantly significant experience for a particular theology may be of many kinds – secular or religious, political or mystical, Christian or non-

Christian. This other source is utterly essential, its theological significance and decisiveness have seldom if ever been properly explored, yet its authority must absolutely not be absolutized. Let us not misunderstand this. There are always 'two sources' – in nothing was pure classical Protestantism more misguided than in the denial of a structure of revelational duality, understood aright. For in a very real way this 'something else', this second source is genuinely a source of revelation. God's revelation to human beings of 'the ways of God' did not cease with the death of the last apostle, just as it is not all contained within the pages of the Bible or the experience of Israelites and Christians. The whole world and the whole of time remain God's world and God's time. 'God has shown' to all (Romans 1.19) and continues to show to all 'in many and various ways' (Hebrews 1.1) the truths with which theology is concerned. It appears in 'natural religion', as well as natural phenomena, in social and political developments, in intellectual and cultural achievement of every sort, in physics and astronomy, in the most intimate personal and spiritual experience, even in the life of the church! Human beings can find God and learn the ways of God through all these things. Nor are they sources of revelation only for those who have not biblical revelation; essentially they relate to the latter not as a substitute but as complement. Christian theology, as distinguished from biblical exegesis, is in fact impossible without both. Nevertheless Christian theology also becomes impossible if the authority of particularities within the 'other source' is absolutized as the central line of truth within the biblical source can in some way be. To absolutize the authority of current political experience was the fundamental error of the 'German Christians' of the 1930s, it may equally be so of some liberation theologians today. To absolutize the authority of any other particular, personal, ethnic or international religious tradition or experience – even the experience of the Reformation or the life of a saint or whatever – is inherently to deny ultimately normative authority to the biblical tradition. Valid Christian theology derives its character from the existence of its two sources but equally from an intrinsic difference between its relationship towards the two: if it either absolutizes the authority of both or relativizes the authority of both, it must destroy itself, just as it does (if less obviously) by denying the existence of the second source. Purely 'evangelical' theology, purified from dependence upon the non-biblical, upon the 'world', is quite simply a non-starter. Biblical revelation is essentially incomprehensible and useless without its sparring partner, but in the constant wrestling match between the two which constitutes Christian theological thinking it is finally always biblical revelation which will prevail – even if it is a biblical revelation which frequently appears strangely different after the wrestling from how it seemed before.

The diversity of theologies derives from the endless diversity of effective sparring partners. In Africa today there would seem to be three chief 'something elses', three basic areas of concern and experience, which can be seen as productive of three principal contemporary types of African theology. The first is African traditional religion. Its content, interpretation, relationship with Christian revelation, as also the actual living of Christians who continue to share in some beliefs and practices, became the dominant sparring partner for scripture in most of the first wave of published work in English or French deriving from East and West Africa.[3] The scientific study by Christians of African religion, whether sympathetic or unsympathetic, may not constitute as such a piece of Christian theology,[4] but the character of any wider interpretation will very easily come to rest on some sort of theological presupposition and must tend to stimulate a Christian theological interpretation of other religions as well as a critique of the historical process of evangelization[5] – whether it be to insist upon the otherness of Christian faith and practice or, alternatively, to argue for a previously unrecognized harmony and continuity between traditional and Christian religion. The typical nineteenth-century western missionary (though there were exceptions) undoubtedly tended to stress the otherness, often crudely enough. The twentieth-century missionary position, both better informed and more naturally sympathetic to *Africana*, has tended to discover the harmony. Edwin Smith was a leader here, and African theologians while often belabouring the one are equally indebted to the other. The Christian theologian cannot furthermore avoid consideration of not just the character and comparability of beliefs, but also the existential and salvific relationship betwen the pre-Christian African and the living God of the Bible. When the so-called 'High God' – *Mulungu, Mwari, Leza, Katonda, Kwoth* or *Nyame* – was worshipped, was Yahweh in truth being worshipped and was such worship truly salvific? How far could the whole wider complex of pre-Christian religious ritual and belief – focused so often upon ancestors or hero-divinities – form part of the salvific relationship between God and human beings? Possessed of his or her own religion, a world of spirits leading up to 'Spirit', did the African need Christ at all? For Byang Kato even to ask such a question was near to blasphemy.[6] For others, like Gabriel Setiloane, it seems not only obvious to ask but only after a great anguish and wrestling with both traditions can it be answered affirmatively.[7]

The second 'other source' is the contemporary pol.tical/social situation in which people find themselves, situations especially of power and powerlessness, of racial, tribal and class conflict, of poverty and affluence, of division, oppression, liberation. From these emerge major moral issues, both personal and collective, together with an underlying view of human social existence, which may in any part of the world provide the central concern for a theology. This has been the case since the 1960s for Latin American liberation theology and North American black theology.[8] The latter passed across to South Africa at the end of the 1960s, in the context of the black consciousness movement and it has ever since provided, not surprisingly, the dominant concern of South African black theologians. For them black theology is African theology. The rather racialist note that has characterized some but not all expositions of black theology in North America has appeared very little in South Africa where 'black' has come to signify pretty inclusively – at least for the time – the poor, the oppressed, humankind's have-nots.[9] Elsewhere on the continent, despite the occasional appeals, this source remains rather under-used. Thus for Mbiti, the relevance of black theology for Africa is 'either non-existent or only accidental', its weakness being an 'excessive preoccupation with liberation'.[10] There has in fact been very little political theology written north of the Limpopo, with the lively exception of two books by the Reverend Canaan Banana, until recently President of Zimbabwe, which do show just that preoccupation which Mbiti would judge excessive.[11]

Our first area of concern provides us essentially with what has come to be known as African theology (in a narrower sense) in East and West Africa – the theology of Idowu, Sawyerr, Mbiti or Pobee – while our second area gives us what has come to be known as black theology south of the Limpopo. Clearly the two are not incompatible and there are South Africans like Gabriel Setiloane and Desmond Tutu who fully share both fields of concern. Part of colonial oppression has been the belittling of the culture of the oppressed. Liberation is not only political, it must also be a cultural achievement, a reassertion of the validity of spiritual and intellectual continuity with the pre-colonial past, and not only for the inhabitants of some backward human dumping ground but for the central thread of South African society and its Christian churches. The central theme of African theology is then itself a theme of liberation and a significant element within a black theology context. Nevertheless effectively the gap here is fairly large. One has only to compare, for instance, John Pobee's *Toward an African Theology* with Allan Boesak's *Farewell to Innocence*, two of the most important recent works, to realize this. For Pobee in Ghana black theology is a very small part of African theology and one not without inconveniences resulting from its North American origins in a situation immensely different from that of West Africa, however much Afro-Americans may want to be sensitive to their West African background. For Boesak, on the contrary, the issues of culture and traditional religion which are so important to Pobee seem remote and very secondary. For him North American black theology, with perhaps an additional injection of Latin American liberation theology, fits the South African black predicament like a glove. Boesak is not, admittedly, fully characteristic of South African theology. Tutu,[12] Buthelezi or Setiloane stand somewhere between Pobee and Boesak, but the basic contrast between the two approaches is very clear; the one is concerned especially with tradition and culture, with religious things and the harmony between religion and society, but not much with the explicitly christological (though Pobee does try to remedy this) or the political; the other is concerned with change, pain, conflict and politics, with at least tinges of a Marxist analysis of society, and very explicitly with sin and redemption, with Christ and the Cross.

There is a third 'second source', less talked of but not necessarily less influential: recent Christian and ecclesiastical experience. As a matter of fact the life and experience of the church herself has in the West been traditionally the principal sparring partner of the Bible in the evolution of theology: the practice of the sacraments, the ministry, the papacy, the actual historical struggles for orthodoxy, the calling of general councils, the emergence of schisms and rival communions, the lives of the saints. All this has been a principal source for theology, without which indeed the pattern of dogmatic theology which most of us take for granted would be quite inconceivable. The dependence of Roman Catholic theology upon the interpretation of ecclesiastical history is more explicit; but for Protestants too, however much some may take a stand on *scriptura sola*, in reality the experience of the Reformation, of Luther above all, but of all the Reformers, provides a 'source' of immense richness for the theological understanding of the ways of God and the nature of the church. It is clear too how much modern European and American theology has been a consequence of, and reflection upon, the ecumenical movement as a fact of Christian life. In a similar way much recent African theological thinking has grown out of explicitly African Christian experiences: reflection upon the missionary/local church relationship from the receiving end; reflection upon Christian life and church ministries in a society where ordained priests are very few, where the village church and the catechist have a character all their own, where the veneration of ancestors, rites of passage, the practice of sorcery are all part of the regular texture of local life; reflection upon outstanding Christian experiences within modern Africa such as the life of Simon Kimbangu and the growth of Kimbanguist and other churches.[13] *Lex Orandi, Lex Credendi*. In African Christianity prayer has certainly come well before theology. The worship and ministry of the local church may well be in practice the most powerful and consistent source in the shaping not, perhaps, of the rather limited field of academic theology but of popular and preached theology in Africa today: the work of Kalilombe, Boulaga, Mveng or Sanon.

Clearly these three areas are far from unrelated; nevertheless each draws upon its own special source of inspiration and the three are in fact quite recognizable with their own particular preoccupations and pit-falls. Thus African theology tends a little naïvely to see the past through rose-tinted spectacles, a golden age of marital and communal responsibility, while black theology tends to over-simplify the present and even to diabolize (as in the famous *Kairos* document) those with whom it contends: a biblically fundamentalist take-over of Marxist categories.

It could well be argued, never the less, that an adequate *theologia Africana*, were it to exist, would need to do justice to all three areas, that it would be a synthesis creatively inspired by a wrestling between the Bible upon one hand and traditional religion, the demands of contemporary political reality, and characteristically African Christian experience in both the mission and the independent churches on the other. Some such synthesis is in fact being encouraged particularly by the development of the Ecumenical Association of Third World Theologians, formed at Dar es Salaam in 1976.[14] One sees it fermenting in a journal like the *Bulletin de Théologie Africaine* sponsored by the Ecumenical Association of African Theologians and edited by A. M. Ngindu of the Faculty of Catholic Theology in Kinshasa. For the present, however, it is to be admitted that in practice what we have are more limited theologies concerned with one or other of these areas, and that a provisional typology may most usefully be related to them.

It is of the paradoxical essence of Christianity both to affirm and to seem to deny the value of what has happened beyond its own explicit boundaries; to affirm a continuity between nature and grace, between the experience of other religions and the Christian experience, indeed the universality of grace in and through all religious experiences, and yet to affirm a discontinuity – an otherness and a transcendence in Christianity which is obscured if the uniqueness of the Christ event is not absolutely recognized together with a deep consequential inability to compromise. No tension is more crucial for Christian theological thinking or for missionary experience. It is the tension between, for instance, the approach of Hendrik Kraemer and that of Dom Bede Griffiths. The temptation is enormous to opt for one side only, and representatives of each tendency are to be found within African Christianity today as they have long been found within missionary ranks. Are the symbols of traditional religion to be venerated or to be destroyed? Sometimes it appears today as if the theologians of the mission churches argue a little too easily for the former, in line with much current western theology, while the leaders of the independent churches insist a great deal too rapidly upon the latter in line with past missionaries from whom upon other grounds they parted company. Historically Christianity has proved both highly intolerant and immensely accommodating and this both in theory and in practice: intolerantly evangelical, accommodatingly catholic. In actual African church life today this may well provide the sharpest cutting edge for contrary lines of direction; here and perhaps everywhere it may also provide the most profound criterion for the constitution of a typology of theologies: a redemptionist model of 'Christ only' as against an incarnationist model of 'Adam renewed'.

In practice not unrelated to this in Africa today is the contrast between academic and popular theology. Mbiti, Idowu, Fasholé-Luke, Pobee are university figures participating in, and being steadily influenced by, a wider world of international theology. They all studied for years in European or American universities. They are co-heirs with postgraduate theologians of every nation to a legacy of theological literature and formal method hammered out by generations of western scholarship. At the most crucial stage of their theological formation they were far from any African church context, having to satisfy instead a western supervisor who had possibly never set foot on the continent. At times, as with Tarcisse Tshibangu's masterly *Théologie positive et théologie speculative* (Louvain 1965), or John Pobee's beautiful little study 'The cry of the Centurion – a cry of defeat',[15] it would be hard to tell that their works were in fact written by an African: they are simply fine examples of western-type scholarship. Their books are written with an international public in mind.

Popular theology arises very differently, and in reality it may be very much more important for the church in Africa today than academic theology. It is found in hymns, the sermons of local ministers and catechists, the devotions of pilgrimages, the existential merging of old religious attitudes with new. In Africa today the poverty of the local church, the multiplicity of languages in which ordinary people actually pray, the limited range of written formal theology, all contribute to widen the gap. Does the one have much influence upon the other, we may ask? Does John Mbiti's *New Testament Eschatology in an African Background* actually find a way through to catechists, or Kimbanguist hymns to the teaching of theologians? The writers of black theology, one may note, seem on the whole less academic, nearer to popular religion than those of African theology. That is, perhaps, simply a consequence of the South African situation and the absence of prestigious 'chairs' for any blacks (though that is changing). It is closer to being a people's theology. The question of the wider relationship between academic and popular theology inevitably links up with that of language:

academic theology is almost entirely written and discussed in English or French; 'popular' theology has nearly always a vernacular as its vehicle. Have we thought enough about the intrinsic relationship of theology and language? It seems to be the case that missionaries in the past often greatly underestimated the difficulty of translating the scriptures into African vernaculars, and that some of the early (and even not so early) translations were almost unintelligible – at least at many crucial points. No language is naturally provided with an adequate vocabulary for Christian use. May not the most crucial theological struggle in Africa today perhaps be that going on in scores of languages to create an intelligible and adequate vehicle of Christian religious expression? This struggle is central to current work in biblical and liturgical translation but surely also to the wider evolution of language across the usage of preaching and common conversation. Far more than a matter of translation it is, finally, one of creation in which theology and language grow together and old words are infused with new meanings. How far will a really living African theology need to be expressed across an African language which alone can be sufficiently in touch with African religious experience, either pre-Christian or Christian? How far is the use of European language a significant bar to the emergence of African theology? Few higher theological colleges make major use of vernacular in their teaching, but there are scores of lower level catechetical schools conducted wholly in a vernacular. It is very probably there rather than in university departments or the writing of Mbiti or Pobee that African theology in its widest sense is really being forged. Will men and women taught their theology largely through a vernacular come out significantly different from those taught through English or French? Their range of quotable authority will surely be narrower, will their insight into the cutting edge of the biblical word at work in the existential reality of the African Christian world be more acute? One can guess, but we cannot really know the answers to such questions.

Finally, if a theology is somehow an amalgam of Bible and human experience, both sides have to be taken afresh with adequate seriousness. Most of what I have been saying has concerned our second source, but what of the first? Lip-service recognition of the Bible is not enough. The Ghanaian Kwesi Dickson has remarked mildly enough in a careful discussion of *Theologia Africana* that 'though there has been a stated interest in biblical foundations, there has not been a clear demonstration of this interest'.[16] In understandable reaction to the previous neglect of African traditional religions as a valid 'source' for Christian theological understanding, it could be suggested that among Christian teachers in university departments of religious studies, a preoccupation with African traditional religion has brought with it a dangerous neglect of the scriptures. They have been taken for granted, their standard texts quoted, their apparent similarities with African religion noted approvingly and even simplistically, but they have too seldom been wrestled with.

Acceptance of the justifiability, indeed inevitablity, of a vast multiplicity of theologies does not after all mean that all such theologies are equally valuable. Even within the New Testament if one cannot say which is the greatest one can, with reasonable confidence, place the Johannine or the Pauline both well above Lucan theology, which is by no means to despise the latter. In theological history one has to recognize not only the peaks but also many lesser hills and ranges, including some which are positively dangerous – unbalanced defective responses to either word or world. A truly great theology will excel upon both sides. A theology which is effectively struggling only with revelation will sink into exegesis or into some form of fundamentalism; a theology which is creatively alive only on the side of the world, is on the way to succumbing to one or another species of ideology. The greatness of Aquinas derived from the quality of his wrestling both with the scriptural and Augustinian tradition on the one hand and Aristotle (together with contemporary mediaeval Aristotelianism) upon the other, within the abrasive context of the medieval university – and in response to what was being studied in the arts faculty as much as what was going on in theology itself. Theology as a creative exercise essentially implies this *both and*. In practice few theologies come near to the ideal, but the less they do so the quicker they need to be discarded.

The strength and central paradox of the Christian religion seem to lie in its combination of unbounded universality with the most absolute particularity of its focal point. This requires an ever ongoing series of analogous particularizations. Every authentic theology must strive somehow to do justice to both dimensions, not only in the objects of its study but also in its whole approach. A theology which does not consent to be a reflective particularization of response to the word but claims some sort of phoney a-historical universality will gravely mislead its devotees as to the limitedness of the theologian's condition; yet equally a theology which so preoccupies itself with a special people or class, a particular moment or concern, that it obscures the absolute unlimitedness of the grace of God in history is twisting the central mystery to its own ruin. A theology can, must, be black, African, Greek or whatever because to live at all it must be gripping, contextualized, enfleshed within the particularisms of the world, yet if it questions for one moment that salvation is wholly unlimited by such particularities, if it does not point again and again beyond them, demonstrating that the word became not just Jew but *Man*, not just *vir* but *homo, anthropos, muntu*, then its road to life becomes instantly instead its very murderer.

One can but try. African theology is and will be subject to all the temptations of its elder brothers and sisters: it may well succumb in part to a false subservience to traditional religion, Marxist ideology, racism or simply its own local ecclesiastical praxis. It will only avoid this by wrestling as profoundly with the word of scripture as with any and every 'other source'. If the emerging diversity of Christian African theology can relate itself integrally to biblical diversity, so that the multiplicity of African experience can both creatively throw light upon the multi-faceted vision of the scriptures and in turn be illuminated by it, then it will be validated as inherently faithful at once to revelation and to the world and will, by so doing, justify itself as truly and absolutely theology.

7

The Choice of Words for Christian Meanings in Eastern Africa

In a brief article on 'The Perils of Translation,'[1] published near the end of his life. Professor Evans-Pritchard glanced at the work of missionaries in Zande and remarked, 'Translating the Bible into an African language is a tough enough task, and one is lost in amazement at the naïvety of people who add to it by trying to translate also the English hymnal with all its cultural idioms, metaphors and nuances into a language which has quite different ones.' One might add Italian hymnals and neoscholastic catechisms. Yet what else were they to do? And aren't the 'cultural idioms, metaphors and nuances' as strongly present in the Bible as in any hymnal? In fact, if the Bible has been translated (which, on the Catholic side, as regards most language groups is still not the case), then most of your major verbal options have already been settled at least until you reach semi-systematic theology, whether scholastic or other. A primary language need for missionaries and a new Christian community is surely something to worship with, hence the speedy appearance of hymnals all over Africa of one sort or another, but most Christian worship is extremely biblical in its content and vocabulary and the illustrations Evans-Pritchard offered were in fact biblical ones. For example, 'The Azande have no flocks and no shepherds and no words for either.' Yet here we come at once face to face with an image which is not at all marginal to the tradition of Christian worship or indeed faith: 'The Lord is my shepherd', or still more crucial, 'Behold the Lamb of God', the paschal lamb. How to teach the paschal mystery without a paschal lamb? It can hardly be done, so rooted is the Christian tradition of meaning in a particular cultural, economic earth. What does the missionary, the theological communicator, do when a language has no words because the society just does not know the things indicated by the words? Africans may not have large flocks of sheep, but sheep are present through most of Africa so this is not the most acute of problems – though it could have been, for instance, on the Pacific island of Tikopia, where there were no animals at all. But if there can be a problem for simple solid things like sheep, how much more intricate are the problems of translating the meaning of 'faith', 'grace', 'baptism', 'spirit' and so forth; equally the technicalities of systematic theology.

Translation is always a problem. No language can exist in advance for a new set of ideas. Half the battles of orthodoxy in the first five centuries arose out of differences of Greek linguistic usage, the difficulty of acceptably redefining *ousia*, *physis*, *hypostasis*, *prosopon*. Christians had to decide their faith in terms of words and concepts whose usage and meaning hitherto had had other purposes and other senses. They then had to do the same thing across the far from identical terminologies of Latin, Coptic, Russian and even English. Christian faith, like any science or body of ideas, creates its own vocabulary anew in every language (and, of course, must renew that vocabulary as language and culture change). It is likely to find its chosen vocabulary in a new language partly by importation. Yet the operative meaning of such borrowed words must inevitably alter in the process, just as the adoption of a native word can never produce identity of verbal function: a new range of reference and partial equivalence there must be. From language to language genuine communication of sense is possible, total equivalence of meaning – verbal or conceptual – is not.

Even languages which have been open to Christian usage for many hundreds of years may remain only partially effective media for the communication of major Christian concepts. And here it can be remarked that Bantu languages may actually in some important ways be better at this than modern European languages, despite all the centuries of Christianization the latter have undergone. Take a pretty basic example: the key title of the second person of the Trinity: the Son. The word in English already denotes male gender. however much we declare theologically that there is no gender in God. This is, of course, in continuity with the original biblical forms.

That does not make it less misleading. Moreover we cannot get very far without giving 'him' a pronoun 'he': 'He came down from Heaven, was born of the Virgin Mary and became man.' Our creed and our preaching reinforce linguistically again and again the doctrinally false conception that the 'Word' was male 'before' becoming man. In most Bantu creeds this does not happen. 'The Son' is *Mwana*, an entirely ungendered noun, and verbs do not have pronouns. The typical Bantu Christian is given no linguistic misinformation implying the masculinity of the Word of God. And then 'became man', *homo factus est*. The Latin *homo*, like the Greek *anthropos*, basically includes no indication of gender (even if, very occasionally – as in Matthew 10.35 and 19.10 – *anthropos* is used with a male connotation just as *aner* – e.g. in Acts 17.34 – seems to include a wider one).[2] Jesus was, of course, male, but it is not God's becoming male which the creed asserts as important but becoming human. Not *vir factus est*, became a male, but *homo factus est*, became man. Now English is ambiguous in that it does not have two words but only one: *man* translates both *vir* and *homo*. So when we affirm 'became man' we are affirming something still unrelated to gender but because of the ambiguity of our language, we can easily think that we are affirming that the Word became a male human being and not a female one: the one sense glides misleadingly into the other. English is here not in continuity with the Greek.

A Bantu language, on the contrary, is. The *Mwana wa Mungu*, the child of God, becomes *Muntu*, and the sense of *muntu* is wholly ungendered. It could never occur to a Muganda, for instance, to affirm that the *Mwana wa Katonda*, became *musajja*, a male, in opposition to *mukazi*, a woman. That is not the faith of the creed and the Bantu language expresses the credal faith correctly while English, French or Italian partially obscures it.

Thus, for instance, the Catholic bishops of England and Wales recently ordered the word 'men' to be dropped forthwith from the eucharistic words of institution. 'It will be shed for you and for all men.' Presumably the reason was the implication that Christ's blood was not shed for women. One may surmise that this novel episcopal anxiety not to include women among men was fuelled by the need to maintain a certain consistency with Rome's reasons for refusing to ordain women. The central argument of the Declaration of October 1976 on the Admission of Women to the Ministerial

Priesthood was that 'we can never ignore the fact that Christ is a man' and therefore 'in actions . . . in which Christ himself . . . is represented . . . his role must be taken by a man'. A woman is no longer, it seems, a man: that is to say the Church has moved from meaning *homo* when it says 'man' to meaning *vir*. Hence, if Christ's blood is shed 'for all men', it is no longer shed for women, so in this context – as the church is not yet prepared to exclude women from salvation altogether – there arises the need to drop the word 'men' and affirm instead that it is shed 'for all'. But once we move down this linguistic path our theological troubles are endless. The bishops did not order the wording of the creed 'and was made man' to be altered. Yet the salvation of 'all', the shedding of blood 'for all' is grounded on the incarnation. If women are not included in the 'man' (Adam) the Word became, then they cannot properly be included in the 'all' of salvation (despite Acts 17. 30–31, which might be held to suggest the opposite). A hasty attempt to cover their flanks in view of feminist pressures and the Roman objection to the ordination of women seems to have pushed the bishops into a theologically quite confused position. But the trouble behind it all is an important weakness in the English language to do justice to something at once philosophical and theological, despite a thousand years of English Christian usage. The weakness was there all the time. We lived with it, as we do with countless other linguistic ambiguities and inadequacies. Theology uses language but frequently transcends it too until, as now, new pressures suddenly place the whole argument in jeopardy. We can be sure that many comparable usages exist in every language into which Christian belief is newly translated. Formal translation is not a matter of perfection but one of establishing a working arrangement, avoiding the grosser misunderstandings, out of which multiple linguistic practice will slowly shape a new linguistic community of understanding but one in essential continuity will all other Christian linguistic communities.

Words could not be there prior to meanings. Of course, today we can look back within most African languages on fifty, a hundred, even two hundred years of linguistic wrestling. Decisions taken today by African Bible translators are done within a context where a language has already been used, and thus effectively reshaped, by Christians over many decades. It would be not only undesirable but completely impossible to ignore that lengthy usage.

In principle, however, the translator into a language in which a belief system has not previously been expressed has four large options to choose between in regard to words with a specifically religious sense: (A) To take a word or phrase of the language he or she is translating into and press some new or extended meaning into it which will then through regular liturgical and catechetical usage become a familiar one. (B) To borrow a word from a language neighbouring that into which he or she is translating and which already possesses a more developed theological vocabulary. (C) To retain the word from the language he or she is transl2.ing out of, simply transliterating it. (D) To abandon this word or phrase as such as being meaningful within one culture but not viable in meaning in another.

Probably, if we examine any considerable body of Christian translation into a new language and society hitherto unaffected by Christianity, we will find that something of all four options has been adopted. It would, I think, be mistaken to claim in principle that any of the four approaches is always wrong or to be rejected. The work of religious translation can only accept the complex nature of every language, the limitation of each, their non-correspondence, but also their continuing capacity to grow. It is to be expected that the new experience and horizons of Christianity with its characteristic concepts and structures will extend the vocabulary of a language, just as the opening up of a society in any other direction will equally bring with it the importation or creation of new words.

It seems reasonable to presume that in no age have missionaries consciously opted for the fourth alternative: simple abandonment of a word or concept as too difficult for this language because too unrelated to the life of its society. Yet Kenneth Cragg has pointed out how this did in fact come near to happening in New Testament times with phrases such as 'the kingdom of heaven' and 'the Son of Man'. While retained in the gospel texts these quickly slipped out of the current idiom of preaching and catechesis. They were allowed 'to lapse in certain territories by virtue of their disservice to their meaning'.[3] He adds that the lesson should not be lost today when in a missionary context other traditional phrases fail to be meaningful. Admitting the force of Evans-Pritchard's difficulty, should the 'Lamb of God' title be permitted to lapse in certain countries from current religious usage, just as the 'Son of Man' lapsed? Should the very fatherhood of God be dropped where the traditional concept of God is feminine not masculine?[4]

In modern Africa missionary translators have certainly made use of all the other three options, in this following in the steps of their predecessors of many earlier eras.[5] This study will in fact be largely one of the rise and fall of preferences in one or other of the three directions. While many key Christian words in any language have always been words native to that language and pre-existing their specific Christian use, others have on the contrary nearly always been carried across unchanged by Christians from language to language, thus expressing in a striking way the continuity of Christian belief and religious culture across the borders of society and language. 'Amen', 'Alleluia', 'Christ' are obvious examples, and there are others not far removed which most modern missionaries have treated as in the same class. They tend to become words of identification rather than of communication. However, in a good deal of Catholic missionary practice they were, for a time, much more. While accepting the necessity of this class and even its importance rightly understood, one may feel that its easy extension to include a wide range of key religious words was likely to do a disservice both to the communication of an intelligible gospel and to its deeper localization. In the late 1950s Fr Walser, a missionary in Uganda, did in fact make this point in the very first issue of the *African Ecclesiastical Review*: 'To adopt simply the transcribed Latin term (batismu, konfirmasion, Patri, grasia, purgatory, induljensia, matrimonio, krisma etc.) is certainly the easiest way for the translator and at the same time it avoids the risk of heresy; but such foreign terms convey nothing to the average African and necessitate, therefore, cumbersome catechetical explanation.'[6] One of the most discernible tendencies in eastern Africa of more recent years has, in fact, been a reduction in the number of such words. I would presume that an imaginative theological translator (as probably a good translator in any other area as well) would first try to follow option A. If that proves unrewarding, he or she may turn to B, a possible borrowing from a neighbouring language. (This approach, as we shall see, was often used at least at first in East Africa, through the adoption of Swahili words into languages of the interior.) If that does not serve, he or she will be left with C, the retention of the word basically in the form provided by the language he or she is translating out of. For Christian missionaries in Africa, of course, this final option could still provide a choice of source languages. Should the modern European vernacular (English, French or Italian) provide the form, or should it be Latin, or Greek or Hebrew? Where Protestants tended to use English or Greek, Catholics would use French or, more likely, Latin.

It is worth observing here that, quite apart from the coming of Christianity, religious words of every sort, including words of great importance, have been carried rather easily from one African language to another. Indeed unwritten languages could be so fluid that it is almost, though not quite, misleading to speak of any African language in the pre-missionary era as a discrete reality at all. Borrowing was particularly common for the name of God where a 'foreign name' was often used. For instance the Masai *Ngai* was taken over by many of their neighbours such as Kikuyu, Chagga and Kamba, who sometimes linked it with an 'original name' to make a double title, such as *Mulungu-Ngai*. E. Dammann comments that 'it is difficult, or even impossible, to find out in detail the conceptions which have resulted in the adoption of a foreign name for the High God'.[7] It may also be noted that the non-comprehensible aspect of religion, the expression of mystery and awe, can be served by the use of foreign, mysterious sounding words – as by the archaic resonances of the King James version. The adoption or retention of such verbal usage is a deeper matter than one of not finding a possible local or contemporary equivalent. The practice of a number of African independent churches in developing a mystical vocabulary can illustrate this.[8] It may well be doubted whether in any congregation an indigenous African word could effect the religious vibrations that can be drawn from an 'Amen' or an 'Alleluia'. Some people, while conceding that this tendency is true of religion in general, might urge that any deliberate encouragement of the dimension of the non-comprehensible in liturgy is still a distortion of Christianity whose true genius is to work through the familiar and the comprehensible, not the mysterious. But that is an over-simplification. Certainly in many ages various branches of Christianity, including the Ethiopian, have tended to make use of either a complete language or individual words which are either archaic or foreign.

After these more general remarks let us turn to consider some examples of Catholic missionary translation in eastern Africa and the issues underlying them. One, relatively minor, issue is that of Catholic/Protestant divergence. While there was always a large measure of common translation practice in most languages, in a few it diverged sharply at certain points, reflecting the wider relationship between the churches. Thus in regard to Luganda, when I arrived in Buganda in 1958, there was still a conflict, not only over words but over the spelling of the same words. 'Catholic spelling' and 'Protestant spelling' were not the same. While this is as such a study of Catholic practice, the interchurch dimension is an important part of its subject and particularly the change which has come since the Second Vatican Council in ecumenical relations bringing with it in many places the joint revision of Bible translations. This and parallel post-conciliar liturgical work in every vernacular have brought many changes in Catholic vocabulary since the 1960s. Consequently we have at times to note the difference between an 'old Catholic' form and a 'new Catholic' one.

For our examination of the choice of words in Catholic missionary translation we will look at a series of key words in eight languages – Swahili, Haya, Luganda, Runyaankole, Ateso, Bemba, Chewa (Cinyanja) and Tonga (of southern Zambia). These range from northern Uganda to southern Zambia. They are chosen for a variety of reasons: Swahili as the base vernacular of East Africa – at least so far as incoming Europeans were concerned. Ateso in northern Uganda is included as a sole non-Bantu example. However the missionaries in Teso were Mill Hill men coming up from southern Uganda (Buganda and Busoga) and the fact that this was an extension of work begun in Bantu areas and initially undertaken largely through Bantu catechists posted among non-Bantu greatly influenced the language choices made, as we shall see. I have included Tonga as a Bantu language from outside the Swahili sphere of influence. The Jesuit missionaries at work there came up from the south, not down from the north-east as had the White Father missionaries in the Bemba area. The original coastal language, if any, behind their line of advance was Zulu or Xhosa. Haya, Luganda, Runyaankole, Bemba and Chewa stand in basically the same relationship to Swahili. Moreover, in all five cases the principal Catholic missionaries were White Fathers. It should be pointed out that White Fathers never worked on the coast of East Africa where

Swahili was a first language, so they had less reason to favour Swahili than, say, the Holy Ghost Fathers. (Ideally it would have been preferable to include an example like Chagga where Holy Ghost Fathers not White Fathers were at work.) I will pay special attention to Luganda, simply because it is the one I know most about.

The four principal issues we will consider are, first, names for God; second, the translation of the word 'spirit'; third, the influence of Swahili; fourth the recent move away from clinging to a foreign-based technical vocabulary to dependence upon native words with an underlying congruity of meaning.

It is striking that in none of the eight languages did Catholic missionaries attempt to impose a non-African name for God, though this did happen elsewhere, if rarely: the Verona Fathers in the southern Sudan apparently made use among some people of the word *Dio*, and the Jesuits in Zimbabwe (formerly Rhodesia) working among the Shona long refused to use the name *Mwari*. When one remembers widely held nineteenth-century missionary views about the debased character of African religion or even about the entire absence of religion in Africa, it is perhaps surprising that they were so generally convinced that they could use an existing name for God without dangerously confusing their converts. By so doing they would seem to have admitted the existence of a basic African monotheism, and to have made a basically positive judgment about African traditional religions and the possibility of linguistic continuity between them and Christianity of vast consequence. It is noteworthy that the church did not take so favourable a view of the traditional religion of the Germanic or Scandinavian peoples a thousand years earlier. No one attempted to use the name of *Thor* or *Woden* for the Christian God. Contemporary African scholars who denounce the missionary rejection of religious continuity[9] might instead occasionally ask themselves – as indeed Okot p'Bitek did – whether their fault was not rather to presuppose too great a measure of conceptual continuity.

In our eight languages the word selected for God was as follows:

Swahili	*Mungu*
Haya	*Ruhanga*
Runyaankole	*Ruhanga*
Luganda	*Katonda*

Ateso	*Katoda*
Bemba	*Mulungu*
Chewa	*Mulungu*
Tonga	*Leza*

The strangest name here may be *Katoda*. It is clearly an importation from Luganda and this brings us face to face with a striking contrast in Uganda between the Bantu and non-Bantu peoples. It is true that, even among the Bantu, missionaries imported a considerable number of very basic words for religious use, mostly from Swahili, such as *dini* itself, *sala*, *soma*, and others which we will meet later, but they also found that some of the key words they were in need of could be found locally, that for God above all. If they were bringing in a new thing *dini*, as they indeed claimed to be doing, it was still the *dini* of *Katonda* or *Ruhanga*, the God already at least obscurely known. Thus the 1898 White Father Luganda catechism is entitled *Eddini ya Katonda*. *Okutonda* meaning 'to create', the catechism could continue for some way within a substantially indigenous way of thinking and terminology: *Katonda yatonda ebintu byonna*. 'God made all things', and so on.

Among the non-Bantu peoples of the nilotic north, however, missionaries found this impossible. They encountered here, or thought they encountered, 'Men without God'.[10] There seemed to be no general belief among these peoples in a monotheistic 'high god'. This is not uniquely a missionary judgment. The African anthropologist and poet, Okot p'Bitek, fiercely agreed. As a consequence, all through the languages of the north they imported more or less alien names for God. In Lugbara, Madi and Alur the Protestants introduced the Swahili *Mungu*, in Langi and Acholi they used *Lubanga* derived from the *Ruhanga* or *Luhanga* of Ankole and Bunyoro. In all these languages the Catholics used *Rubanga* (the *hanga* root in Lunyoro, like the *tonda* root in Luganda, means 'to create'). Now it seems that Lwo-speaking people did know already of a rather nasty little foreign spirit called *Lubanga* who was responsible for tuberculosis of the spine. As a consequence the biblical and Christian Yahweh, not wholly adequately translated into the Nyoro *Ruhanga* but then transferred to Acholi, in an entirely different language group, and repronounced *Lubanga* or *Rubanga*, was carrying with it not only an absence of correct resonance but also a positively false and dangerous intimation. It was a meaning, moreover, of which the missionaries were probably for long quite aware.[11] *Dio* would surely have been preferable.

Very strangely, in Ateso the Protestants did quite the same thing as in the Lwo languages, choosing *Edeke*, again the name of a spirit responsible for tuberculosis of the spine (some say venereal disease). The Iteso did apparently have names – *Akuj* and *Apap* – for a beneficial, if remote, 'high god',[12] but neither group of missionaries tried, so far as I know, to make use of one of these names. So the Catholics introduced *Katoda* from Luganda, which they more recently changed to *Atoda* – a more Ateso looking word.

It is difficult to be sure today how far a pre-existing monotheistic belief and language usage of the people concerned was really decisive even in the choice that missionaries made among the Haya, the Runyaankole and the Ganda. The choice once made for Christians of a particular word could subsequently influence the vocabulary, belief and creation myths even of non-Christians, concentrating a diffuse monotheism or even upgrading a lesser deity across the selection of a single name as Monica Wilson suggested was the case for *Kyala* of the Nyakyusa.[13] We are becoming less confident than scholars of twenty or so years ago that there was, almost continent-wide, a recognizable monotheism within traditional religion.[14] Nevertheless it would be mistaken to swing too far in this direction and the monotheistic belief of most Bantu people at least has plenty of evidence for it.[15] For both Bemba and Chewa, on the other hand, *Mulungu* was either a foreign importation or a secondary name; its use may have seemed natural and safe for the White Fathers advancing inland from their Tanganyikan bases. *Chauta* was at least a more common Chewa name and it is now sometimes used by Catholics. The Jesuits among the Tonga had adopted *Lesa* and this was the primary divine name among the Bemba as well and accepted by Protestants. Bemba Catholics have now recognized this and a few years ago changed from *Mulungu* to *Lesa*. In Buhaya just the contrary has happened. Under the increasing pressure of Swahili in Tanzania, *Mungu* has supplanted *Ruhanga* among Catholics, though Protestants apparently still use neither but *Katonda* instead. We may well see much of this as an example of Robin Horton's thesis about the way conversion to Christianity and Islam was not an entirely revolutionary religious development for nineteenth-century

Africa but rather fitted in to a religious enlargement of scale which was already taking place.[16] In much of eastern and central Africa, so far as we can see, a vast multiplicity of names for God was being quietly replaced during the nineteenth century by a small number of more inter-tribal terms such as *Mulungu, Leza, Iruva*, and *Nzambi*. The coming of both Arabs and missionaries extended the process but also, on occasion went against it. Thus the White Fathers imposed *Mulungu* on the Bemba or held to *Ruhanga* among the Haya, but the advance of *Mulungu* in East Africa (helped by Nyerere's Swahili policy) or of *Lesa* in central Africa has continued none the less and in both cases Catholics have in the course of time conformed.

Catholic and Protestant missionaries seldom discussed this in early times in order to reach a common line, though in many languages they surely did follow each other's example. In some places, however, they made different choices. Where they came to an identical, and unchanging, practice, as with *Katonda* in Buganda – a choice too which has not been subsequently challenged by Africans – the agreement may in itself be some vindication of their choice, yet it would seem that in this case it was essentially a Christian take-over of a Muslim decision already made some forty years earlier.[17] Some scholars would argue that *Gulu* or *Muwanga* might have been a better choice, more probably that of the primal Ganda name for the one God (if such a name really existed). Yet each of these undoubtedly had its disadvantages. Missionaries were looking for the name of an all-powerful, non-human, unique creator spirit. Anything which suggested being one among several, having human habits or cruel habits (like the acceptance of human sacrifice), anything which brought God too much inside the human circle and might suggest a deified ancestor (such as use of the name as a human name or association with spirit possession) would tend to rule out its suitability for adoption. The case of Buganda is in fact in this, as so much else, a particularly interesting one. Unlike most Bantu societies it had a very developed pantheon of gods, the *Lubaale*, and its religion in the nineteenth century was focused upon the temple worship of *Mukasa, Kibuka* and others. They may well centuries previously have been kings. Was *Katonda* too a *Lubaale*? Did he too have a local temple worship? The missionaries – it seems – at first thought not and this may have stood him in good stead in their eyes, yet if so they were in fact mistaken, for there were shrines and priests for *Katonda* in Kyagwe, though their worship was bloodless and far smaller in scale than that of *Mukasa* or *Kibuka*.[18]

Gulu was the name of the sky and had no shrines, but in the Ganda myth of origins did have a wife and may have seemed rather too anthropomorphic a figure. *Muwanga*, god of thunder and earthquakes, (strictly one who fixes the world, sky and earth) was a name (like *Mukasa* or *Kiwanuka*) taken by ordinary people – a strong point against – yet it was only a variant of the *Ruhanga* in fact adopted as the name for God by missionaries in the area to the west of Buganda. In point of fact however, as already indicated, an open choice of names hardly existed for the missionaries to Buganda – the presence of Islam may have been already considerable enough to impose, if required, some degree of monotheization upon the name *Katonda*. But in general the underlying truth would seem to be that in so far as it existed, a diffuse monotheism was seldom tied to a single, unvarying name, unless it was so tied by foreign influence (as with Muslim influence on coastal Swahili and the word *Mungu*). Names were multiple, they came and went; they were often shared by a mythical first man or contained a generic note to include a much wider range of spirits. In the nineteenth century there may well have been a tendency, more pronounced in some areas than others, towards standardization of a sort, linked with other aspects of societal enlargement of scale. It would be foolish in such circumstances to criticize missionaries for their hesitations, especially as their knowledge of both language and religion was inevitably so limited. It seems clear enough that in most cases such names could symbolize something of genuinely shared meaning with the biblical Yahweh. They could also mean much else, but provided there existed something of the former and not just an unfortunate misunderstanding, then with constant Christian usage in an oral culture, the Christian connotations of the word were likely to multiply, the non-Christian ones to dry up.

Translation of the names of the persons of the Trinity has proved more complex. 'Father' and 'Son' would appear easy enough but while this proved true for the latter, difficulties have arisen over the former, though not everywhere. Swahili has *Baba*, Chewa *Atate*, Bemba and Tonga *Tata*. Catholic missionaries around Lake Victoria, however, discovered (or imagined) an additional insuperable problem, an instance of extraordinary doctrinal rigidity. It is this: the word for father in, say, Luganda (as in biblical Hebrew), is always relative to another person – *Kitange* is my father, *Kitawo* your father, *Kitaffe* our father. In Luganda, Catholic missionaries found no difficulty in beginning their translation of the Lord's Prayer *Kitaffe* . . . but in the creed or the baptismal formula, for instance, no particular relationship is implied ('in the name of the Father', not 'in the name of our Father' or 'his Father'), hence they fell back on the alien *Patri*, surely an unhappy rendering of something which should have such an intimate resonance. In Runyaankole and Haya they did the same, though in Haya a local word *Isheichwe* was also at first used. Actually in Luganda they also first attempted to use a native word, only some years later retreating to *Patri*. Father Lourdel's catechism, printed in 1881, has the formula *Ku linnya lya Sevo n'erya Mwana n'erya Mwoyo Mutakatifu*.[19] And what was *Sevo*? Presumably Fr Lourdel's miss-hearing of *Ssebo* – 'Sir', a title of respect often used for one's father. In the 1888 catechism it was replaced by *Patri*.

It is to be noted that the Catholic missionaries working with Luganda, Haya and Runyaankole, and settling for the *Patri* option were not only all White Fathers, but were in particularly close touch with one another – the Buhaya mission being linked with that of Uganda rather than with that of central Tanganyika. Further south the White Fathers did in fact think differently; thus those working among the Ha were prepared to use a relative form of 'Father' in the baptismal formula which consequently runs in that language: *Ndakubatiza kwizina rya Se nirya Mwana nirya Roho mtakatifu*. Bishop Van Sambeek, the proto-bishop of the area, commented in his old age: '*Se* means 'his father' a splendid relative term.'[20] In Luganda it was just such a relative term that Catholic missionaries found themselves unable to accept, settling instead on the formula *Nze nkubatiza ku linnya lya Patri n'erya Mwana n'erya Mwoyo Mutukirivu*. The Protestants never found this a problem but they chose to translate it not as 'his father' but 'our father'. Their rendering went: *Nkubatiza okuingira mu linya lya Kitafe, Nomwana, Nomwoyo omutukuvu*; (in this formula the Catholics strongly criticized the use of the word *okuingira*, a point we need not consider). Luganda was followed in this by several neighbouring languages: Haya and Runyaankole also employed *Patri*, Ateso *Papa*.

In Ankole Catholics have now given up *Patri* for the non-relative *Tata* or the local *Ishe*. In the 1960s I several times asked Baganda why, faced with this difficulty, they too could not use *Tata*, which is in fact employed in Luganda. The reply given is that it is too familiar, almost vulgar – an objection which might be countered by Jeremias's claim that Jesus's own use of *Abba* had something of that very character. I understand that Joseph Kyagambiddwa, the well-known Muganda musician, actually threatened to leave the Catholic Church because of its use of *Patri* instead of *Tata*. Aloys Lugira too proposed this in 1970, suggesting the formula *Mu linnya lya Taata ne Mutabani ne Mwoyo Mutukirivu*. This, he argued, would better express 'filial devotedness and affection' while the 'current translation betrays an under-rating of the vernacular'.[21] In fact the only change the Catholic Church in Buganda agreed to make of recent years was to replace the initial *ku* by *mu*. This was done in 1970. The *Patri* remains an extraordinary and unnecessary oddity (dictated, one may say, by a combination of liturgical fundamentalism and Luganda linguistic perfectionism) yet after a century of baptisms it has had its own hallowing, though today increasingly people are replacing it in practice with *Kitaffe*.

'Son' appears nowhere to have presented difficulties, all our languages except Ateso using *Mwana*. This seems strange, seeing how rather fundamentalistically literalistic our translations tended to be and that *Mwana* meant 'child', not 'son'. It does, however, now come near to representing one of the basic and best elements of consensus in Bantu Christianity – though indeed the idea of the *Mwana* of God coming to earth may in some places have been a pre-Christian conception too.[22]

The Holy Spirit was a far harder problem. Will you look for a word in the line of breath, or wind (*pneuma*) or in the mind, soul and heart, human psychology and physiology (*psyche*)? Swahili's *roho* comes from Arabic and is thereby related to the original hebrew *ruach*. With such good ancestry it may seem surprising that missionaries did not use it more. Among our languages it was only adopted for Bemba, and there it has recently been abandoned together with other Swahili borrowings. But, as we have seen, it was also taken into Ha, and doubtless into some other Tanganyikan renderings. The Jesuits among the Tonga adopted *muya*, a breath word. Elsewhere the tendency was to take a 'soul' word – *mwoyo* (Luganda, Haya and Ateso, the last again a borrowing from Luganda), *mutima* (heart) (Runyaankole). A considerable number of options between local words were open to the first translators; thus in Ankole, while the Catholics took *mutima*, the Protestants stuck to *mwoyo* as in Buganda. In Luganda the words *mwoyo, mutima, muzimu, mukka* and other possibles all exist. It was not easy to decide which to adopt and often the choice, required at a very early stage of the missionary process, may have been somewhat arbitrary. In most places missionaries were careful to avoid the almost ubiquitous *mudzimu* or *mzimu*, the word for the spirit of an ancestor, and just because the veneration of such spirits and their possession of the living is so central an element in African religion. If in the name of God the missionary church mostly opted for continuity with African religious tradition, at this point it opted on the contrary and emphatically for discontinuity: worship of the Holy Spirit was not at all to be seen as an extension of the worship of spirits, ancestral or otherwise, who often possessed their clients. Yet there were exceptions. In Chewa the Catholic missionaries did in fact adopt this word for the Holy Spirit (*mzimu woyera*) and in Shona Anglican missionaries also did so at first but later rejected it as dangerous. When one thinks of the particular prevalence of spirit possession in Malawi, one may wonder whether the Chewa choice too was not a gravely misleading one.

One verbal problem here was that all those spirit words were in the Bantu noun class III (*mu-mi*), like trees and bodies, not in class I (*mu-ba*), the personal class. There was a fear that the use of any word from class III must depersonalize the Spirit.[23] Fortunately this did not result in the rejection of all such indigenous words, but it did lead to some translators attempting to move the word used out of the *mu-mi* class and into *mu-ba*. Thus the Union Shona translation of 1949 wrote *Mweya wa Mwari*. But this was both grammatically offensive and showed an inadequate grasp of the language. All *mu-ba* nouns are personal, but not all personal nouns must be in *mu-ba*. The *mudzimu* of the dead was not impersonal after all but it was everywhere in *mu-mi*. The Protestant Luganda translation correctly left the Spirit of God grammatically in class III: *Omwoyo gwa Katonda*. In just the same way the Word (*Kigambo*) should surely be left – even in John 1 – in the *ki-bi* class. Catholic translators, however, placed both in the *mu-ba* class.

We may note in passing a comparable problem with regard to the word 'Trinity'. The majority of missionaries accepted a straight translation of 'threeness' – *Butatu* or *Utatu* (Swahili, Haya, Runyaakole, Bemba, Chewa and Tonga) but Luganda and Ateso have stuck to *Trinita*. Here as elsewhere Luganda has a specially complicated history. The first attempt, of Lourdel, was *Amapersona* – a very curious word quickly replaced by *Obusatu obutakatifu* which appears in the 1898 catechism. *Obusatu* is also the Protestant form to which they have stuck. The Catholics, however, abandoned it some years later for *Trinita omutukirivu*, returning from a Ganda to a Latin form. The reason for this seemingly retrograde step was probably again that *Busatu* placed the Trinity in a basically non-personal class of nouns (*ka-bu*) and so deprived the Trinity of proper respect. *Trinita* could be placed on the contrary within the *mu-ba* class, as it was. Although they had moved *Mwoyo mutukirivu* from *mu-mi* to *mu-ba* and even treated *Kigambo* in John 1.1 as if it were in *mu-ba* and not in *ki-bi*, it may have seemed too linguistically shocking to use *Busatu* and treat it systematically as belonging to *mu-ba* and not to *ka-bu*: hence they fell back on *Trinita*.

In regard to 'spirit' it ought finally to be noted that in traditional Christian terminology it would seem that a difference in word has long been maintained between what is used for the Holy Spirit and what is most commonly used for the human soul, even if the word used for the Spirit of God is also usable for humans. Thus we have the verbal difference of *pneuma* and *psyche* maintained in *spiritus* and *anima*, *esprit* and *ame*, spirit and soul. This is not the case in any of our eight languages. The translators opted for a single word to translate both, except initially in the case of Bemba where *roho* was adopted for the Holy Spirit, *mweo* for a human soul; but since *roho* has now been replaced by *Mweo mutakatifu* for Holy Spirit, here too there is now uniformity. It may be that this represents a serious failure to get a central element of the Christian theological tradition across in these languages. Yet it has to be added that there is a remarkable unanimity in maintaining this deviation in linguistic continuity, across all the languages considered and both Catholics and Protestants. It may then be, on the contrary, that this should be seen as a deliberate and valuable rejection of the Hellenistic concept of 'soul'. It is after all biblical enough to use the same word for the Spirit of God and the human spirit, and of course the latter has never disappeared from use, despite the greater prevalence of 'soul' language.

In many parts of East Africa, including Buganda, missionary teaching was initially imparted either through the medium of Swahili, or in a local language much affected by Swahili borrowings. Reasons for this were several. Swahili being the coastal language its missionary use preceded that of any other language by several decades. Up-country missionaries were almost forced initially to learn some Swahili, if only to speak with their porters; moreover they had Swahili grammars, dictionaries and Bibles to make use of in coping with their own still unwritten but kindred languages. Furthermore, while Swahili was basically a Bantu language, its very considerable Arabic borrowings related it, in a good many instances, to Hebrew and biblical terminology. (It could be compared with English, as a Germanic language. which has been affected by very extensive Romance borrowings.) It might seem in consequence a godsend and at first that is how many missionaries saw it, holding that 'a Swahili word was a better thing to introduce than an English one where the vernacular was in want of a loan'.[24] In the earlier twentieth century, however, missionaries tended to react away from it, almost as a poisoned legacy – the vehicle of a wider coastal cultural and religious influence which they feared, something 'actually evil'.[25] So they then turned to purging their theological language of Swahili borrowings. The history of Catholic Luganda is particularly illustrative of both developments.

Take the word 'holy'. Luganda, Haya, Bemba (and, as we saw, Ha) adopted the Swahili *mutakatifu*. Others found local words referring to the white or the sacred, except for Tonga which fell back on the Latinizing *musante*. In Luganda *takatifu* was at first only one of many Swahili words employed, including no less than the old Swahili and Muslim form of Jesus Christ *Isa Masiya* or *Aisa Masiya*.[26] This reflectd the extent to which very early Christian teaching was in fact conducted through a garbled Swahili. Between 1908 and 1912, however, there was a systematic removal of unnecessary Swahili-isms from Christian Luganda undertaken by both Protestants and Catholics. Swahili had come to be regarded as an alien and – perhaps also – a threateningly Muslim language, precisely in its Arabic element. *Aisa Masiya* gave way to *Yezu Kristu* for Catholics and *Yesu Kristo* for Protestants. (It seems particularly sad – and absurd – that at this relatively late date the two could not agree on a common form but actually initiated such petty differences. Recently, however, with a joint Luganda New Testament published, Catholics have begun to write *Yesu Kristo* too – a tiny but significant ecumenical step forward.) The same elimination of *Isa Masiya* seems to have happened at much the same time in a number of Tanganyikan languages. It would be of interest to know quite how and where this major decision was taken, a decision involving no less than a change of nomenclature of Christians themselves. In 1900 in Buganda they were called *Bamasiya* and their religion, Christianity, *Obumasiya*; by 1912 they had renamed themselves *Bakristu*. The psychological effect of these changes must have been considerable: indeed it seems that the old for long identified themselves as *abamasiya* in contrast with the young *abakristu*. *Takatifu* was at this point changed to the indigenous *tukirivu* or *tukuvu*, while *kuwabudu* (worship), another Swahili import, was replaced by *kusinza*.

Missionaries in Tanganyika even attempted to remove the Arabic elements from the Christian use of Swahili itself, insisting upon a restoration of pure Bantu forms. Already at the end of the nineteenth century *Isa Masiya* was removed from the old Zanzibar Swahili translation of the New Testament.[27] By the 1930s some were objecting even to *injili* for gospel and suggesting instead a newly devised *utume mwema* ('a good sending') on the ground that 'when expressing new ideas or describing new things, it is surely wiser to use words which may at first be strange to some of one's hearers than to use old words which suggest something quite different'.[28] This is a fascinating argument because one would naturally imagine it was being used to justify the non-use of traditional African words, familiar to new Christians but with a different sense, and the introduction of foreign ones. In fact it was being used to justify the introduction of what one might call 'neotraditional' Bantuisms which will now initially seem 'strange' to Christians, and the rejection of foreign (Arabic) but now very familiar words on the grounds that their underlying senses still 'suggest something quite different'. In the case of *injili* what is in question is actually a pretty basic and still recognizable derivative from the central Christian linguistic tree:

if the Swahili was dependent upon the Arabic, the Arabic was dependent upon the Greek. Nevertheless in the missionary antipathy to Swahili of the early decades of the century, it was felt by many that the word had somehow become too deeply Islamicized to be healthily used by Christians. This judgment did not, however, prevail and *injili* was retained by Christian Swahili.

'Sacrament' and 'faith' offer us the clearest contrast of translatability in the minds of the early missionaries. For the former all eight languages stick to option C – *sakramentu* or some such word. The sense of the specificity of theological meaning was here completely dominant. Interestingly Catholic missionaries appeared to feel much more relaxed in regard to the concept of faith. All here went for option A – a local word signifying believing or trusting – *okukiriza* and such like, with *aiyoun* in Ateso. Not one of the others adopted (or at least retained) option B – the Swahili (Arabic and Hebrew rooted) *imani*.

The elimination of Swahili influence, however, was by no means complete and a few examples of retention should also be considered. 'Angel' presented a problem similar to that of 'spirit'. Missionaries were confronted with plenty of local words for spirits of one kind or another but they were anxious to avoid them all, together with any suggestions of identification between their angels and the spirits of the dead or of natural forces so familiar to Africans. In this predicament they were for once permanently grateful to the Hebrew/Arabic contribution to Swahili, here *malaika*. While no other language in our group permanently accepted that contribution as regards *roho* or *imani*, everyone that could did so for *malaika* (Luganda, Haya, Runyaankole, Ateso, Bemba). The two languages to the far south, outside or almost outside the sphere of Swahili influence, contented themselves with retaining a Latin form: *mungelo* (Tonga), *angelo* (Chewa). And much the same is true as regards the Virgin Mary: *bikira* from Arabic and Swahili was taken over by Haya, Luganda and Runyaankole (where Bemba, Tonga and Chewa preferred *virjine*. Recently, however, in Tonga the latter has been replaced by *mumbulu*, and in Luganda *bikira* by *omubererevu*, in both cases a move to the fully indigenous word).

Again the Arabic/Swahili word for 'grace' (*neema*) – like *malaika* – continued to find favour in several languages, though not in Buhaya where *egabo ya Mungu* was used. Elsewhere it was carried into Luganda, Runyaankole, Ateso and Bemba. (In Tonga the missionaries clung to *gresi*.) In Luganda Protestants did in fact reject *neema* for the local *ekisa* but Catholics did not regard the latter as suitable and decided they had no option but to retain the former,[29] though in practice they have made much use of the latter in less formal contexts. Here as elsewhere, it may be noted, Haya has more recently moved towards the Swahili model adopting *nema* while Bemba has moved away, rejecting it for *ubusuma*.

Let us finally consider three further words as illustrative of the choice between foreign technicality and indigenous word and the predicament pointed out by Fr Walser in 1959: church, baptism and apostolic. All have long possessed a specifically Christian connotation, with any other sense almost forgotten, though each has a fairly clear secular root meaning (assembly, washing, being sent). How have they been treated? For baptism all eight languages, Swahili included, have held on to the original word *baptismu* or some such, just as they have done for 'sacrament'. The same, of course, has been true for many European languages, though not for German. This safety-first line in regard to the word baptism was not, however, quite universal in East Africa as Bishop Van Sambeek interestingly remarked thirty years ago when expressing some discontent with the 'exotic' character of the language in the Ha baptismal formula: 'The word *kubatiza* does not mean anything to a pagan, although by usage our Christians have got the meaning. I know a tribe in Africa where the Protestants came first and introduced for baptism the word 'to wash'. Later on the Catholics came there also and took over the word and still use it. But I wonder if the Catholics, had they come first, would have had the revolutionary courage to wash their Christians instead of baptizing them?'[30]

The pattern of translation of church, *ecclesia*, is different again. In four languages (Swahili, Luganda, Ateso and Runyaankole) the word was maintained as such: *klezia, akeresia*. Bemba, Chewa, Tonga and Haya all tried such local words as *lusangano* (a gathering) in Tonga, *mpingo* in Chewa. The obvious Swahili alternative *kanisa* was associated with Protestants and used by them, not only in Swahili but in Luganda and Runyaankole. This apparently made the Catholics reluctant to use it as this was an area where denominational difference, they felt, required clear manifestation in words. (Actually at the very start of the Buganda mission, in Lourdel's time, Catholics did use *kanisa* in Luganda but they had abandoned it before the end of the nineteenth century.)

Recently, however, the whole pattern has changed. Both Bemba and Haya have here reversed the normal process of moving from a foreign word to a local one, by giving up their indigenous forms and adopting the more distinguishable *eklesia*. At the same time two of the languages which started with the latter have now dropped it for local forms: Swahili has overcome the fear of using the same word as Protestants and accepted *kanisa*, while Runnyankole has replaced *eklesia* by *eiramizo*. Here too the denominational divide in words has been overcome, for Protestants have at the same time replaced *kanisa* by *eiramizo*.

While initially at least the majority of translators opted to retain *baptizo*, and even *ecclesia*, in the case of 'apostolic' the approach was quite different. Here the root meaning of 'sending' and 'someone sent' was at once latched onto in the majority of cases. Curiously the two southern languages, Chewa and Tonga, (the only two which have steadily refused *ecclesia* in all its forms) are the only ones which kept to the word apostle: *ba apostolo* in Tonga, and *wofumira kwa apostoli* in Chewa. In all the others a local word was adopted – *a kitume* (Swahili), *eyava mu batume* (Luganda). In Chewa too the *apostoli* have recently become *atumwi*.

It is clear that in no language did the translators follow a fully consistent line throughout our examples. They shopped around for suitable words, more or less adventurously and knowledgably, they argued among themselves, made some obvious mistakes and at times corrected them, so that in each language a different pattern of selection emerges. Fashions move back and forth. In general Catholics tended to use more European-root words than did Protestants, chiefly because they were less concerned with biblical translation and more with that of a rather hard-edged modern theology. It would be absurd to say that it is always wrong to use imported words; on the contrary, it may on occasion be the wisest course and it may well be, for instance, that the proper name *evangili* rather than some such phrase as *amawulire amalungi* (good news) will prevail in the long run in many of these languages just as it has done in Italian or French as providing an absolutely distinctive word for a distinctive thing. Some of the fashions of recent years may not last, but the general tendency to use local words instead of Latinisms or Swahili imports is surely healthy and will stay, with the exception that Swahili borrowings may grow rather than decrease inside countries where Swahili is the national language; we have noticed how, as Bemba is discarding its Swahili imports, Haya is tending to take them in.

The overall value of the Hebrew/Arabic/Swahili link has surely been a very real one for East African theological translation – despite the rather unbalanced hostility which surfaced for a while in the earlier decades of this century – and the problems have clearly been more difficult both in non-Bantu languages such as Ateso, where Swahili (or Luganda) words could look almost as foreign as Latin ones, and in Bantu languages quite outside the Swahili sphere of influence. On the other hand, the very proximity of Swahili could constitute a temptation for the translator who would feel relieved by it of the task of finding truly indigenous words.

This survey has indicated a considerable degree of change since the 1960s, even for quite basic words, including the very name of God. This is particularly true for Bemba and Tonga, our two Zambian languages: Tonga has pulled away from a particularly large number of Latinisms, Bemba from its surviving Swahili borrowings. Yet in some places there has been considerable resistance to change. The church in Buganda with its many Latinisms (*Patri, batisimu, klezia, sakramentu, musaserdoti, Trinita, komunio, konfirmasion* etc.) has hitherto been most resistant to change, unlike its neighbour in Ankole, although – as we have seen – early in the century, around 1910, it accepted major language alterations, including even that of the name of Jesus, without qualms. However, I understand that in practice words like *klezia* are being increasingly abandoned by the younger generation and replaced by one or another indigenous alternative.

I have referred earlier to an interesting correspondence on the Luganda baptismal formula published in *AFER* almost thirty years ago.[31] It related chiefly to a very precise point indeed – the repetition of the pronoun *erya*. It was clear enough from the correspondence that the formula was syntactically wrong and should be changed; it was also clear that in some other places similar changes had taken place and been easily accepted by the people. Fr Walser, the Mill

Hill missionary who initiated the discussion, mentioned that he had already raised the question thirty years before that (about 1929) and that the White Father Bishop Streicher had then declared that it was now too late for a change! 'Is it too late?' asked Fr Walser in 1959. To that Father Adrian Ddungu replied in 1960: 'It is thought in certain quarters that it is too late to change. This is rather strange. It took centuries in some cases to polish certain expressions of dogma and what was reached after research of centuries was most welcome. Why then, on earth, could we not change something which has been in existence for only eighty years, if the stark truth is that it is inaccurate?'[32] For most of the last thirty years Adrian Ddungu has been Bishop of Masaka. Yet little has been done officially in Luganda beyond exchanging a *mu* for a *ku*.

It is a certain fact that it can be the most Africanized churches which are now most reluctant to change their vocabulary – wedded, we might say, each to its own King James version. Elsewhere, as we have seen, in many other languages, from Tonga and Chewa to Bemba and Runyaankole, a considerable renewal of theological language did take place in the post-Vatican II years as part of a process of more powerful acculturation, liturgical renewal, biblical translation and ecumenical *rapprochement*. Yet African theologians have still done little to analyse African languages theologically. English and French have been their medium of expression. While this allows the international contact they greatly need, it is ironic that it precisely prevents the indigenization they so often and rightly call for in what is, after all, Africa's greatest traditional glory: its wealth of languages. A linguistic outsider like myself can only indicate some of the broad issues in a rough and perhaps not always accurate way as a challenge to insiders to take up anew with a fine comb the work of theological linguistics in African tongues, while learning for myself some lessons about the endless relativity of language.

8

The Post-Conciliar Catholic Church in Eastern Africa

The Catholic Church in contemporary Africa was profoundly affected by the Second Vatican Council (1962–1965), but the Council's impact upon Africa can only be properly understood in the context of two other processes already well developed when it began; one religious, the other political.[1]

It was only in the wake of the Second World War that the scale of Christianization which had been accelerating within the context of the rapid colonial modernization of other aspects of African social life, education above all, became fully evident. The 1950s were the high point of a new, mostly benign, colonialism endeavouring to get the young nations of Africa onto their feet in a western sort of way as quickly as possible. They were also the years when the Catholic missionary movement was at its most confident, most innovative and most numerous in personnel. The Catholic Church in black Africa in the 1950s was advancing rapidly in numbers, in the range of its institutions, in the competence of its ministry. It was still, undoubtedly, overwhelmingly white-led. There had never before been nearly so many foreign missionaries in Africa. They came from more and more countries and in more and more different religious orders and societies, including a quickly growing number of lay people. The appeal of Africa in the 1950s was a very great one and it was being responded to within the Catholic Church on an unprecedented scale – often to the bewildered alarm of Protestant churches and mission societies who were unable to field so many. But it was also, and increasingly, a black-led advance as well. The Catholic missionary effort in Africa had long been authoritarian enough, and in most places it had been distinctly slow in looking for any black inititative at all above the level of catechist. Only in a few areas, most notably the White Father missions around the great lakes, was there an African clergy of any considerable number in 1950. Only there – in the vicariate of Masaka in Uganda – was there, at that date, a black bishop, Mgr Joseph Kiwanuka. By the death of Pius XII in 1958, he had been joined by just twenty more, of whom half were auxiliaries. In 1958, of over 200 Latin dioceses and vicariates, just eleven were ruled by an African. Not one of the latter was in Zaire (then the Belgian Congo), the giant of Catholic Africa, though there were by then over three hundred African priests in that country.

Everywhere major seminaries were being enlarged, new minor seminaries opened, just as new congregations of African Sisters were being founded, new secondary schools established. There was nothing very radical or in wider Roman Catholic terms unconventional in these developments. Neither black nor white in Catholic Africa at that time was theologically or pastorally creative or radical. Seminary teaching was conventionally neoscholastic in the extreme. It is true that a small group of young black priests in Rome and Paris published in 1956 a challenging collection of essays *Des prêtres noirs s'interrogent*. They had been stimulated while abroad by the *nouvelle théologie* of France and Belgium as well as by the new winds of black nationalism. But little indeed of this had got back to the general run of an African diocese by the day Pius XII died. January 1959 saw the publication of an important new quarterly for the whole of English speaking Africa edited from the seminary of Katigondo, Uganda, *The African Ecclesiastical Review (AFER)*. Its spirit represented all that was best in the upsurge of the Catholic Church in Africa which was mounting from year to year: a new openness, certainly; a new concern for the lay apostolate, for an adapted catechetics, for a more participative liturgy, but nothing very radical, certainly nothing to disturb the sleep of the Roman Curia. Moreover for many years the *African Ecclesiastical Review*, despite the genuine efforts of its White Father editor, Joop Geerdes, was almost entirely written by white people. Clearly any sort of ecclesiastical renaissance had far to go.

Nevertheless the material was very much there together with a cautious but increasingly widespread sense of the need for more radical change – a genuine Africanization of this, in all sorts of ways, still terribly western, Latin, unadapted church. The missionary movement to Africa had developed in the decades after Vatican I, in the highest period of ultramontanism, and the missionary societies were ultramontanist almost to a man in their theology. It was a Roman church they were bent upon establishing in the utterly different world of Africa with its thousand languages and tribal division, its poverty and illiteracy, its marriage practices so very far away from those of canon law, its endless network of little villages largely inaccessible in the rainy season, its own amorphous but powerful world of beliefs in ancestral spirits, witches, rain-makers, all integrally related to the cycle of season and human development. The growth of the church did not necessarily mean the decrease of all these things. Indeed as the church did grow faster and faster, the tight early clerical control over its functioning and the lives of its members was inevitably relaxed, so that a new existential mix – Catholic and traditional – became more apparent. Hence the 1950s, if an era of great achievement, was also an era in which the problems of the young church were surfacing more and more obviously and in which, therefore, there was an obviously increasing need for new approaches, for an Africanization of Catholic Christianity instead of a mere imposition of forms long developed elsewhere.

That was, clearly enough, the point reached when John XXIII became Pope and, almost simultaneously, the *African Ecclesiastical Review* appeared from Uganda to call, mildly but insistently, for an African *aggiornamento*. But, of course, all this had now to happen within a far wider secular and political opening of windows: the colonial age was about to end. The Second World War, the decline in power of Britain, France and Belgium, the ideology and activities of the United Nations Organization, the decolonization of Asia, all this and much else had produced pressures which brought the formal period of colonial rule to an end in most of Black Africa in the early 1960s. There was a period of hasty economic, educational and political preparation, both producing and deriving from new nationalisms, taking the form of a range of political parties, some more apparently progressive, others conservative or tribal in base. Effectively, by the later 1950s all the European powers ruling parts of Africa, except for Portugal, had decided that it was better to pull out rather fast in an atmosphere of good will than to fight both black nationalism and world opinion. The Suez Crisis of late 1956 was perhaps the point at which a policy of retaining African colonies for a long time yet was seen to be unrealistic. 1960 was the 'Year of Africa' in which the Belgian Congo became independent in June, Nigeria in December – black Africa's two largest and most populous countries. Twelve other states of West Africa from Senegal to Congo (Brazzaville), formerly ruled by France, became independent the same year. They were followed by Tanganyika (later Tanzania) in 1961; Rwanda, Burundi and Uganda in 1962; Kenya in 1963; Malawi and Zambia in 1964. This meant that the years of the Second Vatican Council and its preparation were years of extraordinary rapid and complete political change: white governors disappeared almost overnight, black presidents took over their residences. Old flags were pulled down, new ones appeared. Upon the surface there was an extraordinary reversal of the previous order of things (a reversal, of course, wholly rejected in the south of the continent, from the Zambezi to the Cape). It was, however, in most places a remarkably peaceful and optimistic reversal. It was believed that this score or more of new states with their western-type constitutions and very small educated élites were truly viable economically and politically. It was obvious, quite apart from the Council or any specific ecclesiastical policy of Africanization, that the churches had to respond to the new situation. White archbishops fitted well enough into the old colonial order. They stuck out like a sore thumb as heads of the church in the new world of Nkrumah, Mobutu, Kenyatta and Nyerere.

Inevitably the political revolution was accompanied by a cultural one. In and for the young universities of Africa, history was being rewritten as something achieved by Africans themselves instead of something done by explorers and colonialists in Africa. African novels and plays were being published – by Achebe, Ngugi and Soyinka. African philosophies of society were being produced by Nkrumah, Nyerere and Kaunda. Friendly as, for for the most part, the new order was to the main mission churches - most of its leaders had, after all, been educated in church schools, while some had been seminarians or even priests – it clearly called for a very considerable change upon their part; a change in personalities at the level of leadership, but a change also in ethos, in priorities, in the sense of relationship to African tradition, culture and identity.

There was, then, an almost millennial sense of renewal in much of Africa in the early 1960s. That sense was, in its central thrust, or at least in the intention of its overt political leaders, secular enough. It could indeed see religion with its multiple separations between Christian, Moslem and traditionalist, between Catholic and Protestant, mission church and independent church, as dangerously divisive, something for which there should not be too much room in the new nationalist political kingdom. The millenarian sense could also take a religious form hostile to the mission churches to produce in Zambia the *Lumpa* Church of Alice Lenshina, in Kenya the *Legio Maria* Church of Simeon Ondeto, and many others too. It was then a moment of excitement, expectation, potential instability. But it was not, except marginally, anti-missionary, and most of the new political leaders realized how much in the fields of education and health they needed the co-operation of the major churches, and in such things the Catholic commitment was second to none.

All this meant that Pope John's announcement of an ecumenical Council in January 1959 and the actual sessions of the Council between 1962 and 1965 found a response in the African situation very different from that almost anywhere else. The mood of the Council, its optimistic image of *aggiornamento* and the opening of windows, fitted extraordinarily well with the wider mood of Africa. Moreover the forward march, the vigour, the increasing sense of need of new directions to be found in the missionary church of the 1950s meant that in an efficient but mostly quite untheoretical way there was an ecclesial dynamism available to be harnessed to the new vision. In the early and mid-1960s other churches mostly had neither the resources nor the sudden sense of a new wind, which the Catholic Church experienced at this point, with which to respond to the new post-colonial situation. In a very real way the 1960s may be seen as the high point of African Catholic history. Previously, especially in British Africa, the Protestant missions had appeared to call the tune – they were both politically more akin to the British colonial state, and intellectually more advanced in tackling the problems of Africanization. The African theologians of the 1960s – Harry Sawyerr, Bolaji Idowu, John Mbiti and others – were mostly Anglicans, Methodists or Prebyterians. The Catholic Church in Africa had, hitherto, largely eschewed discussions of the problems of culture, marital practice and traditional belief with which the more thoughtful leaders of other churches had long been wrestling. But now suddenly, galvanized by the Council upon one hand, political independence upon the other, and increasingly conscious of its own resources and strength, it suddenly entered into the debates and, for a while, with a vigour all its own. The years of the Council and immediately after the Council were, undoubtedly, for many Catholics in Africa a particularly exhilarating time – if often confusing and frustrating too. Of course that was not only true of Africa. It was the suddenness of it in Africa and the apparent providentiality with which the Council and its new guidelines responded to the secular needs of the post-Independence situation which were special.

It is also true, however, that the ethos of the Council came through less easily to many remote dioceses of Africa than to those in more technically developed parts of the world. There were almost no *periti* from Africa and far, far fewer newspapers and journals to spread the news of day to day conciliar happenings. Most African Catholics knew no European language. For a long while the sermons of rural priests and, still more, rural catechists were almost unaffected. Yet as the majority of bishops were Europeans – especially French, Dutch, Germans and Belgians – they were naturally in touch at the Council with the bishops and *periti* of their home countries, so that the missionary church tended naturally to learn from and side with the more progressive forces at the Council, whose message they saw anyway as pastorally appropriate for the dioceses of Africa. Theirs was not a major voice within the Council[2] but they spoke responsibly and they organized themselves effectively, thanks largely to moderate progressives like the Dutch Bishop of Mwanza in Tanzania, Mgr Blomjous, the South African Archbishop of Durban, Denis Hurley, or Jean Zoa, a young African archbishop from Cameroon who had been just a few years before one of the slightly rebellious group of *Prêtres noirs* who had published that symposium in 1956 which had so upset the old hands (several other contributors to the book were also now bishops). Already too, however, a certain division of sympathy was just beginning to appear. If some of the missionary bishops identified easily with the more progressive bishops of northern Europe, there were at least some African bishops whose training had been in Rome and who

127

identified almost entirely with a Roman view of things. Their theology was wholly Roman and a certain caution made them feel that in practice diversification in the immensely subdivided world of tribal Africa could only lead to disaster. The unity of Latin and an unadapted canon law covered over the myriad problems of countries including scores of different languages and cultural practices. Once you began to adapt to traditional culture where would it end?[3] Was polygamy, after all, to be permitted? Already at the Council, but much more evidently since, one of the complexities of the African Catholic quandary has been that the very scale of the case for Africanization and the programme it can quickly lead to provides an argument for its rejection. It is an argument which appeals particularly to some of the most convinced Roman-educated leaders of the African Catholic Church, men like Cardinal Otunga of Nairobi and Bishop Ddungu of Masaka.

The rapid implementation of important areas of the Council's constitution and decrees was, nevertheless, decisive for the future character of African Catholicism. Nowhere, in fact, had the liturgical changes greater impact. It was, in a way, fortunate that the decision to adopt the vernacular in the liturgy came after, and not before, political independence. If it had come in the 1950s, in the colonial period, it would have been hard not to agree to the celebration of mass in an almost unlimited number of tribal languages. Very many were in fact accepted for liturgical use in the 1960s; nevertheless guidance could now to some extent be taken from the policy of the new states, anxious to unify rather than divide. This made it easier for the church to opt for the over-arching vernaculars, like Swahili, for use over a large area. Nevertheless the number of African languages in which mass was being celebrated by the end of the decade was very great and the effect, in the transformation of worship, was enormous. With the vernacular went in many places several other, not unconnected, things: a rehabilitation and exten- sion of lay ministry for the thousands of priestless village communi- ties, a reshaping of catechesis, and a musical revolution – the use of the drum and the development of properly African hymn styles in place of western translations. It may seem odd, but it is probably true, that the most important single effect in Africa in popular terms of the Council has been the change in singing, in hymns, in music, in the use of musical instruments.[4] The pre-Conciliar African church set its heart on the possession of a harmonium. The post-Conciliar African church glories in its use of drums.

The transformation of the liturgy in terms of popular participation was just part of a far wider pastoral revolution. With a Catholic population rising by 5% a year or more, with an already bad and steadily worsening priest–people ratio, with the increasing loss of control over church schools to the state, it was absolutely necessary to rejuvenate the already traditional pastoral shape of the African Catholic Church. Its cornerstone from the end of the nineteenth century had been the village catechist. He, and he alone, had ensured regular prayer and a measure of simple instruction in the vast majority of village churches and primary schools. To begin with, he had been the school teacher himself, but then the two roles had split – the catechist remaining a churchman and a pastor, poorly paid if at all and poorly educated, while the teacher had improved in status, pay and education but had become in due course a government-contracted professional. For a while, in the 1940s and 50s, the Catholic Church had almost completely given up training catechists in its preoccupation with schools and the meeting of government requirements. But then its schools themselves slipped away and the 1960s witnessed a massive rediscovery of the catechist, a reopening of catechist training schools and a series of studies on the practice and even the theology of this form of ministry.[5]

Above the catechist training centres major new regional pastoral institutes, such as those at Lumku in South Africa, Kinshasa in Zaire, Abidjan in the Ivory Coast and Gaba in Uganda were opened. These have been the key institutions of the post-Conciliar African Catholic Church in which every aspect of a new pastoral policy has been worked over. Crucial again was the change in attitude to the translation and use of the Bible. The pre-Conciliar contrast between Catholic and Protestant biblical translations into African languages was striking indeed. In hardly any language had Catholics translated the complete Bible. In East Africa there were just three Catholic translations of the complete New Testament to stand against many complete Protestant Bibles and nearly fifty New Testaments.[6] The Pan-African Catechetical Study week, meeting at Katigondo in Uganda in September 1964, passed as its first and most memorable resolution a plea to the hierarchies of all African territories to work together with the Protestant authorities for the early publication of both the Old and the New Testament in versions adequate both exegetically and linguistically.[7] Meanwhile it required that Catholics be permitted to make use of Protestant editions. This was in reality a truly revolutionary proposal. Hitherto Catholics had been almost everywhere forbidden from reading a Protestant Bible. Within a couple of years of the ending of the Council, The Secretariat of Christian Unity had come to a formal agreement with the Bible Societies and Catholics were joining translation teams set up by the Bible Societies in many parts of Africa.

This illustrates another aspect of what was happening: the rapid transformation in relations with Protestants. Previously these had varied. In some places they were courteous enough; in many others, however, they had been ones of bitter rivalry in which each side thought the very worst of the other. Catholics regarded Protestants as Communists in disguise, Protestants denied that Catholics were Christians; each saw the other as a rival comparable to Islam. The change in the course of the 1960s could in places go very far, particularly in the area of theological education, co-operation in the use of mass media and, as we have seen, scripture translation. Of course, at grass roots level in most places the relations had always been good enough, in that most ordinary families were divided according to what school they had been to. Vast numbers of marriages were mixed marriages between Catholics and Protestants, but as a dispensation was seldom given, this would normally mean their permanent subsequent exclusion from communion. Yet again, as so many other good Christians were excluded from communion for one reason or another (in many cases simply because they had not solemnized their marriage in church but only in customary form), the state of those mixed marriages was in no way outstanding. It was just one of many things which demonstrated how far the formal canonical shape of the church was remote from the reality of popular Christian life.[8]

Finally, the Council brought about a very considerable shift in the concern of the institutional church towards 'development' work. This did not begin with the Council, but it was now much enlarged, particularly because far greater funds were henceforth available from western countries for projects of this kind. *Misereor* and its like became a dominant force in the life of post-Conciliar African Catholics. Hospitals had always been a high mission priority, but to these were now added far more agricultural and co-operative projects of one sort and another. Bishop Blomjous' 'Social Training Centre' at Nyegezi in Mwanza was symbolic of the new concern even if it in fact predated the Council – just as so many of his projects did.

It has in honesty to be said that in almost all the things we have been speaking of, which so characterized the period up to the early 1970s, white priests were taking the lead. In the direction of the pastoral institutes and special study projects, the editing of journals, the organization of renewal conferences, in the writing of books about the renewal of African Catholicism characteristic of the time, it was almost always white missionaries who were still in front: Ton Simons, Eugene Hillman, Bernard Joinet, Aylward Shorter, to mention a few from East Africa. It was certainly a weakness in the whole movement. Up to 1968 in most countries there was still a majority of white bishops. This suddenly changed in the next two or three years, not so much as a result of the Council as of two other things. One was a political realization that a white bishop was now an anomaly. The number of African priests had risen in most dioceses and it seemed politically and pastorally opportune for the missionary to resign and an African to take over. The second factor was different. By the end of the 1960s Rome was becoming alarmed by the radicalization of the reform programme beginning to be proposed in Africa in the wake of the Council by both bishops and theologians, and it noticed that those who were proposing the reforms were in most cases white foreigners. By appointing black bishops instead of white it hoped to relieve the pressure for radical change and – in due course – this indeed happened. As the 1970s advanced the radicals faded away.

The problems, however, did not. The high point of the confident post-Conciliar process of a moderate pastoral Africanization may be seen as the first papal visit to Africa and the most memorable: that of Paul VI in 1969. 'You may, and you must, have an African Christianity,' he declared to the bishops assembled from the whole continent in Kampala for the opening meeting of SECAM, the new official organization of Catholic African bishops. Great things were still expected at that moment, even from SECAM, and episcopal conferences did in fact continue to make quite bold proposals for a while. As a matter of fact, however, the tide of post-Conciliar renewal had now turned. The Council's more straighforward decisions had been implemented to great effect but, despite the fact that they seemed insufficient to resolve the massive pastoral and institutional problems of the African Catholic Church, for which they had anyway not been particularly designed, it was becoming increasingly clear that additional major proposals for effecting an 'African Christianity' were not acceptable.

In fact two clearly opposed models were now on offer and the traditionalist one was chosen: 'traditionalist' in a western and Roman sense. The character of the priesthood was the most obvious issue at stake. The reformers had called increasingly for a far more diversified sacramental ministry with the ordination of married men, including some of the better-trained existing catechists.[9] There were numerous dioceses with hardly half a dozen African priests in them and little sign of many more coming. The number of missionaries was beginning to decline, due both to a falling off of vocations in the West and political pressures in Africa, while the number of the faithful was mounting as rapidly as ever. By the mid 1970s there were many dioceses with hardly one active priest for 8,000 faithful. Moreover even in earlier years when the ratio was far better, the territorial size of dioceses, the poor state of roads and the multiplicity of small villages ensured that most Christians seldom saw a priest. All this was getting rapidly worse, and would do so still more as the rise in petrol prices reduced the possibility of clerical travel. In these circumstances a number of African hierarchies, including Zambia, Central Africa, Cameroon and South Africa petitioned Rome to allow the ordination of married men in order 'to answer the most elementary pastoral needs' (the words of the Central African and Cameroon request). The petitions were emphatically rejected. Indeed the hierarchy of Zambia was abruptly ordered not even to discuss the matter further. This was the point (1969–70) at which the main thrust of post-Conciliar reform in Africa in its logical development came to an end. The alternative model was an increase in the number of seminarians and priests of the traditional type. Here it must be said that in numerical terms much has been done. The number of major seminarians in black Africa was 1,661 in 1960, 2,000 in 1967, 2,755 in 1971, 3,650 in 1974 and it has risen much more since then. By 1975 there were some 3,700 African priests in all. Twelve years later they were over 7,000. This still, however, means less than twenty on average per diocese. In fact they remain bunched in a minority of dioceses – in eastern Nigeria, parts of Zaire, Rwanda, Uganda and Tanzania in particular – and are still exceeding few in many other parts. Even where they are most numerous the priest-people ratio has deteriorated rather than improved under pressure of population growth and the decline in missionary numbers. Pastorally the situation is now, all in all, very much worse than in many parts of South America.

By the mid 1970s a logic of reform had given way to a logic of conservatism. Cautious as the *African Ecclesiastical Review* might appear in theological terms to a European or North American, African bishops could forbid their clergy even to read it. Centres like Gaba were under continual pressure to avoid innovation. An attempt to switch the argument away from the shortage of priests and the consequent 'eucharistic starvation' to develop 'local Christian communities' on a Latin American model essentially failed because it was an idea imposed rather woodenly from above and, moreover, because as a matter of fact such communities already existed and the church would not have been able to survive at all if this had not been the case. The multiplication of papal nuncios (one for each African country or for two together) and their presence at all meetings of Episcopal Conferences ensured that the line the bishops took would be that preferred by Rome. Where there were bishops of more originality or independence, such as Patrick Kalilombe of Lilongwe in Malawi or Emmanuel Milingo of Lusaka,[10] they were forced to resign and move to Europe. In comparison with the African Catholic Church of the 1960s, that of the late 1970s and 1980s had become a Church of Silence.

This was not a merely ecclesiastical development. It relates to the whole African situation in this period. Compare Uganda in the early 1960s with its condition in the early 1980s. There was nothing odd or awkward about holding a large international conference at Katigondo in the Ugandan countryside in 1964. It was a peaceful, well-governed and prosperous country. Twenty years later it had been through a series of increasingly awful despotisms and a civil war. The economy was ruined. Local government had almost broken down. The Gaba Institute had been moved to the more stable atmosphere of Kenya. But what had happened in Uganda had also happened in Chad, the Sudan, Ethiopia, Angola and Mozambique, to name but a few of the more desperate examples. The 1960s were, on the whole, years of moderate progress and economic growth for most of Africa, but after that things went from bad to worse. Zaire had broken down immediately after independence. Elsewhere coups, military governments, tribal conflict, civil war (in places encouraged by South Africa, by the Soviet Union or a western power), the rise in the price of oil, recurrent droughts, all contributed to produce a situation entirely different from that in which the Council had first been welcomed.

There was now no money for conferences, or even for buying books and theological journals, little petrol even for the most elementary pastoral visiting. There was a recurrent state in many places of personal and communal danger. It was not an atmosphere in which the internal reform of the Catholic Church was likely to flourish, but rather one in which the attention of the bishops was concentrated upon survival, upon the immediate strengthening of local support and traditional loyalties. If the anomalies were getting bigger and bigger in strictly theological terms, that was not evident to a laity which had little theological education and only the most tenuous links with other parts of the church. It was not very evident even to the clergy, few of whom read any further theology after leaving the seminary or otherwise kept in touch with the church outside their own diocese. The local isolation of mission, parish and diocese had long been a major characteristic of the Catholic African scene. It diminished somewhat for about ten years in the 1960s. It then set in again. In such a situation the bishops felt strongly – just as East European bishops might feel – the value of the support of Rome. The last thing most would wish to do would be to lessen the Roman link by arguing for a more decentralized church. A few theologians might do so but the bishops, desperate for financial assistance from abroad and a friend to appeal to in their need, would not. They could hardly be blamed for their caution.

The wider state of affairs also contributed to an overall sense of leaderlessness. The multiplicity of countries and the often antagonistic relations between neighbouring countries (for instance between Kenya and Tanzania or Kenya and Uganda, between Malawi and Zambia or Zaire and the Congo) made it difficult for any particular bishop to have a wider than national influence. When there were only a few African bishops in the early 1960s, those who did exist were more widely known. Now no one was, and the inter-territorial organizations intended to facilitate episcopal co-operation, such as SECAM and AMECEA (for Eastern Africa), were able to effect very little. The problems of continental co-operation were simply too great at a religious as at a secular level. Even without a single country the revival of tribal and regional conflict, at times resulting even in civil war, limited the scope for major ecclesiastical leadership, though undoubtedly – to take one example – Cardinal Nsubuga of Kampala exercised an important and truly national role across the many disasters that Uganda suffered. He did this by combining a cautious but courageous personal judgment with the powerful support of his own Ganda clergy and laity. His strength was essentially a local one. He had never studied abroad and had been appointed just after the Council ended. His theological and pastoral attitudes remained those of the church of his youth.

Among the considerable number of young priests and young sisters too there was, undoubtedly, some sense of unrest. There were people who wanted to resume, and indeed deepen, the interrupted 1960s agenda of Africanization. The weakness in the 1960s had been the continued effective dominance of outsiders, a youngish group of enthusiastic but efficient missionaries. If the agenda was to be retaken it would now be by Africans and some attempt has been made to do so, but it has to be said that they lack an institutional base or easy recourse to the media. There is almost nothing of the more or less independent position which European and American theologians can find in the universities and elsewhere. There is also little of a middle-class thinking urban laity to support their proposals. There are also few, if any, genuinely well-known names. African theology is lived rather than published.

What has happened most decisively and continuously in these years is a process that has gone on almost regardless of the Council: the rapid numerical enlargement of the Catholic community. Probably at least twice as many people would call themselves Catholics today in Africa as would have done so in 1960. This is largely the consequence of the population explosion but also of the decline of traditional religion as a distinct allegiance. Catholicism has become the majority religion or the largest minority group in more and more areas. Where there were twenty African bishops when Pope John was elected, there are now more than two hundred; where there were over six hundred African priests there are now over six thousand. Where there was no cardinal there are now twelve, including two curial cardinals, Gantin and Arinze.

Africa could still be almost disregarded in the run-up to the Council. It is now, on the contrary, frequently cited as a major area of church growth and vitality. Many caveats may fairly be made in regard to that assessment. The proportion of Catholics ever contracting an ecclesiastically recognized marriage has fallen very low. A still largely priestless peasant religion is what has prevailed in most places in, arguably, almost as much continuity with traditional religion as with missionary Christianity. Relations with other churches are less close than they were twenty years ago, and gone is the sense that Catholicism is providing a spiritual and intellectual leadership for other Christians. There has been wave after wave of Evangelical born-again Protestants, fuelled from the United States, flowing across Africa in the last few years, and it is influencing even the older better-established churches.

In comparison with this sort of activity, strident and well-financed, the African Catholic Church today often appears inert and listless. It has almost no programme for change or advance. Its bishops are cautiously anxious to displease neither local politicians nor the Roman Curia. Pope John Paul lectures it, but never listens to it. Its theologians, in so far as they exist, are voiceless. Even in Zimbabwe, where conditions are exceptionally favourable, Catholic clerical leadership is now almost non-existent.

South Africa is very different. Some of what has been said applies there too, the shortage of African priests being particularly acute. In some ways the fact that black political hopes were denied, white rule maintained, meant that the progressive development of the 1960s, which began rather later in South Africa than elsewhere, has continued with less of a break. The wise, moderately progressive leadership of Archbishop Hurley of Durban has extended over more than thirty years – one of the very few senior active members of the Council still in office in the late 1980s. But apartheid and the political state of the Republic has inevitably provided for the church within its frontiers a different agenda from that elsewhere, and an increasingly political agenda. To the north the church's agenda has become, for good or ill, rather obviously apolitical. In the south, on the contrary, it has maintained and strengthened its participation in the ecumenical front established by liberal Christians against the racialism and oppression of government policy. For this a good deal is owed to the leadership of a few: to Albert Nolan, a South African Dominican who refused election as Master General of his order so as to continue his witness in South Africa; to Patrick Mkhatshwa, General Secretary of the Episcopal Conference, who has been many times in prison; to Denis Hurley, who has learnt with the times and yet kept ahead to provide again and again a presidency which encourages renewal. South Africa is a predominantly Protestant society, considerable as the Catholic minority now is. The sense of being socially at the centre which the church undoubtedly has in Uganda, Tanzania, Rwanda, Zaire or Zimbabwe is something very different. In South Africa Catholics are still essentially in the margin, at times a highly conformist margin, occasionally a quite creative one – even theologically creative. They are a more urban church than any other on the continent and that may be important for the future. They are also not leaderless.

The general characteristic of Catholicism elsewhere is quite different: it is that of being largely homogeneous with society, especially rural society, immensely numerous but with very little capacity to mobilize its membership for anything other than religious festivals: a profoundly pre-Conciliar church. Yet it was greatly strengthened in its ability simply to be by the central reforms of Vatican II: the reform of the liturgy, the acceptance of the vernacular Bible, the wider validation of lay ministries. Without this much the prospect by the 1970s would have been bleak indeed. Maybe it was just enough to see the African Catholic Church through a long dark tunnel without catastrophic loss. Only in the retrospect of the twenty-first century will it, perhaps, be possible to know. Meanwhile, buffeted by drought and war and waves of either corrupt or over-ideological government, the Catholic Church in Africa stands loyal to the heroic mythology of its missionary past, glad to welcome the diversion of an occasional papal visit, but almost entirely unable to chart a course, analyse its problems or perceive a future.

9

Emmanuel Milingo as Christian Healer

Emmanuel Milingo was appointed Archbishop of Lusaka in 1969 as a rather young man – Zambia's radio priest – aged thirty-nine. He was compelled to resign the see by Rome in 1982 and, after a period of enforced seclusion, now lives and works in Rome. It was in April 1973 that he began a ministry of healing which led to his removal from office. He described the incident in his booklet *Healing* written in 1976. The incident has almost all the main characteristics of Milingo's later work: a woman suffering from a combination of physical and mental disorders (she was unable to eat, heard voices and was frightened of her own child) came to see him. She had, she said, tried traditional western medicine but it had not helped. He now tried traditional Catholic 'medicine' – praying together in a conventional way, confession and mass – and it did not, apparently, help either. He then, by an inspiration, practised hypnosis. While the woman was relaxed and unconscious, he prayed intensely and was thus 'able to reach her soul'. The woman was cured. It was, for Milingo, a case of freeing someone from Satan's possession.

Very soon after this incident healing became central to all Milingo's work and self-understanding. Almost inevitably this brought him into conflict with most of his priests, both white and black, his fellow bishops and – most decisive of all – Rome. A charismatic healing priest has a fairly marginal place in the church and can with reasonable ease be tolerated, even encouraged. An archbishop is different. He rules a diocese and – in the case of the Archbishop of Lusaka – is the Catholic Church's most evident public representative to the nation. He is largely an administrative figure with a rather formalized pastoral and liturgical role. Remember too that Milingo was young, had been archbishop for a fairly short time when this began, that his home and diocese of origin were not Lusaka but Chipata in the east of the country, and that Lusaka had few African priests anyway. The greater part of its clergy consists of European priests, Irish, Polish, and Yugoslav Jesuits. Milingo was, as archbishop, already in a fundamentally isolated position without an integrated group of priests around him who would be naturally inclined to accept his lead or share in his cultural background. The criticisms of him seem basically to have been that he was mixing African tradition unacceptably with Christianity, that he was neglecting other necessary duties, administrative and pastoral. Perhaps the last was the most substantial criticism. There were also unpleasant and quite ungrounded insinuations relating to the misuse of money and sexual misdemeanours. It may be noted that if the attacks on Milingo were in part both uninformed and unfair, it is also true that he himself has had the habit of attacking other people, the more scientifically-minded especially, somewhat immoderately. Thus Aylward Shorter recalls 'a lengthy attack on the human sciences and in particular experimental psychology' back in 1971 when the archbishop was invited to preside over and address the graduation ceremony at Gaba Pastoral Institute in Uganda.[1] Moreover he has written of theologians in a wildly denunciatory tone: 'Their ignorance of him (the devil) has even succeeded to subject most of them to himself. They have unknowingly become his agents. . . . in many ways they have nicely misguided the Church through their scientific and systematic theology.'[2]

Perhaps beneath the more explicit complaints, it was the sheer fundamentalist and seemingly anti-scientific convictions of Milingo, manifest in so much of what he says and does, which were really the main problem. From the Roman point of view he was rapidly judged to be unreliable and a potential source of major trouble. As Milingo himself put it, 'The letter from the Vatican stated clearly that what I was doing was not becoming to a man of my standing as Head of the Archdiocese of Lusaka.'[3] That probably sums up the main case against him pretty succinctly. There was no impartial investigation and no chance to explain and defend himself. It is hard to doubt that he was treated wretchedly and that his fellow bishops were too confused by the issues, too unsure of their theology, and too frightened of Rome to stand up for him in any way. They appear to have been relieved to see him go. It could well be the case that he was unsuitable as an archbiship, even if the mode of his removal was cruel and damaging to the Catholic Church in Zambia as much as to Milingo himself. Our present purpose, however, is not to examine an issue of ecclesiastical politics but a way of healing, and it is to this that we should direct our attention. As a healer he is, in a way, unique. Milingo can well, of course, be compared with a number of famous healers in twentieth-century Africa – men like Simon Kimbangu and Isaiah Shembe – who link together Christianity and African tradition. However while most of them became prophet-founders of independent churches, Milingo has remained a faithful member of a main-line church. He is unique among such healers, furthermore, as someone with a considerable western education who has been able himself to write at length about his ministry. We can, therefore, consider it in a different way from that of Kimbangu or Shembe. Finally, he is unique in having successfully exported his ministry from Africa to Europe.

I have never seen Milingo at work as a healer, nor have I talked with anyone who has been treated by him. Futhermore I have little evidence in regard to his ministry as it has developed in Rome in the last few years. This can be, then, only a partial investigation of his work based almost entirely upon his own writing, seen within the wider context of healing practices in modern Africa. It is at this point worth noting that the earliest booklet Milingo wrote on the subject was the one mentioned above, entitled *Healing*, in 1976. It (at least its first sixteen pages) was written at and for a vast Charismatic Conference at Ann Arbor in the United States, participation in which certainly had a great influence upon him. By this time Milingo was already feeling lonely and misunderstood. In America among charismatics he found for the first time a thoroughly sympathetic audience. But it is clear that already in this booklet, as in his subsequent writings, he is considerably influenced by the viewpoint of this modern western movement. This does not necessarily diminish the accuracy of anything he says, but it does mean that we simply have no extended evidence of a Milingo unaffected by contemporary American and European neopentecostalism. This is still more apparent in his most recent writing. In Rome Milingo has moved increasingly into the Catholic charismatic circle which appreciate and support him, and his writing today – even when ostensibly on a theme like 'Cultural Emancipation and Healing in the Third World' – in fact appears to reflect current American and European charismatic approaches far more than anything specifically African.[4]

The first characteristic of Milingo's healing which we should note is his sense of mission, authority, communion with God. The basis of everything is the absolute confidence of having received a 'gift', as he himself calls it, from God. Until April 1953 he had no awareness of it but from then onwards it has dominated his life. It is something which 'befell' him and which, particularly to begin with, he found hard to explain. He says that indeed at first he did not 'recognize the gift God was giving me'. He remarked in June 1976 that if he had known at ordination 'what the future held in store' for him, he would have been scared to join the priesthood and had he known what 'powers' he would receive, he would have neglected his ordinary studies. Such remarks do not relate to becoming an archbishop, but to the reception of his healing powers and the painful confrontations they have brought upon him. 'Even today,' he continued, 'the Lord, my God, does not show me the immensity and depth of these powers. He continually varies the healing of the sick so that I never get attached to just one way.'[5]

At times Milingo compares himself with Jonah or another prophet. Three points may be stressed in all this. The first is that he always, emphatically and absolutely, insists that his powers are from God and Christ. They are a divine gift. Secondly, the gift is to him personally. It is true that at first he seemed to suggest that such powers might be exercised far more widely within the Catholic Church if people were only willing to do as he did. Probably he would not deny this now, but subsequently the impression he has given has been consistently of a very special gift granted to him personally. Thirdly, the consequence of his view that his healing power is a divine gift is that it is not to be seen as just the exercise of a remarkable natural talent. Nothing seems to annoy him more than the attempt of some to suggest that his work could be explained in natural terms as a matter of hypnosis, rather than supernatural terms.

How has this conviction of mission been communicated to him? In describing the original incident he spoke of how 'suddenly an idea glowed in my mind', and this sense of *ad hoc* inspiration when faced with a patient or when in deep prayer of an 'ecstatic' kind remains the dominant one. As he describes it: 'I am aware of what is happening to me, and I am sometimes even directing questions to God, but I leave the greatest active part to Him. As I enter into prayer, there comes in me a power which puts me at ease and makes me relax . . .'[6]

This form of communication, through inspiration in prayer, is reinforced at times in other ways. First, by dreams, though these do not appear as a very important phenomenon in Milingo's life. In February 1974 he had what he calls 'a strange dream'. 'The Lord Jesus said to me "If they do not believe that the powers you have are God-given, you should take an egg, hold it for a time in your right hand till it warms up. You then break it open and out of it will come a chicken." '[7] The lesson he learnt from this was to do things contrary to the expectations of the laws of nature. Secondly, and probably more important, is the way in which Milingo's sense of mission is regularly reinforced by the experience of conversation with spirits, mostly devils – and to this I will return – but also good spirits, guardian angels. Thus on one occasion he said to some of the latter, ' "May I know your names?" The names they gave me were very rare and strange. I went on to ask, "How can I contact you? Can I rely on your help?" They answered, "Yes, count on us." They were very gentle and obedient to me, and answered every question briefly and courteously.'[8] Such guardian spirits he on occasion identifies with the 'ancestors' of African tradition.[9] He can give precise dates for many of the encounters but, he says, he has written relatively little about his 'experiences with the spirit world' because within Catholic clerical circles he is so emphatically disbelieved. 'Some years back,' he writes, 'I told a group of priests that I was able to speak with the dead and the evil spirits. They almost uttered the word "*Anatemasit*", meaning "May he be cursed".'[10] It is necessary to refer to such experiences at this point as they are clearly an important source for Milingo's understanding of his mission, his confidence in being able to both grasp and battle with the realities of the spiritual world.

This gift of healing related above all, at least to begin with, to those suffering from *mashawe*, a local form of spirit possession to which we shall return. While he calls it *mashawe*, he increasingly explains it in fairly conventional western religious terms as possession by Satan or devils. There was, I expect, even from 1973, some healing performed by Milingo which did not involve explicitly a battle with evil spirits, but this was certainly the decisive element in his work during the years in Africa. Whether it is still so, I do not know. It certainly remains central to his 1984 volume *The World in Between*, which is of course an anthology selected from earlier publications. In many cases the spirit possession was explicit: the person being treated behaves incoherently and when tackled by Milingo the possessing spirit responds to interrogation. He quotes many such conversations, ' "Who are you?" He answered me, "I am the second in power with God." At that moment I realized that I was dealing with a lion.'[11] Again, 'I was recently taken aback by one woman who had five spirits: a Portuguese, a Canadian, a Bemba, a Nsenga-Luzi, and a snake. This woman changed from Portuguese to English, from English to Bemba, from Bemba to Nsenga with such ease, and spoke the languages so perfectly, that she almost drew away my attention from sending away the spirits. I was astounded to the core. And she is such a simple woman when she is normal.'[12] In other cases a general condition, such as childlessness, is imputed to the power of Satan. (Barrenness is one of the conditions with which Milingo has been most frequently concerned.) Certainly Milingo sees his healing work as a whole as part of a fight against Satan, but I doubt whether he regards all his healing as being precisely this, or every case of sickness treated as being, in any way at all, one of possession. For instance the long account in *The Demarcations* (pp. 66–74) of the healing in July 1976 of Mother Theresa Gacambi, the Mother General of the Assumption Sisters in Nairobi who had been involved in a car accident in 1973, is quite without any suggestion of possession or the power of Satan. Again, consider the treatment of Karen Swanson, an American psychiatric social worker in 1980, described by herself at the beginning of *The Demarcations*. She explains her previous condition as follows: 'My blood pressure was severely high. My energy had been depleted for two years. I had an enlarged heart, my left kidney was not functioning properly . . . I had also been in severe pain because of injury to several of my vertebral discs, which X-rays showed were pressing on my spinal nerves, causing severe pains which the doctors told me was irremedial without back surgery.' Milingo's treatment produced an immediate end to back pain and a normal blood pressure. The point here is that in such cases there is no explicit possession, nor –

on the evidence provided – is there any treatment of the case as something caused by the devil. The area of ill health treated by Milingo is a very wide one. In practice he treats anyone who comes to him – in his own words, he has no right to act 'as someone who had given oneself authority to select those to be healed, and those not to be healed'.[13] Of course, as he grew more renowned more and more people came. He claims that by the end of 1977, when he was ordered to stop, he was treating 500 people a week (at that time two groups came on Tuesdays and Thursdays: one group from 2 p.m., the second from 5.30 p.m. to 9 p.m.).[14] It is not entirely clear whether at this period, apart from the more apparently obvious cases of possession, he regarded most of his patients as being in any precise way victims of Satan. It is striking that in the ten cases described in detail in *The Demarcations* (pp. 53–93) there is not one single reference to the devil or spirit possession. These cases extend from 1973 to 1980. *The Demarcations* was published late in 1981 and it may be that by then the archbishop was becoming a little less preoccupied than previously with devils. According to Aylward Shorter, in the last few years, 'Exorcism of demons plays little part in Mgr Milingo's healing services outside the African context.' This, however, does not seem to be true; indeed, recent accounts of services in Rome have focused precisely upon the throwing out of devils.[15] The contrast seems to be rather between individual healings (in which the demonic element is largely missing) and public services where the dimension of exorcism is dominant. Milingo declared emphatically in 1979, 'For seven years I have waged war against the evil spirits.' His 1984 volume undoubtedly remained focused upon this war. It is true that on 14 April 1986 Milingo underwent a further prophetic experience calling him, it appears, to a new concentration upon 'inner healing'.[16] All one may conclude here is that there appears to be an ongoing ambiguity in his work between two rather different models of healing.

Let us turn now to his healing method. It includes various elements. The first and basic one is a profound sense of personal relationship established with his patients, an impression of controlling concern upon Milingo's part which results at once in a deep, calm, normally hypnotic sleep. He tells his patients to relax and close their eyes. They do so and fall asleep – even, he stresses, the babies.[17] In one case he was told afterwards that a sister had only pretended to be asleep and this, clearly, distressed him. The case of Mother Gacambi is enlightening in this regard. Milingo describes what happened as follows: 'As soon as I began to pray, a wave of divine power embraced her. I could see that she was totally responding to prayer. She went into quietude, her face became calm and plain without any wrinkle. She was very much relaxed. I felt soon that she left me alone, she was somewhere. I went on praying, till the time to speak to her. She stood up and shouted: "The water is gone! The water is gone!" As she was saying this she was touching her back.' In this passage Milingo does not say quite explicitly that she was asleep. Mother Gacambi's own account is as follows: 'He just told me to sit on the armchair and he stood beside me and said something to this effect, "Lord, when you were on earth the human bodies were subject to you, make this body be subject to me." And then he put his hand on my head saying: "Mama go to sleep." I literally went to sleep. Peacefully, calmly and completely relaxed . . . that kind of sleep whereby one is half conscious and half asleep. I could at times be able to follow what the Archbishop was saying but I was so content and happy deep down that I could hardly open my eyes! I felt that there was a certain presence and kind of thought the Archbishop was in communion with somebody with whom he was familiar. I continued to hear the Archbishop ordering the various parts of the body, "Heart, in the Name of Jesus pump the blood to all parts of the body . . . thanks be to God. Deo Gratias," and I really felt a current passing through my whole body. As he went on to call the bones of the pelvis to go back to their place I felt a cluttering movement within me. He continued to pray and I could vaguely hear him calling on the Name of Jesus, involving the saints and the Blessed Virgin Mary. He seemed to be in personal contact with them. I came to full consciousness when I heard the Archbishop say, "Mama wake up," and with his hands on mine lifted me up from the chair . . . I realized the session had taken almost two hours and the other sisters in the house had witnessed me in that state of sleeping peacefully.'[18]

Sleep or semi-sleep provides the context for the immediate effectiveness of Milingo's prayer. His prayer is the central and essential element in the method. He would certainly consider anything else done by him utterly subsidiary. It is prayer into which he throws himself with the greatest intensity and which can leave him extremely exhausted. The prayer, as we see, combines a direct calling on God, Christ and the saints with precise reference to that which he is praying for.

At times he adds to this the use of instruments, medicines of a sort – holy water, water mixed with cod liver oil, a cup of tea and so forth.[19] He compares these things with the rod of Moses and Aaron: 'Moses and Aaron were ordered to use a rod to get water from a stone. There was also a possiblity to tell them to just use words.'[20] 'I have no right ask God to make the healing powers more divine than they are.' Again he says, 'Since I received the gift of healing I have never, in dreams, been shown roots or any other way. But I was ever confident that anything I would use as medicine in healing would in fact become medicine. This has in fact happened. Even simple and ordinary water can be given to any one of the sick people and in each one of them this water will heal the disease as found in the sick person. The sick may drink the same medicine but each one will be healed from his own particular complaint. The medicine proper for healing headaches may be given to a person suffering from stomach ache, and he will be accordingly healed. This means that with the power of the Lord, anything, anything, is medicine if it is coupled with prayer.'[21] Clearly then he uses medicine but as little more than stage props. It is in no way a power proper to the particular substance which is important, but the sacramental power received by this substance through prayer to become a symbolic agent of healing. A more important agent of healing is Milingo's own right hand, to which he attributes considerable significance as the working instrument of the divine power within him. His right hand, he says, may 'communicate what people call healing radiations'.[22]

With his hand he is, in many cases, operating by touch – and it would seem that it was particularly the touching of women which stimulated many of the earlier criticisms of him. He prays for every separate part of the body involved and – one presumes – normally touches that part. Many of his earlier cases were ones of barrenness. Milingo claims that when at work healing he is not subject to normal physical emotions. He is 'communing with the world-in-between', neither earth nor heaven. While his body loses weight, it is 'suddenly readjusted to calmness, relaxation and a unique suppleness beyond explanation. It is under the control of a power that turns it in any direction as demanded by the Lord.'[23]

Let us note, finally, that Milingo's charismatic ministry is not strictly confined to occasions of healing. Thus he describes a confirmation service in June 1980 when, as a result of his anointing the confirmands, 'commotion began. Some people fell down. Others cried. Still others were shaking and trembling.'[24]

We have now examined the various aspects of Archbishop Milingo's special ministry as precisely as I am able to do, but I have left to one side what is probably its most contentious aspect – the underlying theory of spirits. To this we must now turn.

There can be little question but that Archbishop Milingo sees a battle with evil spirits as the very core of his work. 'The evil spirits and how to fight them' is the title of easily the longest chapter in his 1984 volume *The World in Between*. The subject is central to his writings from beginning to end, but it seems to take a particularly important place and be treated in a more extensive way around 1978, in which year several of his booklets were published including *The Church of the Spirits, Plunging into Darkness* and *Precautions in the Ministry of Deliverance:* in fact all his most spirit-orientated writing.

Milingo claims to identify, or at least closely relate, his understanding of spirits with that of African tradition. The relationship between the two we will consider in more depth later, but we should note at once that he actually speaks of them in ways characteristic less of African tradition than of western tradition as reinterpreted of late within the exorcizing wing of the charismatic movement. He and the two traditions are all agreed that there exist a multitude of spirits, bad and good, in close contact with humankind. For Milingo both kinds of spirits frequently possess people in one way or another. Milingo frequently speaks of 'the devil' in the singular, of pacts with the devil, gifts from the devil, possession by the devil, agents of the devil, and so forth. But he speaks as often of a multitude of devils ('it took up more than two years to deliver a sixteen-year-old girl from twenty-five devils') as of individually named devils (Lucifer, Astaroth, Naba, et al.).[25] It is clear that for Milingo the spirits are unambiguously either good or very bad, and it is mostly of the latter that he speaks. As spirits, he remarks, 'they can only operate in the physical world through someone or something physical'.[26] The requisite intermediaries are of two chief sorts which we must clearly distinguish. The first are people possessed by devils more or less involuntarily: the many cases of spirit possession which undoubtedly included a considerable proportion of Milingo's patients in Zambia. Treating such cases of possession involves the interrogation of the spirits prior to their expulsion. This is a major source of his knowledge of devils. It is to such occasions that he is referring when, for instance, he writes, 'On the 2nd October 1973, I talked to three senior demons who had in their company two others who were the spirits of evil men.'[27]

For Milingo exorcism is, or should be, a central part of a priest's ministry. In this he places himself directly under the authority and example of Jesus. It is Jesus who provides him with the power to throw out evil spirits: 'In the realm of exorcism we human beings are not standing in the ordinary arena. We are in the world of the spirits, and so in order to stand firm and face the enemy, we need to be clothed properly – hence the need of God's grace.'[28] At this point Milingo may be out of fashion with most modern theology, let alone modern science, and his preoccupations with exorcism may well be embarrassing for church authority, but he is not out of line with either the New Testament or central Catholic Christian tradition and he is, of course, very much in line with quite a range of twentieth-century charismatics.

The second type of person Milingo sees as subject to the devil is considerably more problematical. These are the active agents he is discussing particularly in *The Church of the Spirits:* witches, possessed mediums, and such like. In the first and later phases of his ministry there appears to be little reference to witches but they are almost dominant in the concerns of the middle phase – the late 1970s – and, it has to be noted, discussion of them is very much included in sections of the 1978 writings included in the volume of selections republished in 1984. 'I have talked with the witches and I have dealt with the dead. I have gone beyond theory.'[29] This is the basis of Milingo's claim to be listened to, though whether all or most of what he says in this connection really comes from individual conversations within his own experience, rather than from a body of accepted lore, African and western, one can hardly say.

'A witch,' he tells us, 'is a person who is a faithful and committed disciple of the devil . . . a witch, in this strict sense, is the devil incarnate . . . witches rarely agree to submit themselves to healing prayer.'[30] The devil, it seems, operates both by direct possession and through the ongoing client status of a witch. These two may well actually conflict, indeed 'those possessed by the devil will fight tooth and nail against all those human beings who are witches (needless to say the devil is causing as much harm in society as the witches). The reason why the witches will be revealed by the possessed is because there is no place for two kingdoms in the one they have possessed . . . what I have found out from experience is that there is no unity among those in the devil's kingdom.'[31] 'The Church of the Spirits,' Milingo declares, 'is a group of people who have been given spiritual power by the devil, and whose aim is unquestionably to wage war against the holy people of God.'[32] They make perverted use of the Bible and of Christian prayers and take 'courses', they may be baptized in a river in the name of Satan, they may be given medicines to drink at odd times (i.e. before dawn), they may not be allowed to live with wives or husbands, they may in due course get 'all sexual satisfaction' from marriage to the devil. Their way of life becomes 'a complete sharing of self with the devil',[33] the pact between them being finalized when on a given night the devil comes with some specific sign. It is not quite clear to me whether, when Milingo is describing the formation of these 'agents' of the devil he is, in his own mind, talking of what elsewhere he calls witches, or whether he sees these as being in some way different. Essentially, at least, their characteristics would seem the same.

For this kind of belief Milingo has no authority in the New Testament nor within the greater part of the Christian tradition but it is – of course – essentially and in many details the belief behind the European 'witch craze' from the fourteenth to the seventeenth centuries, and it is fairly close to many traditional African ideas of the witch. In Zambia and neighbouring countries of central Africa – though, of course, in no way exclusively – the fear of the witch as an immediately present, thoroughly evil and very effective person, who may well be identified within one's own village by someone skilled to do so, has surfaced again and again in twentieth-century witch-eradicating movements. Witness the story of Tomo Nyirenda in 1925, Mchape in the 1930s, the accusations of the *Lumpa* Church in the 1950s, Chikanga still more recently and much else.[34] When

Milingo goes so far as to write, 'The devils . . . confessed to me that this woman had been given to them by Mrs . . . , who is their agent in one of the townships of Lusaka,' he is approaching perilously near the very recognizable role of a central African witch-finder, though he has come to brand the witch-finder as 'the greatest witch' of all.[35] In the opinion of Aylward Shorter, 'Archbishop Milingo imposes a fundamentalist demonological theory on the phenomena of African spirit mediumship. It is a theory which has more in common with the *Malleus Maleficarum* of fifteenth-century Europe than with any tradition to be found in Africa.' This criticism is, I believe, a little wide of the mark. Milingo certainly does not impose a demonological theory upon all African spirit mediumship. He agrees with tradition in distinguishing between witches and spirit possession and is indeed not greatly concerned with traditional mediumship at all – something not identical with possession. He certainly insists that mediums may be in touch with good spirits (which he equates at times with ancestor spirits) as well as evil ones. It is true that he tends to see 'the possessed medium' as someone 'controlled by the devil', even if as 'the devil's transmitter' he is to be distinguished from the witch who is 'an incarnate devil'.[36] But the point which needs to be stressed is that, however similar his witch conceptions seem to those of the *Malleus Maleficarum*, they are at least equally close to the current local form of African traditional belief in witchcraft. But it is important to stress that this group of ideas appears relatively marginal to Milingo's work as a whole, even if it seems to have temporarily taken a considerable hold on his imagination around 1978. Yet it is a theme to which he keeps returning.

Shorter contrasts Milingo's interpretation of the spirits with 'the morally neutral spirits of African tradition'.[37] He argues that while Milingo agrees with tradition in emphatically asserting the objective personal reality of the spirits, he in no way agrees with it in interpretation of their nature. Shorter is challenging Milingo as a priest-anthropologist, and it may well be that Milingo's bitter words about 'priest-graduates and postgraduates of African anthropology . . . (who) come to us as specialists, fit for teaching their science in high institutes of learning and universities'[38] are in fact aimed at Shorter. Is Shorter in fact quite right about this? Certainly, most spirits – even 'alien spirits' – were not seen traditionally as unambiguously evil, though witches and spirits connected with them (e.g. the spirits of dead witches) were, and there were others too (the local *cibanda*) who were clearly maleficent rather than 'morally neutral', even if the note of nastiness may not be nearly as metaphysically unambiguous as the word 'devil' would suggest. African traditional conceptions were in general morally charged, even if ambiguously so, rather than morally neutral.

The so-called *mashawe* with which Milingo was, at least initially, so much concerned, are – it would seem – fairly new intruders within the Zambian scene, immigrant spirits from Zimbabwe, but they are not much different from the local *cibanda* or the contemporary form of *ngulu*. Clive Dillon-Malone, also a priest-anthropologist, has recently made a remarkable study of another contemporary Zambian healer, Peter Mulenga and his *Mutumwa* Church.[39] Mulenga's concerns are remarkably similar to those of Milingo and understandably so – for both are responding to the needs of the contemporary Zambian urban population. Dillon-Malone has examined very carefully the nature of *ngulu* spirits and shows how while the more old-fashioned *ngulu* (he calls them *ngulu 1*), if dangerous and difficult, could be honoured and welcomed, nowadays a new kind (*ngulu 2*) are far more prevalent, which are regarded as, on the contrary, thoroughly malevolent and need to be driven out of people at all costs. They are Milingo's *mashawe*. The *Mutumwa* Church identifies them, no less than does Milingo, as demons in league with Satan. Both agree that the only effective treatment is a strong dose of Christian exorcism.

Undoubtedly the *Mutumwa* Church remains closer in its idiom to African tradition and indeed to a deep ambiguity in the nature of such spirits than does Milingo. Nevertheless what they have in common seems far more than what may separate them. 'The reason people are suffering now is that Satan came down on earth and brought *ngulu* spirits with him' declares Mulenga in a service of exorcism and he, like Milingo, appeals to the authority of Jesus in his work of casting them out. The gap between old-fashioned tradition as perceived rather neutrally by the classical western anthropologist and Milingo's ideas drawn from his commitment to the struggle may seem very great, so that Milingo may appear as really someone imposing a mix of western Christian charismatic demonology upon Africa, but the position is in truth more complex.

The social reality of contemporary urban Africa effectively links the two together – and that, of course, is why Milingo could be so phenomenally successful as a healer in Lusaka. The healing ministry of Milingo, to be properly understood, has then to be placed within both the Christian and the African traditions, but especially within both as widely interacting in the context of modern African society. Society itself, as well as the healer, is fusing the two traditions, and the healer, when successful, is so precisely because he is responding to both the fusion and the confusion of the former. But the popular healer does, of course, not merely respond to but also moulds society's understanding of its maladies. Milingo needs to be compared not only with Peter Mulenga, but with Edmund John – not an archbishop by any means, yet the brother of one – the extraordinary Anglican healer and expeller of devils in Tanzania in 1974 and 75,[40] with Catholic Tanzanian priests who have subsequently done much the same,[41] or with Bishop Samuel Mutendi and other 'prophets' of Zimbabwe in the spirit churches.[42]

Martinus Daneel in his study of faith healing in the Zion Christian Church of Bishop Mutendi in Zimbabwe argues that there is a 'remarkable similarity between the *nganga* and the prophet activities',[43] in regard to diagnosis, in that both find the cause of illness in 'the disturbed communal society' and the relationship of the spirits precisely to issues of social custom and their disturbance; in regard to treatment, however, while the *nganga* essentially goes along with what the spirits want, the prophet on the contrary regards them as 'evil spirits' (*mweya yakaipa*) who must be overcome by the power of God. 'The prophet' says Daneel, 'recognized and deals with the psychological causes of the patient's trouble in terms which are familiar to the latter. Therapeutical treatment, however, reveals to what extent the prophet dissociates himself from the type of solution prescribed by the traditional doctor.'[44] Hubert Bucher in his more recent study *Spirits and Power* has reinterpreted Daneel's evidence to argue that there is really no such significant difference between *nganga* and prophet: 'Whenever prophets come to the conclusion that illness or misfortune have befallen a client because of the legitimate claims which a deceased ancestor or his living representatives have against him, they use the traditional standardized patterns of conflict as an explanation and recommend the appeasement of the irate ancestral spirit as the only solution, exactly as any traditional diviner would do.'[45] Bucher (now a bishop in Zimbabwe) sees this as part of what he calls the 'South Americaniz-ation' of African Christianity – the development of a religious culture which, while superficially displaying a number of Christian characteristics and using a good deal of Christian idiom, remains 'tied to the traditional cosmology'.[46]

I do not think I can agree fully with this view. While there is a good deal of truth in it, it is also undeniably the case that some at least of the Zionist bishops and prophets in question are not merely giving new names to old powers but also – while not denying the reality of the old powers, of which both they and their patients remain only too conscious – are asserting the far greater power of an independent and merciful God invocable in the name of Christ. Christ in such circumstances does not just fit into an existing cosmology any more than he can just abolish it. He realizes his lordship in human lives in, through, and over it. Of course for many Zionist prophets this may hardly even begin to be at the heart of either their personal religious experience or the message they proclaim, but for others it would appear clearly enough to be so.

For Milingo the case is, anyway, significantly different. Neither his underlying diagnosis nor his methods can possibly be equated with those of Daneel's prophet healers. There is really nothing to suggest that he has taken over the diagnosis of the *nganga* in regard to a link between spirit and society (though he may on occasion appear to share the *nganga's* diagnosis in regard to witchcraft). Now it is precisely that link which prevents the traditional spirit, even when rather viciously maleficent, from being properly termed 'evil': he is being nasty for a good reason. The Zimbabwean rural Zionist prophet still largely accepts this, if not entirely, but Dillon-Malone's account of a *Mutumwa* diagnosis hardly includes it at all. What seems here to be happening is that – particularly in the urban context and with the disruption of the traditional social order – while the spirits remain (as do witches) as explanatory causes of illfortune, the spirit-society link which grounded their underlying morality disappears. Hence *ngulu* 1 gives way to *ngulu* 2, Milingo's evil *mashawe*. The spirits then become, inevitably, evil, malevolent beings who should no longer be placated or honoured but only ejected by some greater power. They are in fact ripe socially for reinterpretation Bible-wise, shall we say, as devils and thus only fit for appropriate Christian treatment: exorcism. This is what Mulenga offers and Milingo still more emphatically. Milingo's explanation of possession has nothing left of older African tradition and is one wholly in terms of the diabolical plans of evil beings. If it is a bit beyond the point of evolution reached by Zambian society, the two are on the same line and the one relates very effectively to the other.

What has happened is that Milingo, Edmund John and others share fully in the belief in the reality of individual possessing spirits, just as the Zionist prophets do. Both then are able to minister wholeheartedly to people who feel themselves possessed because to that extent at least they share in a basic cosmological model (as the New Testament also does), but Milingo and Edmund John share it much less than do the prophets. The traditional spirit-society link has been replaced by them by an alternative justificatory under-girding for the activity of spirits: the New Testament model of strictly diabolical possession. *Nganga*/Zionist prophet/Mulenga/Milingo thus stand within a line of coherent development, spanning both social change and two different but not wholly incompatible religious systems. Each is needed to throw light on the cosmology, diagnosis and therapy of the others, but no two should be simply identified. Yet in their different ways and to varying degrees, Mutendi, Mulenga and Milingo are all standing on a common frontier as they endeavour to cope with real and urgent human needs and to do so with some measure of acceptance of traditional cosmology while modifying it by the imposition of biblical models and an intense, if perhaps fundamentalist, sense of an essentially invincible authority to heal and make whole in the name of Christ.

It may well be true that you will encourage the phenomena both of spirit possession and of witchcraft fears if you seem to countenance them authoritatively. Acccusations of witchcraft multiply immediately an expert is available willing to identify and deal with witches. Yet the increase of the phenomenon of possession in central Africa in recent decades is too well known to be ignored, too serious not to require treatment. People who do not accept that it is to be explained by the objective independent reality of spirits can, of course, hardly follow Milingo's road. Yet, as they have little effective alternative to offer the patient, they should perhaps be cautious about rubbishing the not unsuccessful methods of those who do believe.[47]

Emmanuel Milingo as Christian Healer

Archbishop Milingo is, undoubtedly, on any terms a remarkable healer, operating effectively across a strange mix of cultural frontiers. He has an immense confidence, willingness to give himself to his patients, and flexibility in method. He radiates an assurance of power which overwhelms his patients and a still stronger sense of dependence upon a God who is present here and now and able to help. His basic mission of healing, which he himself stresses again and again he does not fully understand, seems separable in fact, if less easily in his own mind, from the narrower preoccupation with a war against evil spirits. Separable again, and very much less important in his practice, is the matter of witchcraft or 'agents of the devil' as developed chiefly in the 1978 booklets. Dangerous as one may judge his preoccupation with the latter – and it could be that it was this development as much as anything which brought on Rome's decision to require his resignation – it is fairly marginal to his work as a whole. Probably he does not himself distinguish these things in the way that we have tried to do. His is an experimental rather than an analytic approach. It may well be that he was not, all in all, a very convenient archbishop for Lusaka but it seems sad – to say the least – that his quite extraordinary powers and intensely committed ministry, well suited as it seems to be to some at least of the most striking needs of contemporary Africa, should now be offered to people in Europe but hardly at all to those of his own continent.

10

Mission, Church and State in Southern Africa: The First 150 Years

For almost two hundred years, from the age of Dr Van der Kemp and Dr Philip to the age of Dr Banana and Dr Tutu, southern Africa has presented what we may well regard as a *locus classicus* for the relationship of church, state and mission – the complex and diverse interaction of politics and religion within a missionary context. The story, of course, begins well before Dr Van der Kemp. The earliest of all Christian missionaries to these parts, the Jesuit Fr da Silveira, arrived at the court of Monomotapa just after Christmas 1560 and baptized the king and his mother soon afterwards. Three months later he was murdered. Fr Silveira had earlier baptized another would-be Constantine on the coast. His views of conversion were clearly simple enough and they certainly included what – in medieval terms – was a quite traditional model of church-state relations. The subsequent punitive Portuguese expedition under Barreto actually had a Jesuit priest, Francisco de Monclaro, as Barreto's special adviser and practically speaking deputy commander.[1] The missionary mix-up of church and state is, then, an old one here as elsewhere, and there is surely much which would seem to justify those churchmen, not to speak of politicians, who in modern times have time and again called for a complete separation of religion from politics. Yet time and again, too, however much they may reject the simplicities of the old-fashioned alliance between church and state, there have been church leaders in southern Africa to insist that, when it comes to substantive issues of freedom and justice, there is an absolute inseparability between the church's mission and matters political.

Dr Johannes Van der Kemp, the London Missionary Society's first representative in South Africa, arrived at Cape Town in March 1799. If he was not quite the first Protestant missionary in the area, being proceeded by some Moravians, he can well be taken as effectively the founder figure of the modern missionary movement in southern Africa. A very fine founder figure, I believe, he was, if one both maligned in his time and still to this day greatly under-appreciated. Though Van der Kemp had intended to work among the Xhosa, still well outside the area of European rule, he soon realized that the Hottentots[2] were in much greater immediate need of his assistance. The need in question was socio-economic not evangelical. They had been reduced by the advance of the colonists to a most miserable condition: either landless wanderers or slaves (or near slaves) on a Boer farm. Van der Kemp saw his work, not only as the Christian conversion of the Hottentots, but as a struggle for their political and economic rights. 'The Hottentots should be perfectly free' he declared in a conversation with Governor Janssens in October 1801.[3] Despite the account of detractors, it was always part of the intention of the settlement he established at Bethelsdorp to ensure the economic advance of the Hottentots, and the loathing which Van der Kemp quickly inspired in many of the colonists derived precisely from the political and economic significance of his understanding of mission: he was diverting their labour market and arguing that the Hottentots had rights just like the Europeans. Let us recall too the special service he held at Bethelsdorp in 1807 of public thanksgiving for Parliament's prohibition of the slave trade, in which all people, old and young, were assembled and, mindful of 'the horrid usage of the poor slaves still in bondage in this colony' agreed to be urgent in prayer that 'this great evil' be wholly done away with. Here liturgy and political liberation were, from the start of our history, fused into one.

However much, and however rightly, Van der Kemp saw himself as an evangelical missionary, there is no doubt that the colonists saw him – and not unreasonably – as a very political one. Indeed his successor, John Philip, declared emphatically that the missionaries were 'the only real protectors the Hottentots have in South Africa'. This role Philip endeavoured to extend to many other peoples. In southern Africa the political priest is, then, as old as the mission. His self-understanding entailed the church's commitment to defend the weak against the strong in all circumstances and by any lawful means available: appeals to government and public opinion, locally and in Europe; the publication of the misdeeds of the powerful, the use of church resources to protect the oppressed, offer them employment and teach them not only such skills as improve their economic position but also the political skills of self defence. Faced, as they saw it, with oppressing colonists and oppressed natives, Van der Kemp and Philip did not believe that they could somehow maintain a role of neutrality, in order ultimately to reconcile the two. Rather they took sides and coupled this with the voice of prophecy, calling in straight Old Testament terms for the liberation of the oppressed. 'I could not forbear to warn him,' Van der Kemp wrote, after a conversation with Governor Janssens, 'of the displeasure of God who most certainly would hear the cries of the oppressed.'

It is clear not only that Van der Kemp and Philip were highly unpopular with the white community as a whole, but that many missionaries at the time, and still more subsequently, rejected their approach. It is with certain issues pertaining to this ongoing debate, almost schism, within the church that I will now turn. Even within the London Missionary Society Robert Moffat may be taken as an example of an outstanding missionary who disliked Philip for being a great deal too political. But let us take the controversy which broke into print between the Wesleyans and Philip in the 1830s as illustrative of the central issue. The relevant documents were published by William Shaw in his *A Defense of the Wesleyan Missionaries in Southern Africa*. Philip's view was that it was the missionary's task to 'defend the weak against the strong' and to be seen to be doing so. For the Wesleyans this was unacceptable in that it meant taking sides between white and black; it could even mean the missionaries 'placing themselves at the head of one of the contending parties', becoming partisan when they should remain ever available as 'mediators'.[4]

It is interesting to find in this argument so very much the same issues as divide Christians today. 'Liberation' involves entering into the struggle, 'reconciliation' means standing apart and above it. Yet then, as now, the objection to becoming partisan in matters political was almost inevitably selective. In regard to conflict between Africans there was seldom the same inhibition about taking sides. Moffat admittedly tried hard to avert a battle with the so-called 'Mantatees', but when it became inevitable he acted as the very 'generalissimo' of the combined force of Bechuana and Griquas.[5] There is no doubt at all on which side he stood. The Methodists too became clearly partisan when it was a matter of defending the political rights of a chief with Methodist sympathies against one without.[6] What was objected to in Philip was the extension of such attitudes to white-black relations, at least when it meant adopting a position consistently unfavourable to the claims of the powerful.

After the death of Philip in 1851 there were undoubtedly other missionaries in southern Africa, particularly perhaps men connected with Lovedale, who shared his basic view, but they were, I think, rather few and mostly rather remote from the centres of ecclesiastical power. John Colenso, the angular, perennially out-of-step Anglican Bishop of Natal was in the 1870s and until his death in 1883 in this, as in so much else, the great exception. His unflagging efforts on behalf of justice for Langalibalele, chief of the Hlubi, and then for Cetshwayo and the Zulu kingdom, were immensely impressive and incurred the bitter anger of most white people in Natal. But they were wholly isolated. He enjoyed no support from any sector of the ecclesiastical community. The consciousness of being a force for secular liberation, so strong in the missionary movement in the immediate wake of the anti-slave trade campaign, had lost any critical sense of direction when faced with the colonizing euphoria and more complex oppressions of the high era of imperial advance, though it could be resurrected among Free Churchmen in regard to the barbarities of the Congo Free State. Among Anglicans, as among Roman Catholics, it seems – however – to have been particularly lacking until, in the early twentieth century, it was revived as one aspect of the more socialist side of Anglo-Catholicism. What was dominant was rather a sense of establishment, of being – if not officially, then unofficially – the colonial state-church. If political matters were to be touched upon it should never be in a way that could publicly embarrass authority, but only within the chosen and confidential circle of the governor's garden party.

In the conclusion to his fine recent study of Colenso Jeff Guy writes, 'We cannot of course use the principles upon which Colenso based his actions: with hindsight we can see their limitations.'[7] I feel obliged to take issue with that judgment. The principles with which

Philip worked in the Cape from 1820–1850 and which actuated Colenso in his struggles for justice in Natal and Zululand in the 1870s were, as I see them, roughly as follows: they accepted the legitimacy of the existing government under which they lived – that is to say of British government in the Cape and Natal – but maintained that if it was legitimate government, it had also to be just government, and in fact they had in Britain a public opinion which in principle supported them. They saw, however, that the majority peoples of both colonies were treated most unjustly and they believed it to be the duty of the church to struggle in every way open to it to right that injustice, though such a struggle inevitably involved taking sides over immediate issues, and taking sides against the powerful. It would have been quite impractical, indeed almost nonsensical, to go further and challenge the validity of colonial government as such. They did, however, equally accept the legitimacy of the government of independent African states – Philip of the Xhosa, Colenso of Zululand. They opposed as both unnecessary and unjust the wars with them and the elimination of their independence. They by no means accepted arguments that the supposed injustices prevalent within such states justified British intervention. They were, then, in a basic manner more genuinely opposed to the under-girding logic of current imperialism than they themselves quite recognized.

Their struggles had little success. Those of Philip had some, not inconsiderable, temporary effect, both political and economic, as friends and enemies fully recognized at the time. But it was largely swept away after his death. Colenso, despite the ceaseless toil of the last years of his life and the impression he made on Lord Carnarvon the Secretary for the Colonies, when he visited London in 1874, in fact almost entirely failed in his immediate aims. It is easy to assert that this had to be so, that it was the inevitable consequence of the inner law of a temporarily invincible imperialism. I do not believe it. What is remarkable is the weight which their isolated voices yet acquired and the consequent intense hatred generated among the colonists. Without them things could have been considerably worse for the oppressed, but equally, if they had been less isolated in their protests, things might have been far better.

Philip was the less isolated of the two. He retained the confidence of many London Mission Society missionaries in the field, and of the society itself in London, even if he lacked support from other churches. He was a masterful man and the real improvements, legal and economic, which the coloured community experienced in the 1820s and 1830s surely owed much to his unceasing activity on its behalf. Once dead, however, Philip was not replaced. Moreover, the Anglican Church, far the most powerful church in England and increasingly so in South Africa in the second half of the nineteenth century, made almost no attempt then or later to challenge injustice. Following Philip there was a void. Colenso was notoriously isolated. If he had had the support of other clergy in his protests over Langalibalele and the Zulu war things might well have been very different, but his criticisms of pentateuchal inaccuracy had already forfeited him the support of most of his fellow Christians in all his endeavours. Philip could, arguably, be said to have represented the missionary church as such. Colenso in no way did so. From the death of Philip the church had next to nothing effective to say about injustice in southern Africa for a very long time.

It was in that context that the foundation of Rhodesia took place. The collusion of missionaries in settler politics was seldom greater and with some Rhodesian missionaries of the 1890s, both Protestant and Catholic, we may feel ourselves very nearly back to Monclaro. Consider one mild exception, Bishop Knight-Bruce, a man who in his own opinion and a more general view, distanced himself from Rhodesian colonialism in a way many other missionaries did not. Nevertheless his approach as a whole, while uncomfortably ambiguous, went along all in all pretty smoothly with the plans of Rhodes. His one little whimper – in a speech at Vryburg in December 1888 – against Rhodes' short-term scheme to provide some extra rifles for the Matabele – was quickly dealt with and Rhodes twisted him round his finger so effectively as to make of the bishop, in Rhodes' view, 'our cordial supporter'. Indeed, Knight-Bruce then wrote to Lobengula stressing his own friendship and adding that Rhodes and Rudd 'are friends of mine' and that 'no other people would be better friends to your country than these' (12 March, 1889). Yet in his Vryburg speech he had declared that 'with the Matabele I have nothing to do; they are no business of mine whatever'.[8] The main point of the speech had been to press for an English protectorate over Mashonaland for just the sort of reason that Colenso had rejected in the case of Zululand; if, theoretically, an English Protectorate was not precisely what Rhodes was wanting, in practice such an appeal could only strengthen Rhodes' hand. The gospel of liberation, as Knight-Bruce had reinterpreted it, in fact led exactly to the pioneer column and so to the Shona rebellion of 1896.

Mr Rhodes was an atheist but he understood better than most the uses of organized religion and by numerous land grants and other little forms of assistance he tied the missionaries of many churches and societies to his juggernaut with remarkable effectiveness. The failure over many years of both the London Missionary Society and the Jesuit missionaries in Matabeleland to produce conversions had convinced the missionary community that the destruction of Matabele power was needed for the success of evangelization. The basic point remains that while the majority of missionaries in early Rhodesia would most certainly have repudiated the attitudes of Philip or Colenso and claimed that their task was a purely religious one, they in fact linked the gospel with politics in no uncertain way: they acquiesced in being, in a more or less collective manner, a colonial state-church, at once privileged and captive.

It is against this background that we need to view the work of John White and Arthur Shearly Cripps. White, a Methodist, entered Rhodesia in the early 1890s; Cripps, an Anglican, in 1901. Two men of outstanding ability and courage, they managed between them to resurrect the Philip-Colenso tradition within the altered circumstances of the first half of the twentieth century. They do so indeed somewhat piquantly. White, the Free Churchman, is able like Philip to exercise something of an episcopal role. As President of the Southern Rhodesian Missionary Conference in the 1920s he challenged colonial authority in a way that no authoritative ecclesiastical voice had done since Philip's death. Cripps, the Anglican lone wolf, on the other hand, was quite unable to carry his church with him, and in fact officially severed himself from the missionary connection as Colenso had been severed. The Bishop of Cape Town had repudiated Colenso, his successor could now repudiate Cripps. Indeed, although Cripps could speak with unrivalled vehemence, poetic insight, and even at times considerable tactical skill, he had a sort of idiosyncratic impracticality which did ensure his effective isolation. The St Francis of Zimbabwe, only given the essential isolatedness of the true prophet, could he be regarded as representing the missionary church in its relationship with the state. White was a different type. While he remained Cripps' close friend and ally, he was a man of great practical experience, the founder of Waddilove Institute and much else, the leading member of the leading Protestant church in the country. It was just because he was so experienced and successful and balanced that he could be elected President of the Missionary Conference and make of it for a few short years an almost effective challenger of government malpractice.

The missionary, White told the Conference in his presidential address, 'is bound to be revolutionary', 'he must not be afraid of nationalism' but until nationalism itself is strong enough to guard the interests of Africans the missionary should 'assume the role of Trusteeship for these people'. He must speak out, declared White, as did Isaiah and Amos. Moreover a united missionary church could do so effectively: 'United we can do almost anything we choose. . . . The United Church of South Africa, did it realize it, holds in the hollow of its hand the destiny of this land'.[9] No wonder such words drew the fire of Godfrey Huggins (the Prime Minister of Southern Rhodesia)! White's hopes were very high, his power was very brief. The missionary church was not united and, faced with government criticism, White was not even elected to the Conference executive in 1930. 'Did one single Missionary Conference member stand up and say a word on his behalf?' asked Cripps afterwards, 'Faugh! the mangy forcible feeble crowd.' It was, he said, 'the betrayal of a great cause . . . the sad breaking up of the noble companionship of the Order of Knights of the Round Table'. It was not the first such betrayal, nor would it be the last. The missionary church in Rhodesia would not begin to speak again with the voice of White until the 1960s, and it would then be chiefly the Catholic episcopate and its *Justice and Peace Commission* which would do so.

A dozen years earlier than that, however, back in South Africa, faced with the new nationalist implementation of apartheid, there was a new burst of prophetic dissent. Michael Scott and Trevor Huddleston were Anglican priests very much in the tradition of Colenso. Indeed Geoffrey Clayton, Bishop of Johannesburg and then Archbishop of Cape Town, authenticated the continuity by doing his best to silence both. As with their predecessors their immediate success was slight. Here as always the lone voice will irritate the state but not affect its policies; yet the lone voice will at least prevent the total corruption of the church and a book like *Naught for Your Comfort* – still, perhaps, the greatest Christian literary protest against racialist oppression – has greatly affected the heart of the church itself.

Even Geoffrey Clayton found it hard not to turn prophetic in the world of Verwoerd and from the 1950s with Ambrose Reeves, Joost de Blank, Colin Winter and Kenneth Skelton, the Anglican episcopal voice did at long last begin to appropriate the tradition of John Philip. Furthermore, with the *aggiornamento* of the Catholic Church and the rebirth of liberation theology in a Latin American context, bishops like Denis Hurley and Donal Lamont began to carry the torch across to the place where, I would argue, it should have been burning brightly all along – the Great Church itself. Today, in a different but equally important transference, principal responsibility for the prophetic voice is being passed at long last from white to black, to Desmond Tutu, Allan Boesak, and others like them. Moreover, they enjoy a wider measure of church support – from the South African Council of Churches, the Catholic bishops and elsewhere – than any of their predecessors. Perhaps something like John White's 'United Church' is at long last almost beginning to be realized. The agenda before them in South Africa and the agenda too in the lands to the north of them is in some ways changing, or likely to change, very considerably, but oppression is not limited to colonialism and it may be as difficult, but as necessary, to speak prophetically in the Zimbabwe or the Mozambique of the 1980s as it ever was in the years of white rule. It would be naïvely mistaken to imagine that the initial – or even enduring – good intentions of the governments of 'majority rule' suffice to ensure that the church can now simply co-operate with the state and must not also stand apart, berated if need be by black rulers as formerly by white, to continue challenging injustice and double-talk.

I fear this has been a far too compressed, partial, in some sense one-sided, survey of the relationship of the church, state and mission in southern Africa across two centuries. There are many most interesting dimensions I have not discussed at all. The excuse for the one-sidedness can only be that there has been throughout the period a single long-drawn out (if often conveniently ignored) central issue: the control of power by a small immigrant minority of the population for the vast economic and political advantage of that minority and to the grave detriment of the majority. Faced with that central issue everything else must fade into insignificance, at least in such a survey as this. Moreover the churches have for historical reasons been so easily and naturally identified with that minority that they had a grave additional obligation, over and above the general obligation to stand up for justice, to make it crystal clear here that their message and fellowship should not be identified with the message of imperialism and the fellowship of the privileged.

It has not, I hope, been mistaken in a historical study of church-state relations to concentrate upon white people. For better or worse it was a missionary church, ruled by white men, which confronted or co-operated with white-led governments. But it is no longer so. Tutu and Boesak are not missionaries and they cannot easily appeal as their predecessors did from Philip to Huddleston to the churches, the newspapers, the public opinion of Britain, though they can, of course, rightly look for support from the world church in their local struggle. They are no longer missionaries from afar, endeavouring to protect a colonized people; they are that people, its rightful religious leaders demanding justice in the name of their brethren. Yet they are also the heirs and successors of the men I have spoken of. They have entered into a long existing contest of church and state. When Desmond Tutu as a boy was mightily impressed to see Father Huddleston respectfully raise his hat to his mother in a street of Sophiatown, the mantle of Elijah was already on its way to the shoulders of Elisha and Huddleston ensured that the stance he was taking would not end with him. But we do not have to wait to the 1950s to observe the transfer taking place. When in 1911 Matthew, an Anglican catechist in Chiduku, part of the young mission of St Faith's, Rusape, appeared before a government commission of enquiry into allegations that the local District Commissioner had been forcing Africans to labour for white farmers, he stoutly declared: 'I consider it my duty should I hear of any irregularity by officials of the Native Department to report to the head of the mission . . . If the Native Commissioner acted wrongly I should like to see him punished.' The evidence was accepted and the Native Commissioner officially censured.[10] The priest at St Faith's was Edgar Lloyd, friend and disciple of Cripps. Here already the mantle of Elijah, the prophetic sense of political responsibility, the

165

obligation of the churchman to speak out for justice's sake, was being passed across.

Or let us go a great deal further back – to what was really the very first generation of native southern African Christians: the Hottentot and other coloured members of the London Missionary Society settlements at Bethelsdorp, Theopolis and Kat River: people like Jan Boesak, the first president of the Church Council at Theopolis, Andries Stoffels, or indeed Mrs Van der Kemp or Mrs Read, the early missionaries' Hottentot wives. Some of these people were gathered at Kat River in April 1830 to greet Dr Philip, who was visiting the settlement, and to express their gratitude both to him and to God for Ordinance 50, passed by the Cape government in 1828, which had in principle established the legal equality of the Hottentots. Person after person rose to express his sentiments: 'The hearts of the people were full, and they spoke with propriety and great effect, because they spoke about what they understood and what they felt . . . the appropriateness of the allusions made by many of the speakers to Old Testament history, the comparisons they drew between their own state and the people of God on various occasions, and particularly their reference to the children of Israel in Egypt, were very striking. The hand of God was distinctly *recognized* in their deliverance.'[11] Perhaps the theology of Allan Boesak in the 1980s is not, after all, so very different from that of the Boesaks of the 1830s. The prophetic mantle had already begun to pass from white missionary to black Christian.

From beginning to end of our story there is a continuity of mission, sense of responsibility and, even, method. The mission in question is that of seeking justice, especially for the poor. It is seen as an absolute responsibility for the church, most particularly in circumstances such as those of southern Africa where, from first to last, there has occurred the systematic oppression of its native inhabitants by more powerful intruders from abroad. The principal method used throughout in bringing this mission to effect has been quite simply that of asserting the truth, providing evidence to destroy the cover-up which, time and again, has been used to hide the reality of what is going on. Let us recall the two volumes of Philip's *Researches in South Africa*, the 900 pages of Colenso's *Extracts from the Blue Books*, Cosmas Desmond's *Discarded People*, the reports of the *Justice and Peace Commission* in the 1970s in Rhodesia, and so much else. Oppression thrives on lies. The primary task of the church in a situation of oppression is to expose injustice by publication of the whole truth. To do so is a prophetic task. 'What does the Lord require of thee,' asked the prophet, 'but to do justly, and to love mercy, and walk humbly with thy God?' (Micah 6.8). It was the text for one of Colenso's greatest sermons, preached at Pietermaritzburg on 12 March 1879. A hundred years later, in the 1970s, I heard another great Natal ecclesiastic, Archbishop Hurley, speak memorably to the selfsame text. There has indeed been within the church of southern Africa an authentic tradition of prophecy, fully in line with the prophets of the past but equally accurately directed at the real evils of today.

But how often has it appeared? One could not dare to say that the church in southern Africa in the nineteenth and twentieth centuries has acquitted itself well in the fulfilment of this task. In many circumstances it has done almost nothing; in some it has warmly abetted the doing of injustice. It has never spoken with a united voice, at least for any length of time. It has frequently repudiated its truest prophets. By and large, painful as it may be to say so, the churches in southern Africa have appeared complacent with injustice, tied by privilege, class and race to government, and far too willing – having plunged deep into the political in their relationship to the state – to offer to its victims the apolitical gospel which both capitalists and Marxists delight to expect from religion. Nevertheless, it does need to be added that many missionaries whose political stance left much to be desired were truly liberating in their deeds in the field of education, medicine and the translation of the Bible.

There were, I think, four religious attitudes we can discern in this story. There was, first, the conviction that mission and church should have as little as possible to do with the political. There were missionaries, mostly little-known ones, who were consistent in this position but for the most part, on analysis, it turns out to be a too selective separation, admitting the acceptability of political involvement in many ways and circumstances, particularly an involvement of complicity with those here and now in power.

Secondly, there was the basically Constantinian conviction that church and state should rightly stand together in institutionalized co-operation; the moral alliance of two God-given authorities. It was the view of Roman Catholics in Portuguese Africa, not only in the distant past but also very much in the years subsequent to the concordat of 1940. It has been, in the last half century, the view of most leaders of the Dutch Reformed Church in South Africa. In British Africa it was the view of many an Anglican and not a few Free Churchmen. Constantine might take the form of the King of Portugal, Dr Malan, the British governor, Mr Rhodes or – even – Mr Smith. Beneath local diversity the same basic attitude is to be found. It is a comfortable attitude and perhaps not to be wholly and always rejected, but it provides one of the gravest of Christian temptations in the many situations where government itself is highly oppressive.

Theoretically quite separate from it is the 'reconciliation' approach, our third position. Here the church and the missionary are supposed to retain their political independence in order to mediate in conflict from the outside. It appears to provide a most attractive alternative to our first two attitudes, yet in practice it may be hardly less grave a temptation. It was that of William Temple in the General Strike of 1926, of Pius XII in the Second World War and the genocide of the Jews. It merges at times with the apoliticism of our first attitude, the establishmentarianism of the second. The stance of reconciliatory independence too often signifies irrelevance, while it is further easily undermined at the social level by a wider identification of church leaders and the political establishment. Its consequence is in most such cases the emasculation of the church's voice in the face of oppression. Of course it is true that liberation must lead to reconciliation and bear the need for reconciliation strenuously in mind: if it does not, the liberation achieved will be but the start – as it so often is – of a new oppression. Of course, it is true that, theologically, we can ultimately not separate the two. And, of course, it is also true that there are many cases of grave human conflict which cannot possibly be correctly interpreted simply or chiefly as between oppressor and oppressed, but rather ones of mutual oppression, in which a simplistic liberation perspective will not only not enlighten but may, on the contrary, help further to bolster a false consciousness in one or other of the protagonists. In this Northern Ireland is a classic example. Nevertheless, there are also many situations of highly one-sided oppression, and South Africa has long been one of the worst. In such situations while liberation does not replace reconciliation, it does require structural implementation as a prior condition to reconciliation. Almost certainly the greatest perennial weakness of the political action of good Christians derives from an over-concern for instant reconciliation while the structural changes required by justice are overlooked.

Our fourth and final possibility is, then, that of taking sides when major issues of justice are at stake, of being committed to liberation before reconciliation. This has been, as I have tried to show, the consistent road of a small but remarkable minority of churchmen in southern Africa from Van der Kemp to Tutu. In contrast with it our three other possible attitudes, theoretically distinct, in practice largely merge to offer a seeming acceptance, if not blessing, of the status quo, only too characteristic of church leadership as a whole.

If this picture I have painted seems a gloomy one, I can only say as a sort of extenuation that everywhere and always the church has been very largely a corrupt and ineffectual body, that the doctrine of the faithful remnant remains applicable in every age, but that a single Shearly Cripps is worth a thousand temporizing nonentities. It is hard to justify, or judge of, Christian history here or anywhere in other terms. The little that is gold may be just, just enough to carry on the tradition of authentic Christian witness, to be in the city of Sodom Abraham's ten just men.

11

Why the Church in South Africa Matters

'Why South Africa?' is a question frequently put to those outside the country who show a very special concern with its problems. Are they really so different, or so much worse, than those of a host of other countries in this confused world? Has South African society, and the church within it, some very special relevance for Christians in other parts of the world? This chapter is the attempt of one British Christian to say why we should answer 'Yes' unhesitatingly to those questions. To do so we must put the South African situation into a far wider context.

Oppression, systematic discrimination against 'second-class' citizens, torture, the murderous elimination of dissidents are common features of many countries in the world today. One has only to think of Kampuchea, Ethiopia, Equatorial Guinea and Uganda, to name four of the bloodier tyrannies of recent years. It is but the start of a long list. The world is an increasingly oppressed condition; horribly divided and in conflict. But the characters of oppressions and conflicts differ. While opposition to inhumanity is finally undivided, it can only be effective if it is based on as clear an understanding as possible of each type of humanity – its historical causes and current mechanism, the ideology used to justify it, the external forces which profit from it and maintain it in existence. Some are blinder, more arbitrary, more wholly irrational, maybe briefer; others are more systematic, more thought out, more subtly defended, more lasting. The oppression of Amin falls into one category, that of Soviet intervention in Afghanistan into a second, that of the South African state system into a third. While our most immediate horror may well be for the holocausts perpetrated by Amin or Nguema, they have a madness which more or less ensures that they will not last too long or be effectively significant for the future structures of our world. The more thought out and rationalized, the more legalized, the more moralized, a system of oppression is, the more money there is in it for someone, the more it requires among the free the most exacting sustained analysis and inflexible opposition. This is true alike of Marxist tyrannies and of anti-Marxist varieties of the South African or Salvadorean type.

It is good to begin by outlining the particular characteristics of South Africa which both make of it a quite special case and slot it in various ways, into a global context. We shall list six. The first, and the core of the whole thing, is of course not just the racial division of its population but the systematic structuring of society, economically, politically, and educationally, in terms of race. And this is not as a matter of habit or of individual prejudice but of the dominant theory of society and of a mass of meticulously detailed law, much of it recently enacted, all of it sharply enforced. No other country in the world has so clear a racial divide within its citizenry, but the clarity of that divide is itself not a matter of race but of law. Many other countries face racial conflict, breed racial prejudice, and in various ways practise racial discrimination. But elsewhere this is a matter of public regret. Nowhere is it a matter of legal principle. This sets racial conflict in South Africa clearly apart from racial conflict elsewhere and makes of it indeed a specifically different phenomenon – transforming it from disorder into a symbol.

Secondly, South Africa is an integral part of the African continent. It is no island of its own. No major geographical feature separates it from the rest of Africa. Nor, on the side of the large (black) majority of the population, is there a racial separation. Nor is there any decisive historical one. The white conquest of most of today's Republic of South Africa in the nineteenth century was simply part of the wider scramble for Africa. The Zulus and the Xhosa, like the Ashanti and Benin, were conquered by British arms. The subsequent transference of power over black natives to white settlers was achieved by Act of Parliament in Westminster. Neither the past nor the present South Africa can be seen apart from the history of imperialism and anti-imperialism in the wider continent. The oppressed majority in South Africa is but one wing of the great black population of Africa as a whole. Poor as most African countries are at present, volatile as their political systems may be, their numbers and potential importance for global history are vastly greater than those of white South Africa. The turbulent tide of black independence, development and self-expression was not stopped at the Zambezi. Nor will it be at the Limpopo. A decade here or there and that tide will have flowed irresistibly on.

Thirdly, South Africa still (just) remains a country within the western democratic tradition. Its constitution, its parliament, its party system, its universal franchise (for whites), its courts, its universities and newspapers – all these things make historical sense, and only make sense, within the tradition of western Europe. It is impossible for Europeans not to think of South Africa very differently from say, Iran or Vietnam. This cultural and political affinity does, of course, reflect a racial affinity. The ancestors of the white rulers of the country today came from Holland, from France, from Britain or from Germany. And it is because they did so and then continued for long to be governed from Holland or from Britain that the institutions of western Europe were implanted so firmly and so recognizably at least within the white segment of South African society.

Fourthly, South Africa remains a crucial member of the western economic system. British, American and West European investment in the country is enormous and growing. The same companies operate across western countries. There is a constant interchange of personnel as well as of finance. This, of course, both vastly increases the responsibility of western countries for what goes on in South Africa and inhibits effective action to right what is wrong, lest in one way or another their own economies should suffer. At present western investors profit as much as South Africa from cheap black labour, long black hours, and no black vote for the parliament which makes the laws that govern them.

Fifthly, South Africa in church-going terms is an extremely Christian country, both on the white side and on the black. Christians do not control the world today and their responsibility for what happens in many countries, large and small, may be next to nothing. If the government of Russia or Albania misbehaves, Christians may and do condemn what is done (and it may indeed be done to their direct disadvantage) but it is not being done within their own family. Christians share responsibility for Constantine in a way they do not for Nero. What is done in South Africa is done emphatically by

Christians, many of them members of the same churches or families of churches that exist elsewhere. Moreover it is seriously defended in Christian theological and moral terms, by 'leading' members of white South African society. Hence the reputation of Christianity, its very word to the world, is at stake here in a way that cannot be the case in Albania or Afghanistan.

Sixthly, and finally, South Africa is increasingly taking on the characteristics of the 'national security state'. This is a fairly recent development and it is worth being clear about it because in some ways it is altering the focus of attention. South Africa's traditional contradiction has been the attempt to reconcile a liberal western political system for whites with the exclusion from that system of eighty per cent of the population, so as to ensure that the twenty per cent should always control the eighty per cent. Verwoerd's philosophy of apartheid was the most laboured attempt to overcome this contradiction through the discovery of the 'bantustan'. If profoundly unconvincing as an *apologia* for what is actually going on, it temporarily filled the gap between theory and practice and enabled well-wishers to argue for the wait-and-see policy: what would come of the Transkei or Kwazulu? The more unsatisfactory they have looked in practice, and the more wholly incapable they are of saying anything to Soweto and the basic urban problems of South Africa, the more apartheid is seen finally to have run out of steam. At the same time the collapse of white rule in Mozambique, Angola and Zimbabwe removed South Africa's legal protective buffer states and the internal contradiction between democracy and racial domination has itself become a security risk both theoretically and practically. The consequent shift has been away from what measure of civilian democracy survived the piecemeal repressive legislation of thirty years of Nationalist government to a system more and more characterized by dependence upon the military coupled with the tight control of civilian patterns of expression: the 'police state' in fact, of Paraguay or Guatemala. As liberal safeguards are progressively removed it becomes – almost but not quite paradoxically – easier also to remove a few of the irritations of 'petty apartheid' which were really required to feed the ego of the poorer members of a white 'liberal democratic' society. As ordinary whites increasingly lose what political power they formerly possessed and the control of power is withdrawn to an inner laager, an oligarchy of the security, political and big business bosses, it becomes practicable, and internationally desirable, to soften the hard dividing lines between white and non-white: to remove the 'whites only' notice from the park bench. Superficially, that is to say, the development of the national security state can go with a diminution in overt racialism (just as Salazar's Portugal did not need to be overtly racialist to hold its black population ruthlessly under control), even though this diminution has itself produced an increasingly threatening white back-lash.

All this is straightforward enough. Democracy has, after all, an authentic meaning. If it is abused for too long by those simply repeating its rhetoric, then it dies. If it cannot be shared with blacks then it cannot for long be shared with whites either. White domination and privilege (the true, underlying commitment of most of the ruling minority) can better be maintained by a basic shift of model and it is that shift which has now largely taken place. Nevertheless, at least for the time being, chunks of the liberal tradition are still there, not in themselves to be despised, and still partly usable: just as anything remaining from Chile's old liberal tradition was still to be used for what it was worth to fight Pinochet's tyranny, or what there was of legal objectivity in Russia to fight Soviet tyranny. The weapons may be weak, and in South Africa weaker than they were, but we use what is at hand. Let us remind ourselves too that the progressive taking over of 'liberal democracy' by 'national security' is not a phenomenon peculiar to just a few states. It is probably happening to some extent in almost every western state subject at present to major political pressures.

These factors, coming together in South Africa and nowhere else in anything like so acute a form, oblige the rest of the world, and Christians in particular, to wrestle with the South African case and its meaning for them in a way that they hardly have to with some more immediately blatant examples of miserable oppression. There is a world-wide spiritual and moral struggle facing mankind in these final decades of the twentieth century. Within this moral struggle South Africa and its image bear what is quite possibly a decisive role. Our world is growing more sharply divided than ever before between rich and poor, haves and have-nots, the 'North' and the 'South'. Very roughly speaking, the rich consist of the white world plus elsewhere a privileged coloured élite; the poor consist of the non-white world plus the lowest strata of older white societies. Furthermore, and still more roughly, the white rich world is very largely co-terminous with countries which at least in regard to their past and their cultural traditions are regarded as Christian, while the non-white poor world is, by a large majority, non-Christian. Japan is one obvious exception to such a simple characterization. Another is presented by the deprived masses of Latin America and black Africa: have-nots, but in large part Christian. To the significance of that we shall return. Yet the overall image remains one paradoxically in contradiction with what – in gospel terms – the Christian image surely should be: a fellowship, not of the rich and the powerful, but of the poor of God.

Is the poor, southern, non-white world also to become anti-Christian because the white, capitalist world is claimed as Christian? Such a scenario is certainly not wholly devoid of plausibility. Let liberation theology be 'excommunicated' in Latin America; let the black millions of central Africa be alienated from the churches by a prolonged white-black conflict centred upon a South Africa firmly backed by the United States and western Europe; let the basic Christian communities of the southern continents be deprived of the eucharist, and starved of life; let a diminishing priesthood retreat into the realm of the sacral, reasserting its segregation from the laity, and its concern with more important spiritual matters than torture and starvation; let an other-worldly and authoritarian form of Christianity be proclaimed again as the only one fully acceptable to Rome; and we are almost there. It is not impossible.

Now the whole nature of the South African situation, as it has been engineered by its white overlords, is such as to provide a paradigm for this scenario: a microcosm almost capable of forcing the macrocosm into its image. For the spokesman of the South African official mind, the world is indeed so divided. On the one side, the white, Christian, capitalist West, of which South Africa is a bastion and integral part; on the other, Communism. And that is not, of course, only a South African view. It is one held by numerous sincere conservative 'western' Christians. Moreover, still more interestingly, it has been the Russian view. The Kremlin and Pretoria have not disagreed in their pragmatic analysis of the contemporary situation. For both, Christianity goes (or should be made to go) with capitalism, in its present multi-national form above all, and with the world hegemony of the white Euro-American states. Whether Christianity is in this context 'true' or whether it is 'false' almost ceases to matter. Its function becomes the same amd is one inherently set against the inescapable immediate aspirations of the large majority of mankind.

If theirs were an adequate analysis, things would be grave indeed for Christianity. In fact, thank God, it is deep down, despite its plausibility, a fearful travesty of reality. Russia is not a genuine friend of the third world oppressed – in Afghanistan, Equatorial Guinea (where it backed Nguema's regime, a particularly horrible little dictatorship), Ethiopia or anywhere else. South Africa is not a standard bearer of freedom, democracy or Christianity. It is the poor, the black, the oppressed who form the great majority of Christians in South Africa as in so many other parts of Africa, Latin America and Asia. Nevertheless in the eyes of many in the international academic world, in the international leftist movement and in the world of international capitalism it does not appear such a travesty, any more than it does in the eyes of the rump of white middle-class 'western' Christians. It is too convenient to their spiritual comfort, their particular type of intellectual myopia, their accustomed rhetoric, their economic advantage. However profoundly mistaken, there has long been something of a consensus, an integral element within the mental substructure of twentieth century orthodoxy, shared by both 'left' and 'right', to see the whole pattern of modern world history, intellectual conviction and group commitment in what is really a very simple binary model of 'left' and 'right'. With 'left' goes 'Communism', 'Marxism', the rights of oppressed people (particularly non-white people), the rejection of religion, the 'revolution'; with 'right' goes 'capitalism', 'the West', white supremacy, religion, Christianity. This latter group will promote the political model of liberal democracy in white societies but in less-than-white societies it will promote instead the national security state. 'White' and 'less-than-white' are not here precisely racial categories: Portugal and Spain have lately been permitted to move from one to the other; Chile, however, was taken in the 1970s in the opposite direction. What is so profoundly shocking (shocking to agnostics, very often, as well as to 'conservative' Christians) about, say, the theology of liberation or the grants of the World Council of Churches to liberation movements, is that they undermine the intellectual categories assumed by the 'orthodox' of both left and right, including the politicization of Christianity in the service of the 'right'. That is why, equally, right-wing agnosticism (a very widespread phenomenon) has, so often, politically to be hidden: 'attending church occasionally' may be an almost necessary characteristic of the successful right-wing politician, Thatcherite or other, lest he flout the categories.

Beneath layer upon layer of intellectual junk passed down in the accepted traditions of western middle class Christianity, agnostic academe and Marxist myth, what is in truth valid at the core of this analysis of the world predicament is little more than the existence of two rival power-blocs, operating from different bases and with different types of strength. The heart of one is American big business and its wider network, the multinationals. The heart of the other is the Soviet Communist Party, heir to traditional Russian nationalism at least as much as to the institutionalization of early twentieth-century European revolutionary movements. Each controls in different ways massive military and economic machinery. Each justifies itself in ideological terms which are in fact entirely subservient to military and economic operations and objectives. We may have reasons to dislike or fear one less than the other, but the differences between them have certainly in principle next to nothing to do with religion, with human freedom or with justice for the oppressed. Genuine struggle for religion, for freedom or for justice in the world must include El Salvador as well as Afghanistan, Czechoslovakia as well as South Africa, and it must in a real way be a struggle against both power blocs.

The significance of South Africa lies, for both sides, in the opportunity provided by the catching up of a local struggle into the global one, the reality of both being at the same time obscured by its smoke-screen translation into religious and ideological terms derived from this false consciousness common to left and right, and of its nature profoundly misleading as to the true spiritual lines dividing today's world. The local struggle is that of a rich, white minority to maintain its political power and consequent economic privilege over a poor black majority. This is not just a class conflict: rich/poor. If it were, it could and would be defused in all sorts of ways, but which in fact are largely ruled out by the profound psychological preoccupation with race and the effective re-drawing of class division on race lines. The identification of class and race immeasurably hardens the lines of division and increases the fears and bitterness upon either side. The racial re-ordering of class does not, though, mean that this is not a class conflict. It is. And the particular character of the South African economy (the world's greatest gold producer, etc.) and geography (the Cape routes, etc.) slot South Africa into the world order in an important way, and the dominating South African class into the dominating class within the western economic and political system. South Africa's dominated class is, as a consequence, at least potentially, an ally of the West's enemy: the Soviet Union.

Black people were far worse treated in Nguema's Equatorial Guinea than in Vorster's South Africa, and Russia and Cuba did their best to ensure the survival of Nguema's unspeakably awful regime, just as they – and they alone – enable Mengistu's appalling tyranny in Ethiopia to survive. Nevertheless, as the conditions of Equatorial Guinea were not widely known throughout the world, and as Nguema was himself a black man, representing no philosophy worth even two minutes' consideration, but simply a maniac addicted to torturing his fellow human beings, Soviet support for Nguema had little wider significance, beyond confirming the wholly opportunistic character of Soviet policy decisions. Western support for South Africa is different. Too big and rich to be ignored, its oppression, precisely principled on racial grounds, is necessarily an affront, not only to its twenty million black citizens, but to the three hundred million black people outside its frontiers. A West/South Africa alliance coupled with a Soviet/African National Congress alliance could then appear as proof positive of the thesis that there is a global confrontation linking Soviet and black interests upon the one hand, and western and white racialist interests upon the other.

But the identification does not end there. Soviet propaganda remains deeply anti-religious, white South Africa has continually justified its stance in Christian terms and its leaders are manifestly church-going Christians harping – like Russia's – upon the Christianity/Communism chasm. South Africa has thus become the most practically effective piece in the validation of the binary thesis for world interpretation:

Why the Church in South Africa Matters

Russia	*West*
Communism	*capitalism*
atheism	*Christianity*
black liberation	*white domination*

The more this model can be seen pragmatically to work, the more it will work: it can be self-fulfilling, with each side conforming to expectation. And, of course, as already suggested, it is simply taken for granted by a sort of twentieth-century orthodoxy and its upholders that they do so conform. Most lamentably of all, time and again white church leaders blatantly demonstrate by their words and actions that they too absolutely presuppose this model, whereas if they have one function in the world today, it should be to confound the model. Yet the model is confounded – by the people. In objective fact, as already stressed, it does not provide a true interpretation of the world at present in regard either to power politics or, and this matters much more to us, to religion. The realities of church life in the latter years of this century are simply not so, but far otherwise. The churches have, in the last few decades and above all in Africa, witnessed what is already appearing as one of the decisive achievements of all church history – a major breakthrough into the non-white, non-dominating, non-capitalist world. Just as the white establishment seems in the deafness of its affluence to be more remote than ever from the gospel message, the non-white world in its wide-awake poverty seems to have taken to itself the figure of Christ as never before. Christianity's present vitality is quite simply to be found among the poor of Latin America, central and southern Africa, parts of Asia. Most bishops in South Africa Catholic or Anglican, white or black, appear to share the wearisome sense of responsibility for clerical propriety common to most bishops the world over. But all together they have not half the spiritual or historical significance for the church of the 1980s that Desmond Tutu has. He is no mere aspiration, no day-dream. He is a fact. He is Christianity in South Africa, while his less vociferous colleagues are but over-dressed, timid administrators, of little more significance in terms of the spiritual combat of a globe in agony than the countless butchers, bakers and candlestick-makers who marry in their churches, vote for the National or opposition parties and do not positively torture their fellow men but are not tortured either.

Desmond Tutu does not just represent a South African reality, but a far wider one: the reality of the Christian consciousness, of the thirst for justice within millions of hearts, Christian, black and poor. The geographical vitality of popular Christianity has shifted very rapidly in the second half of the century, even if there are plenty of hierarchs who have hardly noticed it. Christianity is no longer the religion of the western European dominator, any more than it is the religion of the Soviet dominator. It is, increasingly, the religion of the non-European dominated. It would seem that in the South African ethos the vastness and significance of the ecclesial change, between, say, the early 1950s and the 1980s has not really been appreciated. The canonical institutions do not look so very different from the way they looked thirty years ago; their control continues for the most part to belong to the white élite, but the reality of Christian life is now simply different and if the Catholic institution cannot conform to that changed reality (cannot, in the case of South Africa, recognize that its principal homeland is its eighty per cent black, not its twenty per cent white membership) then the tide will simply sweep on in other courses, leaving that institution – as it has done many a time before – high and dry.

Still, conceivably, Moscow and Pretoria may together get their way. All this new life may still be crushed between the upper and the nether mill stones, between the generals and the multinationals and the bishops on the one hand, the generals and the commissars and the purveyors of atheism on the other. If that should happen, then the greatest achievement of the twentieth-century church – its breakthrough, after centuries of encapsulation, to the non-white world – would be lost. But Desmond Tutu and his like stand up as the sign in the present of hope for the future. And they stand up precisely in South Africa, as South Africans: in the place where all they stand for (the integration of blackness with Christianity and freedom, and of what is good in the tradition of the West with what is good in the tradition of Africa) has been most explicitly and systematically denied.

It is surely not surprising that the church in a racialist society should so largely and long have succumbed to racialism. It tallies with too much Christian history. The weakness of so much ecclesiastical protest against apartheid has been the manifest racial discrimination practised by the church herself. There is very often in Catholic life, in all sorts of fields and countries, a divorce between official statement and ecclesiastical reality which must puzzle the observer, whether he be an outsider or insider, but seldom more so than here. Yet if in one way such a gap must be puzzling, in another the absence of such a gap might be held to be even more surprising, for the church is – in part of its nature – a corrupt body, sharing the corruptions of the society it is part of. Were it not so, it would in some extraordinary way have to be divorced from the mankind of which it must be the inner light. The precondition to offering light is, in a strange way, that one is first part of the darkness, part of the problem. It would be miraculous if in a very racialist society the church were not to some considerable and damaging extent racialist too. And church life is not miraculous. Everywhere it partakes of the sickness of society. How could it not do here? Of course it has done, and it does. But the corruption of a church can become such that it only receives, it ceases to give: it becomes but an ecclesiasticized image of the mess around it. What we look for in a living church is not the absence or exclusion of sin, but surges of life, of repentance, of hope, of prophetic vision, a sense of spiritual struggle with the 'weapons' of Cross and Resurrection used. We look too for at least some partial and provisionally effective overcoming of the major evils of the contemporary world within a fellowship which offers by its sheer existence a sign of the power of God's grace, manifest already, ultimately invincible. Does the church in South Africa do that to its own society and to the wider world – a world which shares the responsibilities, problems and ultimate fate of South Africa?

The witness that one expects of the church in South Africa has, it seems to me, to be of at least three different, if interlocked, kinds. First and foremost it must be, and be seen to be, what it most deeply claims to be: a fellowship of men and women, classless and raceless, a manifest *koinonia*, a church in which the body and blood of Christ are shared by black and white, in which white Christians receive the Lord's body and blood from black hands, as black do from white, a body of people in which this experience of divine condescension achieving human unity is realized in that at least some of its members when outside ecclesiastical walls are quite obviously and decisively influenced in the pattern of their personal and social behaviour by the eucharist.

Secondly, it must be a church which is so clearly and publicly identified with its poorer and therefore black members that no observer can doubt which sort of person this institution most cherishes.

Thirdly, a church is inevitably itself a power institution, and the Catholic Church is more so than most. The character of its hierarchy matters. It is necessary to the church's public witness that the black majority does not have some mere token presence within the hierarchy of ministry and power, but an effective participation within it, so that the church precisely as an institution, as a responsible decision-making body, to some genuine extent confronts rather than mirrors a racially discriminatory world. The Catholic hierarchy is in public eyes very much the 'sacrament' of the church to a wider society and so the colour of its skin, the marks of the police truncheon on its middle-aged shoulders, the comfortable suburbs in which it is not allowed to sleep, may be much more meaningful than the verbal message it utters. The bishops have, time and again, protested forcefully against formal injustice. But it would not appear to an outsider to have woven that protest into anything at all of a confrontatory life-style. It could, on the contrary, be argued that its life-style still remains in all sorts of ways racialist while its statements alone are anti-racialist. The wide Catholic world today has for its criteria the day to day life of Archbishop Helder Camara, the life and death of Archbishop Oscar Romero. Their behaviour has been so much more important than their words. No South African Catholic bishop yet has been imprisoned, deported or placed under house arrest, though their General Secretary, Patrick Mkhatshwa, has suffered both imprisonment and torture. One bishop in prison is worth a score outside. He will be remembered, they will not. And what is the church but a chain of remembrances forged around an initial sacrificial death? – 'Do this in remembrance of me.'

There is a necessary and explicit peak of Christian witness which is certain to be minority witness: a sort of personal and prophetic playing out amid contemporary agony of gospel truth, an approximation to the high hill of Calvary, to which very few are called. But in every living church some are, and the survival – certainly the healthful survival – of the many depends upon the witness of those few. South Africa has indeed provided witness of this sort. A handful in all maybe, but perhaps, for the needs of evangelical warfare and the soul of the world, sufficient to give the lie to the Moscow/Pretoria model of the current human predicament. The church's power is symbolic, 'spiritual' power and that power is carried along the line by the few who are ready to suffer 'even to death'.

There seem in scripture to be two patterns for the destiny of the little flock within the body of dull mediocrity and hard disobedience which so often constitutes the city of men and even, alas, the people of God. One is that the little flock, small though it may be, is just sufficient as salt and light to save the whole, to rescue its neighbourhood from the judgment of destruction: if there be but ten. The other pattern is that the remnant is indeed saved but through the flood, by exodus. It goes out. The mass is lost. The society goes under. The mills of God have ground it so very small. The city of God can and must find some new temporary environment. It will go on but the empire, the kingdom, the republic will not. We cannot ourselves choose or predict the pattern of our own destiny. We cannot know in South Africa which it is to be. We do know that witnesses are there because through the bonding of word and action, accepted suffering and unflinching perseverance, the sense of lived identity with the gospel of divine and human reconciliation, we have recognized the authenticity of their prophecy. In the life of the Afrikaner Naudé, of the Xhosa Tutu, we have seen clearly enough the breaking down of every middle wall of partition, the hallmark of Christ's presence. A small host of witnesses have demonstrated the fallacy of identification between whiteness, Christianity, capitalism, the oppression of the poor. They have spoken to their own society of its discarded people, and they have spoken to the world too. To be able to speak thus from the ground of personal and ecclesial experience in the eye of the storm is to make clear the truth of the gospel and the relevance of even our poor, broken, corrupted church to the loosing of bonds and the reconciliation of people.

12

Our Daily Bread

'Give us this day our daily bread.' As they were eating, Jesus took bread and blessed and broke it, and gave it to his disciples, and said 'Take and eat; this is my body' (Matthew 6.11; 26.26). Bread. Bread. If Catholic Christianity is *par excellence* a sacramental religion there is no point at which this is more true than here: the sacramentality of bread, daily bread, which becomes the eucharistic body of Christ and symbolic focal point for the church's communion of which it is indeed the formal visible enactor. Disrupt the pattern of meaning here and the most inner logic of Catholicism is disrupted. And yet in some African languages and almost all African societies such disruption has, in point of fact, been imposed by the church's chosen translation and, still more, insistence upon wheaten bread for communion.

Take Luganda. The invocation of the Lord's Prayer, 'Give us this day . . .' is rendered: *Tuwe lero emmere yaffe eya buli lunaku gye twetaga*. Bread is rendered 'emmere' which means indeed food in general but in particular the staple food of the Baganda, *matoke*, steamed banana. It is an appropriate translation. When, however, we move to the eucharist a different word is used: *Bwe bali balya, Yezu n'addira omugati*. Jesus took and blessed *omugati*, 'bread' in the specific western sense. *Omugati* is a European food, a loaf made of wheat not grown in the country. It is sold in shops and when people can afford it and it is available, a popular enough addition to the menu. But it is not *emmere*, except rather marginally. It does not signify anything central in the life or work of people here. Above all, it is not the same word as that used in the Lord's Prayer. A verbal dichotomy is thus created between these two texts which is both wholly untraditional and quite undermines the symbolic social significance of eucharistic consecration. Divide the breads and the basic symbolization of Christian concern with the material, with the world of work and daily need, is simply cut away, to be replaced by the esoteric, a symbolic otherness, of sacred and profane.

It is, nevertheless, by no means clear that the alternative linguistic solution, adopted for instance in Swahili, makes better sense. Here *mkate* (bread in a precise wheaten sense) has been employed in the Lord's Prayer as well as the words of the Last Supper. Verbal continuity is thereby maintained but at the cost of gravely damaging the natural sense of 'Give us this day our daily bread' by imposing upon it a word for something never eaten in many households and marginal in almost all.

Of course, the problem is clear enough. I remember my first Christmas in Uganda. It was in Soroti in 1958. I visited the Mill Hill Fathers' mission there on Christmas Eve and found them diligently breaking and rebreaking the wafers to be consecrated in the Christmas masses next day. A fresh supply had not arrived in time from Holland and so – if communion was to be extended to all the many hundreds of people expected – there was no alternative way of ensuring that their needs were met. Behind the verbal problem lies, then, the material problem. The eucharistic bread must, by church law, be made from wheat, but wheat does not grow in Uganda. If this is not a divine requirement for sacramental validity, it is a quite monstrous imposition. But if it is a divine requirement, how silly God must be! A quite unnecessary material limitation in regard to the most central and necessary sacrament of ecclesial existence would effectively make it impossible for the church to exist in non-temperate climes in non-modern conditions. Thus the non-wheaten existence of Christianity and its celebration of the sacrament of the Lord's Supper for centuries in South India, prior to the sixteenth century invasion of the Portuguese, must just have been one long mistake. Here, if anywhere, the westernizing rigidity of church law and traditional Catholic theology should be apparent in all its absurdity.

This very simple matter provides, perhaps, the clearest of all examples of what is at the heart of Christian acculturation. Orthodox Catholic Christianity did for a long time quite unconsciously transcend biblical fundamentalism in accepting that Christian life had to move on, being mentally and morally reshaped across history;

but it then lost its nerve, creating a sort of absurd mediaeval fundamentalism of its own, determined – one could say, a little simplistically perhaps – by the economy, intellectual convictions and ecclesiastical ideals of late eleventh-century western Europe, the age of the Hildebrandine reform. From then on ossification set in. It is logically and practically impossible for a genuinely African Catholicism to develop maturely on the basis of a first-century biblical fundamentalism, an eleventh-century mediaeval Catholic fundamentalism, or a nineteenth-century Victorian fundamentalism, even if there are elements within each of those three which do cohere well enough with the culture of contemporary Africa. Yet life is larger than logic and the reality of African Christianity – just as of Christian vitality anywhere else – is that, again and again, it has leapt logical barriers. One really could not have guessed that out of the rather crabbed and puritanical activity of the Victorian missionary would have come in so relatively short a time such buoyant churches. The Catholic tradition has not, of course, only in Africa been subject to contradictions. It has been so everywhere and attempts to reform public doctrine, canon law and pastoral practice have never been more than very partially effective, entrenched as the most disagreeable abuse has been by clerical pretension, cultural conservatism, class stratification and simple misunderstanding of the requirements of fidelity to tradition. One sort of fundamentalism or another, scriptural or ecclesiastical, has again and again negated the Catholic conviction that the Spirit of God remains within the people of God, enabling the church if it will to pass across new and unforeseen frontiers of time, space, culture and language.

If it will. Fundamentalist ossification is inevitably destructive of the vitality of the body. Christianity has advanced. It has also retreated. It is no more to be heard in the Hippo of Augustine or the Carthage of Cyprian. The church in Africa remains today, despite its too facilely trumpeted growth and vitality, tied by the mental and ministerial bonds of less imaginative formulations of the western mind. Bread and its vernacular form remain simply a central symbol of a far wider church refusal to take its own better logic with any seriousness while being over obsequious to the lesser logic of its more clerical formulations. Despite an existential ability to leap logical gaps, in the longer run such refusals have rent and do rend the life of the church and the web of its meaning almost irreparably.

Insistence upon wheaten bread is closely comparable with insistence upon a celibate priesthood (or, at least, a canonically unmarried priesthood – celibacy cannot so easily be insisted upon). The latter is, of course, still more uncatholic in that it flouts the explicit witness of the New Testament as well as that of the early church and of all other churches, eastern and western. Now, while the inner principle of Catholicity requires a refusal to be tied down, or cut short, by scripture alone, it equally requires a loyalty to, and positive continuity with, the scriptural principle. Compulsory clerical celibacy's moral destructiveness is evident, not only in a wider ambiguous attitude to scripture it forces upon one, not only in the devaluation of marriage it presupposes, but in the pastoral and institutional malformation it leads to and the moral duplicity it encourages. In a seminar in Lesotho, when I had been arguing for the ordination of married catechists and some local priests had been disagreeing fairly emphatically, two young nuns came up to me in the coffee break. Could they ask me a question? Of course, I replied. 'Why do those priests argue most for celibacy who keep it least?' I was staggered by the frankness of those two nuns and the realization of what the real situation must have been like to make them comment so openly. That was in 1971. The shortage of priests throughout Africa and the moral malfunctioning of Roman law in African society was already obvious enough. But the scandal of clerical promiscuity has grown greatly since then. There was an Archbishop of Lagos years ago who earned golden opinions in Rome by declaring in a synod speech that 'back home' celibacy was no problem. At that very time one of his few priests was knifed in bed by an irate husband, and hurried out of the country by an embarrassed church. Today when such things happen bishops more often turn a blind eye – even to front-page newspaper articles. Catholic life in dioceses in too many parts of the continent is being poisoned, the priesthood dishonoured and the laity alienated by clerical promiscuity. If my vocation forty years ago was to serve especially the African clergy (and, in consequence, I have never had other clerical status than that of a Ugandan diocesan priest) then perhaps the last service I may render it is to lament the conspiracy of silence over what is now encouraging conversion away from Catholicism either to Islam or to charismatic Protestantism. Friends, think again. The eucharistic famine of the rural church is getting ever worse. Give us in our village church daily bread – not an irrelevant law of celibacy, nor the bad smell of priestly promiscuity.

African Christianity does exist and yet it is continually being weakened by fetters of incomprehension. In many areas of marginality where there is a strong alternative, particularly an Islamic alternative, the likelihood is that it will in consequence fade away quite rapidly. The failure is one of imaginative love. It is a failure of the hierarchs and the Roman curial bureaucrats actually to care for the condition of the younger churches in their concrete reality. It is also a failure to understand the nature of the Catholic tradition itself in its true inwardness. For the current failure John Paul II is guilty as much as anyone, but he is heir to a long tradition of Roman centralist incomprehension.

The freedom of the Catholic Christian tradition has for centuries been replaced by the requirements of a clerical ultramontanist viewpoint. That viewpoint, despite its apparent beguiling image of unifying strength and confidence, has been more than any other single factor responsible in the second Christian millenium for the division of the church, its inability to relate convincingly with modern society and a sense of institutionalized lack of compassion. The damage it inflicted upon northern Europe – and southern too – in the past it is now inflicting upon Africa and Latin America. While the opening of windows produced by the Second Vatican Council did undoubtedly immensely assist the acculturation and consolidation of African Catholicism at a crucial time, the loss of nerve in subsequent years has maimed its impact.

In eastern Zimbabwe, in Makoniland, there is a little church which in its quite humble way could serve as an alternative model, a David closer to true Catholicism than the Goliath of Roman clerical institutionalism. The church and community of St Francis was founded in the 1930s by an Anglican catechist, Francis Nyabadza, who had quarrelled with his mission, principally over its tolerance of alcohol. The *ecclesiola* of St Francis came to consist of the Nyabadzas, one or two neighbouring families, and a group of 'sisters' – a convent of nuns, sharing a community life of prayer and work very similar to that of small rural monasteries all over the Catholic world. Francis began to say mass, precisely in the form he had seen his High Church Anglican missionaries follow. He and his flock were excommunicated. When he died, he was succeded as priest, the *Baba* of the community, by his son Basil. Basil, a supporter of the liberation forces in the war of Independence, was murdered one night by unnamed men in front of his church in 1977. Today his son Francis is the *Baba* at St Francis. He leads the morning and evening offices, celebrates mass, preaches to his little congregation while being at the same time a farmer and businessman. He lives in the house beside that lovely little village church with his wife, children and mother, where his father and his grandfather lived.

St Francis is still in formal communion with no other church in the world. Informally it surely shares in the world *koinonia* of the one *Catholica*. To be there for a great festival, to attend the long services, to listen to and participate in the intensely moving singing of the sisters and laity, to watch the profoundly reverent actions of Francis at the altar, to share in the simple meal in the courtyard afterwards, all this is an unforgettable experience. Here is a fully 'independent' African church, yet one faithful to even the smaller details of Catholic tradition in a way that few Catholic congregations in rural Africa can possibly be. Of course, its Catholic authenticity derives not only from its married priest but also, quite especially, from the convent of the sisters as also from the unobtrusive presence among them over long years of one white woman who went to Zimbabwe as a missionary but moved from the mission of St Faith to the church of St Francis, Patricia Chater. Here, in a quite humble form, are the diversity of elements constituting between them a witness of credible Catholic authenticity. Yet the fact remains that for the Roman Catholic Church our daily bread may not be given to Africa in this way. The priest is married. It is not that the message of celibacy is derided at St Francis. The sisters, including Patricia, are there to show it. St Francis does demonstrate that celibacy and its characteristic Catholic forms can be cherished on African soil while at the same time remaining faithful to the witness of the New Testament, in continuity with the Old, that priesthood and marriage can and should flourish within a single life and the ministry of a local church. While by no means the only requirement for the flourishing of African Catholicism, this is perhaps, more than any other single one, a *sine qua non*.

Over twenty years ago, urging this same point, as I had already been doing for several years, I wrote a little beseechingly: 'In the ways of the Holy Spirit the church too has her special moments within the complex flow of human history . . . in fifteen years it may be too late, and in fifty church historians will lament the great opportunity for ever missed' (*Church and Mission in Modern Africa*, 1967, p. 13 and p. 237). Today I am inclined to judge that this may well have been true. The moment has been missed and may in a very real way be irretrievable. But for myself I have ceased to make of my life little more than an extended appeal for church reform. Instead, having fallen back on the more detached role of historian, I have to note the near inevitability of this failure of ecclesial nerve. The rhetoric of Vatican II and the needs of the poor were unlikely to be sufficient to alter something still so central to the Roman ecclesiastical system and about which it had not compromised since the eleventh century. There was perhaps anyway too large a measure of romanticism within the optimism of a quarter of a century ago – the appeal of an area of seemingly near medieval rural religiosity to draw us away from the cold secularizing winds of European urban modernity. The missionary has almost inevitably to be someone of rather simple faith. It could be attractive but deceptive to escape the world of demythologizing and immerse oneself instead in a world where one could make a very good case for remythologizing. Back in Europe, not only the demands of a more detached historiography, but also of contemporary theology weigh on one to challenge an African-centred vision in the 1960s which combined the radicalism of ecclesiastical reform with the undergirding of a still fairly traditional faith.

Yet it is hard not to lament. The odd and unexpected confluence of African rural religion, the high tide of the missionary movement, the exuberance of the era of political independence, and the enthusiasm of the Vatican Council made African Catholicism seem a feasible, bewitching mixture of gospel freedom, medieval enrootedness and third world contemporaneity. Perhaps in a much less formal way it may still prove to be so, defying canon law and a great deal else, the religiosity of the grass roots, the Catholicism not of the eucharist but of the catechist. The shape of the future is denied to all of us. It will be for the historians in the twenty-first or twenty-second century, looking back upon our day, to judge where wisdom lay and whether African Catholicism proved this time around, for better or worse, a chimera or a reality.

Notes

1. African Catholicism: Revival or New Arrival?

1. See N. Wiseman, 'The Anglican Claim', *The Dublin Review*, July 1939; J. H. Newman, *Apologia pro vita sua*, ch. III. For the present state of the controversy see W. H. C. Frend, 'The Donatist Church – forty years on', *Windows on Origins*, ed. C. Landman and D. P. Whitelaw, Pretoria 1985, pp. 69–84; R. A. Markus, 'Christianity and Dissent in Roman North Africa: Changing Perspectives in Recent Work', *Studies in Church History 9, Schism, Heresy and Religious Protest*, ed. Derek Baker, Cambridge University Press 1972, pp. 21–36.

2. W. H. C. Frend, *The Donatist Church*, Oxford University Press 1952, p. 88.

3. Derwas J. Chitty, *The Desert a City*, Blackwell 1966, p. 7.

4. *The Donatist Church*, p. 106.

5. One may note the recognition of comparability in, for instance, Peter Brown's 'Christianity and Local Culture in Late Roman Africa', *Religion and Society in the Age of Saint Augustine*, Faber 1972, pp. 279–300.

6. Though modern African Christianity in its Protestant forms has a strong urban root in coastal West Africa beginning from Freetown, see, for instance, A. F. Walls, 'A Christian Experiment: the Early Sierra Leone Colony', *The Mission of the Church and the Propagation of the Faith*, ed. G. J. Cuming, Cambridge University Press 1970, pp. 107–129.

7. J. Waliggo, *The Catholic Church in the Buddu Province of Buganda, 1879–1925*, Ph.D. dissertation, Cambridge 1976.

8. Robin Horton, 'African Conversion', *Africa*, 1971, pp. 85–108; Humphrey J. Fisher, 'Conversion Reconsidered: Some historical aspects of religious conversion in black Africa', *Africa*, 1973, pp. 27–40; Robin Horton 'On the Rationality of Conversion', *Africa*, 1975, pp. 219–35 and 373–98; Humphrey J. Fisher, 'The Juggernaut's Apologia: Conversion to Islam in Black Africa', *Africa*, 1985, pp. 153–73; R. W. Wyllie, 'On the Rationality of the Devout Opposition', *Journal of Religion in Africa*, XI, 1980, pp. 81–91; see also Richard Gray, 'Christianity and Religious Change in Africa', *African Affairs*, January 1978, pp. 89–100.

9. John Mbiti, *African Religions and Philosophy*, Heinemann Educational 1969; Bolaji Idowu, *African Traditional Religion*, SCM Press

Notes

1973; Gabriel Setiloane, 'How the traditional world-view persists in the Christianity of the Sotho-Tswana', *Christianity in Independent Africa*, ed. E. Fasholé-Luke, R. Gray, A. Hastings and G. Tasie, Rex Collings 1978, pp. 402–412.

10. Walbert Bühlmann, 'The Church of Africa from the Council of Jerusalem to Vatican II', *Concilium*, 1966, vol. 3, no. 2, p. 28.

11. J. F. Faupel, *African Holocaust*, Geoffrey Chapman 1962, pp. 129–30.

12. J. A. Rowe, 'The Purge of Christians at Mwanga's Court', *Journal of African History*, 1964, pp. 55–72; D. A. Low, 'Converts and Martyrs in Buganda' *Christianity in Tropical Africa*, ed. C. G. Baeta, Oxford University Press 1968, pp. 150–164.

13. Faupel, p. 167 and p. 193.

14. The phrase was that of the CMS missionary, Walker; see Michael Wright, *Buganda in the Heroic Age*, Nairobi 1971, p. 104.

15. Waliggo, p. 154.

16. Waliggo, Chapter 4; Adrian Hastings, 'From Mission to Church in Buganda', *Mission and Ministry*, Sheed and Ward 1971, p. 144–176; Adrian Hastings, 'Ganda Catholic Spirituality', see above pp. 69–81.

17. See such studies as Ian Linden, *Church and Revolution in Rwanda*, Manchester University Press 1977; Ian Linden, *Catholics, Peasants and Chewa Resistance in Nyasaland 1889–1939*, Heinemann Educational 1974; Brian Garvey, *The Development of the White Fathers Mission among the Bemba-Speaking Peoples, 1891–1964*, Ph.D. thesis, London 1974.

18. Adrian Hastings, 'The Council came to Africa', *Vatican II by those who were there*, ed. Alberic Stacpoole, Geoffrey Chapman pp. 315–23, Adrian Hastings, *A History of African Christianity, 1950–1975*, Cambridge University Press 1979.

19. Johannes Fabian, *Jamaa*, Evanston 1971; Willy De Craemer, *The Jamaa and the Church*, Oxford University Press 1977.

20. Faupel, pp. 180–4; Waliggo, pp. 202–22.

21. See, for instance, Aylward Shorter and Eugene Kataza, eds, *Missionaries to Yourselves: African Catechists Today*, Geoffrey Chapman 1972.

22. Oskar Wermter, 'The Ancestor Spirits: "Test them, to see if they come from God" (I John 4.1)', Paper for Zimbabwe Catholic Bishops' Conference, 27 March 1985.

23. Charles Nyamiti, *Christ as Our Ancestor*, Harare 1984.

24. J. Kumbirai, 'Kurova Guva and Christianity', *Christianity South of the Zambezi, 2*, ed. M. F. C. Bourdillon, Harare 1977, pp. 123–30.

25. Cf. Wermter; Eli Magava, 'African Customs connected with the Burial of the Dead', *Christianity South of the Zambezi, 1*, ed. J. A. Dachs, Harare 1973, pp. 151–158.

26. For an approach to the pastoral problem of possession, see Michael Singleton, 'Spirits and Spirit Direction: the Pastoral Counselling of the Possessed', *Christianity in Independent Africa*, pp. 471–478.

27. St Augustine, Sermon 311, quoted Frend, *The Donatist Church*, p. 175.

28. Enarratio in Ps. 88, ibid. pp. 103–4.

29. George E. Brooks, 'The Observance of All Souls' Day in the Guinea-Bissau Region: A Christian Holy Day, An African Harvest Festival, An African New Year's Celebration, or all of the above (?)', *History in Africa*, 11, 1984, pp. 1–34.

30. M. D. D. Newitt, *Portuguese Settlement on the Zambezi*, Longmans 1973, pp. 78–9.

31. Emmanuel Milingo, *The World in Between*, C. Hurst and Company 1984.

32. See the fine chapter, 'Afer scribens Afris: the Church in Augustine and the African Tradition', in R. A. Markus, *Saeculum: History and Society in the Theology of Augustine*, Cambridge University Press 1970, pp. 105–32; also much in Peter Brown, *Augustine of Hippo*, Faber 1967, especially pp. 408–18.

2. The Gospel and African Culture

1. See A. F. Robinson, 'Doing Research in Africa', *African Affairs*, April 1985, pp. 279–90; Michael Twaddle, 'The State of African Studies', *African Affairs*, July 1986, pp. 439–45; Richard Hodder-Williams, 'African Studies: Back to the Future', *African Affairs*, October 1986, pp. 593–604; Patricia M. Larby, 'Resources for African Studies: The Role of Libraries', ibid., pp. 605–8; James Currey, 'The State of African Studies Publishing', ibid., pp. 609–12.

2. Matthew Schoffeleers, 'Black and African Theology in South Africa: A Controversy Re-examined', *Journal of Religion in Africa* XVIII, June 1988, pp. 99–124.

3. See, for instance, Matthews A. Ojo, 'The contextual significance of the charismatic movements in independent Nigeria', *Africa*, 1988, 2, pp. 175–192; Matthews A. Ojo, 'Deeper Christian Life Ministry: a case study of the Charismatic Movements in Western Nigeria', *Journal of Religion in Africa*, XVIII, June 1988, pp. 141–62.

4. For this see, for instance, Paul Gifford, ' "Africa shall be saved". An appraisal of Reinhard Bonnke's pan-African crusade', *Journal of Religion in Africa*, XVII, February 1987, pp. 63–92.

3. Were Women a Special Case?

1. Jane Sales, *Mission Stations and the Coloured Communities of the Eastern Cape, 1800–1852*, Balkema, Rotterdam 1975, p. 38.

2. S. Akama, *A Religious History of the Isoko People of the Bendel State of Nigeria*, Ph.D. thesis, Aberdeen, 1981, II, p. 231.

3. M. Wright, *German Missions in Tanganyika 1891–1941*, Oxford University Press, East Africa 1971, pp.89–92, and p. 118.

4. Jane Sales, op. cit., pp. 44–5; F. L. Bartels, *The Roots of Ghana Methodism*, Cambridge University Press 1965, pp. 20–1; F. K. Ekechi,

Missionary Enterprise and Rivalry in Igboland, 1857–1914, F. Cass 1972, p. 24.

5. B. Garvey, *The development of the White Fathers' mission among the Bemba-speaking peoples 1891–1964*, Ph.D. 1974, pp. 112–13.

6. The 'Partial Who's Who of the early Christians of Buganda' provided by John Taylor, *The Growth of the Church in Buganda*, SCM Press 1958, pp. 261–73, includes 88 names of whom only 5 are women.

7. Jean Farrant, *Mashonaland Martyr*, Oxford University Press, Cape Town 1966, pp. 124–6, p. 184.

8. S. Akama, op. cit., pp. 226–8.

9. *The Journals of Elizabeth Leeś Price, 1954–1883*, ed. Una Long, Edward Arnold 1956, p. 373.

10. James Buchan, *The Expendable Mary Slessor*, St Andrews Press 1980, p. 74–5.

11. See, for instance, Kenneth Little, *African Women in Towns*, Cambridge University Press 1974, pp. 147–8.

12. Note, for instance, the worries of the perceptive Moravian missionary, Traugott Bechmann, in Tanzania – M. Wright, op. cit., p. 106.

13. Monica Wilson, *Rituals of Kinship among the Nyakyusa*, Oxford University Press 1957 (but material gathered 1934–8), p. 251.

14. J. Waliggo, *The Catholic Church in the Buddu Province of Buganda, 1879–1925*, Ph.D. dissertation, Cambridge 1976, pp. 291–2.

15. Sylvia Leith-Ross, *African Women* – a study of Ibo of Nigeria, 1938, pp. 125–6, quoted in E. A. Ayandele, *The Missionary Impact on Modern Nigeria, 1842–1914*, Longmans 1966, p. 337.

16. M. Perham, *Native Administration in Nigeria*, Oxford University Press 1937, p. 219.

17. Janet Hodgson, *Princess Emma*, Ad. Donker, Cape Town 1987.

18. See F. Coillard, *On the Threshold of Central Africa*, London 1897, and Martin Jarrett-Kerr, *Patterns of Christian Acceptance*, Oxford University Press 1972, pp. 78–86.

19. Taylor, *Growth*, p. 270.

20. Waliggo, pp. 113–15.

21. T. O. Ranger, *Poverty and Prophetism*, unpublished paper 1981, p. 10.

22. Jedida Asheri, *Promise*, African Universities Press 1969, p. 11.

23. Mia Brandel-Syrier, *Black Women in Search of God*, London 1962; David Muzorewa, 'Through Prayer to Action: the Rukwadzano women of Rhodesia', T. O. Ranger and John Weller (eds), *Themes in the Christian History of Central Africa*, Heinemann Educational 1975; Filomina Chioma Steady, 'The role of women in the churches in Freetown, Sierra Leone', *Christianity in Independent Africa*, ed. E. Fasholé-Luke, R. Gray, A. Hastings and G. Tasie, Rex Collings 1978, pp. 151–63.

24. Caroline Oliver, *Western Women in Colonial Africa*, Greenwood Press 1982; Patricia Chater, *Grassroots*, Hodder & Stoughton 1962; Patricia Chater, *Caught in the Crossfire*, Zim Publishing House, Harare 1985.

4. Mediums, Martyrs and Morals

1. R. Firth, *Rank and Religion in Tikopia*, Allen and Unwin 1970, pp. 33–34.

2. For example cf. the role of Nuer prophets like Ngundeng, E. E. Evans-Pritchard, *Nuer Religion*, Oxford University Press 1956, pp. 303–10, or that of Dinka prophets, G. Lienhardt, *Divinity and Experience, The Religion of the Dinka*, Oxford University Press 1961.

3. T. O. Ranger, *Revolt in Southern Rhodesia, 1896–7*, Heinemann 1967, p. 224.

4. J. R. D. Cobbing, 'The absent priesthood: Another look at the Rhodesian Risings of 1896–7', *The Journal of African History* (1977) XVIII, pp. 61–84; D. N. Beach, ' "Chimurenga": The Shona Risings of 1896–7', ibid. (1979) XX, pp. 395–420; D. N. Beach, 'Revolt in Southern Rhodesia', *The International Journal of African Historical Studies* (1980) XIII, pp. 103–8.

5. Note, nevertheless, that in reply to Cobbing's 'Absent priesthood' Ranger has promised us a further article to be entitled 'The priests and prophets return'.

6. J. B. Peires, 'Nxele, Ntsikana and the origins of the Xhosa religious reaction', *The Journal of African History* (1979) XX, pp. 51–61.

7. Jane Hodgson, *Ntsikana's 'Great Hymn'*, Centre for African Studies, University of Cape Town 1980.

8. B. Sundkler, *Bantu Prophets in South Africa*, Lutterworth Press 1948.

9. S. G. F. Brandon, *The Trial of Jesus of Nazareth*, Batsford 1968, pp. 146–8.

10. See for example D. R. Catchpole, *The Trial of Jesus*, Brill, Leiden 1971.

11. G. W. H. Lampe, 'Martyrdom and Inspiration', *Suffering and Martyrdom in the New Testament*, ed. W. Horbury and B. McNeil, Cambridge University Press 1981, pp. 118–35.

12. J. G. Frazer, *The Golden Bough: A Study in Comparative Religion*, Macmillan 1890.

13. E. E. Evans-Pritchard, 'The divine kingship of the Shilluk of the Nilotic Sudan', *Essays in Social Anthropology*, Faber 1962, pp. 66–86.

14. Lienhardt, op. cit., p. 316, p. 141.

15. Ibid., p. 146.

16. Ibid., p. 300.

17. R. G. Mugabe, *The Role of the University in the Process of Social Transformation*, Public Lecture Series 1, University of Zimbabwe, Harare 1983, p. 5.

18. R. Craig, *Social Concern in the Thought of William Temple*, Gollancz 1963.

19. 'The Church and the Labour Party', *The Economic Review*, 1908, quoted in J. Fletcher, *William Temple: Twentieth Century Christian*, Seabury Press, New York 1963, p. 180.

Notes

5. Ganda Catholic Spirituality

1. An essay of reminiscence largely written in 1975 for a seminar on Spirituality at the School of Oriental and African Studies but much revised since. It was published in the *Journal of Religion in Africa* VIII, pp. 81–91, and now also incorporates two paragraphs from chapter 3 of my *Church and Mission in Modern Africa* (1967).

2. The Luganda form for Monsignor Streicher.

3. By the time the church was built he was no longer superior of the local mission, but Vicar Apostolic.

6. African Theology

1. See Adrian Hastings, *A History of African Christianity 1950–1975*, Cambridge University Press 1979.

2. A primary source of contemporary African theology is, of course, the journals. See in particular the *Bulletin de Théologie Africaine* (BP 823 Kinshasa XI, Zaire); the *Révue Africaine de Théologie* (also Kinshasa), *AFER* (PO Box 908 Eldoret, Kenya); *The African Theological Journal* (Makumira, Tanzania); *The Journal of Theology for Southern Africa* (Department of Religious Studies, University of Cape Town) and *Missionalia* (31 Fourteenth Street, Menlo Park, 0081 Pretoria). For a general analysis of the question of African theology by African theologians reference may be made to two studies by Charles Nyamiti, *African Theology, its nature, problems and methods* (1971) and *The Scope of African Theology* (1973) both published by Gaba Pastoral Institute, Eldoret, Kenya; to the more recent work of John Pobee, *Toward an African Theology*, Abingdon 1979; to Sidbe Sempore OP, 'Conditions of theological service in Africa: preliminary reflexions', *Christianity in Independent Africa*, ed. E. Fasholé-Luke, R. Gray, A. Hastings and G. Tasie, Rex Collings 1978, pp. 516–30; E. Fasholé-Luke, 'The Quest for an African Christian Theology', *The Ecumenical Review* 1975, pp. 259–69. See also Aylward Shorter, *African Christian Theology*, Geoffrey Chapman 1975. The latest general studies are Kwesi Dickson, *Theology in Africa*, Darton, Longman and Todd 1984, Gwinyai H. Muzorewa, *The Origins and Development of African Theology*, Orbis 1985, and John Parratt (ed.), *A Reader in African Christian Theology*, SPCK 1987.

3. See, for instance, Kwesi Dickson and Paul Ellingworth (eds), *Biblical Revelation and African Beliefs*, Lutterworth Press 1969; John Mbiti, *New Testament Eschatology in an African Background*, Oxford University Press 1971; Harry Sawyerr, *Creative Evangelism*, Lutterworth Press 1968; Bolaji Idowu, *Towards an Indigenous Church*, Oxford University Press 1965; Mark Glasswell and E. Fasholé-Luke; (eds), *New Testament Christianity for Africa and for the World. Essays in Honour of Harry Sawyerr*, SPCK 1974.

4. One may think of Bolaji Idowu, *Olódùmarè, God in Yoruba Belief*, Longmans 1962; John Mbiti, *African Religions and Philosophy*, Heinemann

1969; John Mbiti, *Concepts of God in Africa*, SPCK 1970; J. Omosade Awolalu, *Yoruba Beliefs and Sacrificial Rites*, Longmans 1979; Emefie Ikenga Metuh, *God and Man in African Religion*, Geoffrey Chapman 1981.

5. See Gabriel Setiloane's *The Image of God among the Satha-Tswana*, Balkema, Rotterdam 1976, or Samuel Kibicho, 'The Continuity of the African Conception of God into and through Christianity: a Kikuyu case study', *Christianity in Independent Africa*, pp. 370–88.

6. Byang H. Kato, *Theological Pitfalls in Africa*, Kisumu, Kenya 1975.

7. Gabriel Setiloane, 'How the traditional world-view persists in the Christianity of the Sotho-Tswana', *Christianity in Independent Africa*, pp. 402–12.

8. For black theology in North America see James H. Cone, *A Black Theology of Liberation*, Lippincott, Philadelphia 1970; Geyraud S. Wilmore and James H. Cone (eds), *Black Theology, a documentary history 1966–1979*, Orbis 1979 – a very useful collection; also Calvin E. Bruce and William R. Jones, *Black Theology II*, Associated University Press 1978.

9. Basil Moore (ed.), *Black Theology. The South African Voice*, C. Hurst and Company 1973; David Bosch, 'Currents and Cross currents in South African black theology', *Journal of Religion in Africa*, vol. 6, no. 1, 1974, pp. 1–22; *Relevant Theology for Africa*, Report on a consultation at Mapumulo, Natal, September 1972; Allan Boesak, *Farewell to Innocence*, Orbis 1977 (published in Britain as *Black Theology, Black Power*, Mowbray 1978). Reference may be made to many articles in the *Journal of Theology for Southern Africa* and *Missionalia*, particularly the three 1981 issues of *Missionalia*, and also to Louise Kretzschmar, *The Voice of Black Theology in South Africa 1971–1980*, Raven Press, Johannesburg 1982. The most powerful recent expression of black theology is, undoubtedly, the *Kairos* document of 1986.

10. John Mbiti, 'An African views American Black Theology', *Black Theology, a documentary history 1966–1979*, pp. 477–82.

11. C. S. Banana, *The Gospel according to the Ghetto*, Mambo Press, Zimbabwe 1980; *Theology of Promise*, College Press, Zimbabwe 1982; see also Laurenti Mageza, 'Towards a theology of liberation for Tanzania', *Christianity in Independent Africa*, pp. 3–15; Adrian Hastings, 'Christianity and Revolution', *African Affairs*, July 1975, pp. 347–61; John Pobee's chapter on 'The Ethics of Power' in *Toward an African Theology*, pp. 141–56; Matthew Schoffeleers, 'Black and African Theology in South Africa: A Controversy Re-examined', *Journal of Religion in Africa* XVIII, 2, 1988, pp. 99–124.

12. Desmond Tutu, 'Whither African Theology', *Christianity in Independent Africa*, pp. 364–9; 'Black Theology/African Theology Soul mates or Antagonists?', *Black Theology, a documentary history 1966–1979*, pp. 483–91.

13. Much of the work of Harry Sawyerr and Gabriel Setiloane really falls into this category; see also *Personalité africaine et Catholicisme*, Paris 1963; Josiah Kibira, *Church, Clan and the World*, Gleerup 1974; Nathaniel

Notes

Ndiokwere, *Prophecy and Revolution*, SPCK 1981; Diakanua Ndofunsu, 'The role of prayer in the Kimbanguist Church', and P. Abega, 'Liturgical Adaptation', both in *Christianity in Independent Africa*, pp. 577–96 and 597–605; the series of articles in *Concilium*, June 1977, entitled 'Les Eglises d'Afrique, Quel avenir?' and very much else.

14. V. Fabella and S. Torres (eds), *The Emergent Gospel*, Papers from the Ecumenical Conference of Third World Theologians, Dar es Salaam, August 1976, Orbis 1977; S. Torres and K. Appiah-Kubi (eds), *African Theology en Route*, Papers from the Pan-African Conference of Third World Theologians, Accra, December 1977, Orbis 1979.

15. John Pobee, 'The cry of the Centurion – a cry of defeat', *The Trial of Jesus: Cambridge studies in honour of C. F. D. Moule*, ed. Ernst Bammel, SCM Press 1970, pp. 91–102.

16. Kwesi Dickson, 'Theologia Africana', *New Testament Christianity for Africa and for the World*, p. 203.

7. *The Choice of Words for Christian Meanings in Eastern Africa*

1. E. E. Evans-Pritchard, 'The Perils of Translation', *New Blackfriars*, December 1969, pp. 813–15.

2. I owe these references to Dr Alan Lowe.

3. Kenneth Cragg, *Christianity in World Perspective*, Lutterworth Press 1968, p. 57.

4. For other, related, aspects of missionary language policy in different parts of Africa reference may be made to Nicholas Omenka, 'The role of the Catholic mission in the development of vernacular literature in eastern Nigeria', *Journal of Religion in Africa* XVI, 2, June 1986, pp. 121–137; William Samarin, 'Protestant missions and the history of Lingala', *JRA* ibid., pp. 138–63; Patrick Harries, 'The Roots of Ethnicity: Discourse and the Politics of Language Construction in South-East Africa', *African Affairs*, 87, 346, January 1988, pp. 25–52.

5. See Rodney Venberg 'The Problem of a Female Deity in Translation', *The Bible Translator*, April 1971, reprinted October 1984, pp. 415–17.

6. F. Walser, 'Theological Precision in African Languages', *African Ecclesiastical Review*, 1959, I, p. 47.

7. E. Dammann, 'A Tentative Philological Typology of some African High Deities', *Journal of Religion in Africa*, II, 2, 1969, p. 94.

8. See, for instance, chapter 22, 'Holy Words', of vol II of H. W. Turner, *African Independent Church*, Oxford University Press 1967, or 'Signs of a different language', B. Sundkler, *Zulu Zion and Some Swazi Zionists*, Oxford University Press 1976, pp. 141–4.

9. See, for instance, Samuel Kibicho, 'The Continuity of the African Conception of God into and through Christianity: a Kikuyu case study', *Christianity in Independent Africa*, ed. E. Fasholé-Luke, R. Gray, A. Hastings and G. Tasie, Rex Collings 1978, pp. 370–88.

10. See J. K. Russell, *Men without God*, Highway Press 1966; Okot p'Bitek, *The Religion of the Central Luo*, East African Literature Bureau

1971; reference may be made to the discussion of Jacob A. Loewen 'Translating the Names of God: How to choose the right names in the Target Language', *The Bible Translator*, Practical Papers vol. 36, no. 2, April 1985, pp. 201–7.

11. cf. Okot p'Bitek, 'The Concept of Jok among the Acholi and Lango', *Uganda Journal*, 1963, pp. 15–29.

12. J. C. Lawrence, *The Iteso*, Oxford University Press 1957 p. 182.

13. See Monica Wilson, *Communal Rituals of the Nyakusa*, Oxford University Press 1959, pp. 16–18; pp. 156–9.

14. For that confidence see Bolaji Idowu, *Olódùmarè, God in Yoruba Belief*, Longmans 1962; John Mbiti, *African Religions and Philosophy*, Heinemann 1969; John Mbiti, *Concepts of God in Africa*, Longmans 1970; Emefie Ikenga Metuh, *God and Man in African Religion*, SPCK 1981; for more sceptical approaches see Okot p'Bitek, *African Religions in Western Scholarship*, Kampala 1970; P. R. McKenzie, 'Yoruba Orisa Cults', *Journal of Religion in Africa*, 1976, pp. 189–207 and Donatus Ibe Nwoga, *The Supreme God as Stranger in Igbo Religious Thought*, Nigeria 1984.

15. See, for instance, Edwin Smith (ed.), *African Ideas of God*, Edinburgh House Press 1950; Gunter Wagner, 'The Abaluyia of Kavirondo' and J. J. Maquet 'The Kingdom of Ruanda', *African Worlds*, ed. Daryll Forde, 1954, Oxford University Press pp. 27–54 and pp. 164–189.

16. Robin Horton, 'African Conversion', *Africa*, April 1971, pp. 85–108.

17. See Noel King, *Religions of Africa*, New York 1970, p. 40.

18. J. Roscoe, *The Baganda*, 1911, p. 312 (rev. ed. F. Cass 1965).

19. I owe this information, together with much helpful comment, to Fr John Waliggo.

20. J. van Sambeek, 'The Baptismal Formula in Luganda', *AFER*, 1959, 2. pp. 120–1.

21. Aloys Lugira, 'African Christianity', *AFER*, 1970, p. 141.

22. See T. O. Ranger, 'The Mwana Lesa Movement of 1925', *Themes in the Christian History of Central Africa*, ed. T. O. Ranger and John Weller, Heinemann Educational 1975, pp. 45–75.

23. Clement Doke, 'The translation of the Holy Spirit in Bantu Languages', *The Bible Translator* 1966, pp. 32–8.

24. B. H. Barnes, CR, *Johnson of Nyasaland*, London 1933, p. 108. He is talking of the 1890s and of a view which W. P. Johnson himself utterly disagreed with.

25. Ibid., Johnson's own view.

26. I owe these references to Fr Waliggo.

27. The old Zanzibar Swahili translation of The New Testament had *Isa Masia* until 1896; cf. H. van 'T Veld, *Towards a Revised Translation of the Bible in Swahili*, London 1966, p. 75.

28. G. W. Broomfield, 'The Re-Bantuisation of the Swahili Language', *Africa* 1931, pp. 75–85, cf. K. Roehl 'The Linguistic Situation in East Africa', *Africa*, 1930, pp. 191–202. For wider issues of Swahili language policy see Marcia Wright, 'Swahili language policy, 1890–1940', *Swahili*,

XXXV, 1965, pp. 40–8; John Iliffe, *A Modern History of Tanganyika*, Cambridge University Press 1979, especially pp. 208–10 and 529–30, and – for its use in Zaire – Johannes Fabian, *Language and Colonial Power: the appropriation of Swahili in the former Belgian Congo, 1880–1938*, Cambridge 1986.

29. There is an interesting editorial on the subject in the Catholic vernacular paper *Munno* for June 1911.

30. *AFER*, 1959, 2, p. 121.

31. F. Walser MH, 'Is our Luganda Baptismal Formula theologically correct?', *African Ecclesiastical Review*, 1959, 1, pp. 47–9; W. Matthijsen, J. van Sambeek and E. Bundschuh, 1959, 2, pp. 120–2; E. Eneku and J. Kamya, 1960, 1, pp. 65–7; Adrian Ddungu, 1960, 2, pp. 153–6.

32. *AFER*, 1960, p. 155.

8. The Post-Conciliar Catholic Church in Eastern Africa

1. See Adrian Hastings, *A History of African Christianity 1950–1975*, Cambridge University Press 1979; also Adrian Hastings, 'The Council came to Africa', *Vatican II by those who were there*, ed. Alberic Stacpoole, Geoffrey Chapman 1986, pp. 315–23.

2. George Conus, *L'Eglise d'Afrique au Concile Vatican II*, Nouvelle Revue de Sciences Missionnaires, Immensee, Switzerland 1975.

3. See for instance, Vincent J. Donovan, *Christianity Rediscovered, An Epistle from the Masai*, Fides/Claretian, Notre Dame, Indiana, 1978 and SCM Press, 1982; Eugene Hillman, *Polygamy Reconsidered*, Orbis 1975. Fr Hillman's original paper with the same title was published as an appendix to *Pastoral Perspectives in Eastern Africa after Vatican II*, AMECEA, Nairobi 1967, pp. 127–38.

4. See, for instance, Boniface Luykx, *Culte chrétien en Afrique après Vatican II*, Immensee, Switzerland 1974; A. M. Jones, *African hymnody in Christian worship*, Mambo Press, Gwelo, Zimbabwe 1976.

5. See, for instance, Aylward Shorter and Eugene Kataza (eds), *Missionaries to Yourselves: African Catechists Today*, Geoffrey Chapman 1972.

6. J. Bessem, WF, 'Scripture Translations in East Africa', *African Ecclesiastical Review*, July 1962, pp. 201–11.

7. The full proceedings of the Pan-African Catechetical Study week are to be found in *AFER*, Vol 6, no 4, 1964.

8. Adrian Hastings, *Christian Marriage in Africa*, SPCK 1973; Benezeri Kisembo, Laurenti Magesa and Aylward Shorter, *African Christian Marriage*, Geoffrey Chapman 1977.

9. Adrian Hastings, *Church and Mission in Modern Africa*, Fordham University Press, New York, and Burns and Oates 1967; Adrian Hastings 'Celibacy in Africa', *Concilium*, October 1972, pp. 151–6; Adrian Hastings, 'The ministry of the Catholic Church in Africa 1960–1975' in *Christianity in Independent Africa*, ed. E. Fasholé-Luke, R. Gray, A. Hastings and G. Tasie, Rex Collings 1978, pp. 26–43; Raymond Hickey, *Africa: The Case for an Auxiliary Priesthood*, Geoffrey Chapman 1980.

10. Emmanuel Milingo, *The World in Between*, C. Hurst & Company 1984.

9. Emmanuel Milingo as Christian Healer

1. Aylward Shorter, *Jesus and the Witchdoctor, An Approach to Healing and Wholeness*, Geoffrey Chapman 1985, pp. 189–90.

2. Emmanuel Milingo, *Healing*, a thirty-eight page booklet, undated (but clearly produced in 1976) p. 21, cf. *The Demarcations*, Lusaka 1981, p. 134.

3. *Healing*, p. 8.

4. Considerable parts of *Healing* are incorporated in *The World In Between*, C. Hurst & Company 1984. 'Cultural Emancipation and Healing in the Third World' is an unpublished forty-three page lecture delivered in 1986. It appears to represent the latest major expression of Milingo's thought. Note its very considerable dependence on recent charismatic books like Ellen White, *The Desire of Ages*, M. Glazier, and George Maloney, SJ, *Centering on Jesus*, M. Glazier 1982.

5. *Healing*, p. 11.

6. *The World In Between*, p. 124.

7. *Healing*, p. 9.

8. *The World In Between*, p. 90.

9. *Ibid.*, p. 42.

10. *Ibid.*, p. 118.

11. *Healing*, p. 13.

12. *The World In Between*, p. 43.

13. *The Demarcations*, p. 87.

14. *Ibid.*, p. 61.

15. Aylward Shorter, *Jesus and the Witchdoctor*, p. 188; Cal McCrystal, 'The Casting Out of a Bishop', *Sunday Times Magazine*, 7 December 1986, pp. 30–9.

16. *The World In Between*, p. 120; 'Cultural Emancipation and Healing in the Third World', pp. 28–9, p. 33.

17. *Healing*, p. 7.

18. *The Demarcations*, pp. 71–2; compare the account of the healing of a woman doctor in Rome in 1983, 'Cultural Emancipation', pp. 31–2.

19. *The Demarcations*, p. 89.

20. *Healing*, p. 3.

21. *Ibid.*, pp. 14–15.

22. *Ibid.*, p. 2.

23. *Ibid.*, p. 20.

24. *The Demarcations*, p. 47.

25. Cf., for instance, *The World In Between*, pp. 38–9. All further references to *The World In Between* on this subject are to extracts from one or another of the 1978 booklets.

26. *The World In Between*, p. 42.

27. *Healing*, p. 12.

28. *The World In Between*, p. 57.

29. *Ibid.*, pp. 36–7.

30. *Ibid.*, p. 99.

31. *Ibid.*, p. 45.

32. *Ibid.*, p. 32.

33. *Ibid.*, p. 47.

34. See T. O. Ranger, 'The Mwana Lesa movement of 1925', T. O. Ranger and John Weller, *Themes in the Christian History of Central Africa*, Heinemann Educational 1975, pp. 45–75; Andrew Roberts, 'The Lumpa Church of Alice Lenshina', R. I. Rotberg and A. A. Mazrui (eds), *Protest and Power in Black Africa*, Oxford University Press, New York 1970, pp. 513–68; Alison Redmayne, 'Chikanga. An African diviner with an international reputation', in M. Douglas ed., *Witchcraft, Confessions and Accusations*, Tavistock Publications 1970, pp. 103–28; J. C. Chakanza, 'Provisional Annotated Chronological List of Witch-finding movements in Malawi, 1850–1980', *Journal of Religion in Africa*, XV 3 (1985), pp. 227–43; Adrian Hastings, *African Christianity*, Geoffrey Chapman 1976, p. 63.

35. *The World In Between*, p. 36; 'Cultural Emancipation', pp. 9–10.

36. Aylward Shorter, *Jesus and the Witchdoctor*, p. 190; 'Cultural Emancipation', pp. 10–15.

37. Shorter, op. cit., p. 189.

38. *The Demarcations*, p. 134.

39. See Clive Dillon-Malone, 'The Mutumwa Church of Peter Mulenga', *Journal of Religion in Africa*, XV, 2, 1985, pp. 122–41 and XVII, 1, 1987.

40. Adrian Hastings, *African Christianity*, pp. 62–3.

41. See the account in Shorter, op. cit., pp. 190–5.

42. M. L. Daneel, *Zionism and Faith Healing in Rhodesia*, Mouton, The Hague, Paris 1970; Hubert Bucher, *Spirits and Power*, Oxford University Press, South Africa 1980.

43. *Zionism and Faith Healing in Rhodesia*, p. 43.

44. M. L. Daneel, *Old and New in Southern Shona Independent Churches*, I, Mouton, The Hague, Paris 1971, p. 463.

45. *Spirits and Power*, p. 171.

46. *Ibid.*, p. 14.

47. For a picture of the phenomenon of possession from the viewpoint of those who believe themselves to be its victims see Gerrie ter Haar and Stephen Ellis, 'Spirit Possession and Healing in Modern Zambia: an analysis of letters to Archbishop Milingo', *African Affairs*, 87, 347, April 1988, pp. 185–206. And for one attempt to cope with the spirit-possessed made by someone who does not himself believe in spirits as other than socio-psychiatric phenomena, but recognizes that you can hardly help individuals if you simply deny their categories of thought, see Michael Singleton, 'Spirits and Spirit Direction: the Pastoral Counselling of the Possessed', *Christianity in Independent Africa*, ed. E. Fasholé-Luke, R. Gray, A. Hastings and G. Tasie, 1978, pp. 471–8, and for a critique of this approach see Shorter, op. cit., pp. 184–5.

10. Mission, Church and State in Southern Africa: The First 150 Years

1. See the full account in Eric Axelson, *Portuguese in South-East Africa 1488–1600*, C. Struik, Johannesburg 1973, Chapters 8 and 9.

2. The generally used nineteenth-century name for the semi-nomadic Khoi peoples who had long inhabited the western Cape but who had by then mostly lost both language and liberty.

3. For this and subsequent quotations from Van der Kemp and Philip, see Jane Sales, *Mission Stations and the Coloured Communities of the Eastern Cape 1800–1952*, Balkema, Rotterdam 1975. For Philip see also Andrew Ross, *John Philip (1774–1851), Missions, Race and Politics in South Africa*, Aberdeen University Press 1986. For Van der Kemp see also Ido H. Enklaar, *Life and Work of Dr J. P. Van der Kemp, Pioneer Missionary in South Africa*, A. A. Balkema, Cape Town 1988.

4. William Shaw, *A Defense of the Wesleyan Missionaries in Southern Africa*, J. Mason, London 1839, p. xviii.

5. Cecil Nothcott, *Robert Moffatt*, Lutterworth 1961, p. 99.

6. William Shaw, *A Defense*, p. 49.

7. Jeff Guy, *The Heretic*, A study of the life of John William Colenso 1814–1883, University of Natal Press 1983, p. 359.

8. *Gold and the Gospel in Mashonaland*, ed. Constance Fripp and V. W. Hiller, Chatto and Windus 1949, pp. 137–8, 140, 322.

9. These and the following quotations are taken from T. O. Ranger, *State and Church in Southern Rhodesia 1919 to 1939*, Harare 1963; see also C. F. Andrews, *John White of Mashonaland*, London and re-published New York 1969; D. V. Steere, *God's Irregular: Arthur Shearly Cripps*, SPCK 1973; Murray Steel, ' "With Hope Unconquered and Unconquerable . . ." Arthur Shearly Cripps, 1869–1952', in T. O. Ranger and John Weller, *Themes in the Christian History of Central Africa*, Heinemann Educational 1975, pp. 152–174.

10. T. O. Ranger, 'Religion and Rural Protest: Makoni District, Zimbabwe, 1900 to 1980', unpublished paper.

11. Philip, quoted by Sales, op. cit., p. 108.

Index

Abeokuta, 40
Achebe, Chinua, 125
Ajayi, Jacob, 37
Akama, Samuel, 40
Alexandria, 3, 18, 84
All Africa Conference of Churches,
   29, 46
Amin, Idi Dada, 7, 12, 30, 170
Angola, 30, 133, 173
Ankole, 107, 112, 120
Arinze, Francis, Cardinal, 136
Ateso, 105, 107–8, 112–14, 117–8
Athanasius, St, 3–4, 18
Augustine, St, 2–3, 10, 12, 17, 19–20,
   186
Ayandele, Emmanuel, 37
Azande, 98

Bakongo, 59
Balandier, Georges, 1
Banana, Canaan, 90, 156
Bannabikintu, Luke, 7
Barabbas, 61
Barotseland, 46
Bazzekuketta, Athanasius, 6–7
Beach, David, 57
Bemba, 105, 107–10, 112, 114–5,
   117–21
Bentham, Jeremy, 9
Bethelsdorp, 40, 157, 166
Bigada, 71
Birabwa, Isabella, 48
Blomjous, Joseph, 127, 131
Boesak, Allan, 32, 91, 164–6
Boesak, Jan, 166
Boulaga, F. E., 92
Brandon, S. G. F., 60–1
Bribrina, Berebolo, 41–2

Bucher, Hubert, 152–3
Buddu, 5, 8–10, 19, 48, 69, 76
Budo, 40
Buganda, 4, 6–12, 14, 22, 26, 37, 40–1,
   45–7, 72, 77, 105, 109–10, 112–13,
   115–16, 118, 120
Bühlmann, Walbert, 6
Bukalasa Seminary, 7, 14, 48, 70–1, 77
Bunyoro, 107
Burkhill, T. A. 53
Buthelezi, Manas, 32, 87, 91
Bwanda, 71, 75

Calabar, 41–2
Camara, Helder, 182
Cameroon, 127, 132
Cape Coast, 40
Carnarvon, Lord, 160
Carthage, 2, 18, 186
Carr, Burgess, 27, 31
Chaminuka, 57
Chater, Patricia, 51, 189
Chaza, Mai, 49
Chewa, 105, 107, 113, 117–19, 121
Chikane, Frank, 32
Chikanga, 149
Chilubula, 41, 49
Chipata, 139
Church Missionary Society (CMS),
   6–7, 39–40, 42
Clayton, Geoffrey, 163–4
Cobbing, Julian, 57
Coillard, Francois, 46
Colenso, John, 43, 159–62, 166–7
Constantine, Emperor, 2, 172
Cragg, Kenneth, 102
Craig, Robert, 52–3, 66

Index

Cripps, Arthur Shearly, 162–3, 165, 169
Crowther, Samuel Ajayi, 39
Cyprian, St, 2, 4, 17–18, 20, 186

Dammann, E., 104
Daneel, Martinus, 152–3
Da Silveira, Goncalo, 156
Da Trindade, Pedro, 18–19
Ddungu, Adrian, 71, 121, 128
De Blank, Joost, 164
De Monclaro, Francisco, 156, 161
Desmond, Cosmas, 166
Dickson, Kwesi, 95
Dillon-Malone, Clive, 151, 153
Dinka, 63, 67
Donatism, 1–2, 7, 11–12, 18
Dupont, Joseph, Bishop, 41

Emma, Princess, 46
Egypt, 1–3, 11, 19
Enugu, 13
Equatorial Guinea, 170, 176, 178
Ethiopia, 11, 30, 133, 170, 176
Evans-Pritchard, E., 63, 98, 102

Fasholé-Luke, Edward, 94
Fiambarema, 40
Firth, Raymond, 56–7
Fleischer, Fr, 48
Frazer, Sir James, 62–4
Freetown, 39
Frend, W. H. C., 4

Gaba Pastoral Institute, 129, 133, 139
Gacambi, Mother Theresa, 143, 145
Gantin, Cardinal, 136
Gayaza, 40
Geerdes, Joop, 123
Ghana, 27, 40, 91
Griffiths, Dom Bede, 93
Guinea-Bissau, 17
Guy, Jeff, 159

Ha, 111, 115
Hannington, Bishop, 6
Haya, 105–6, 108, 111, 113, 115, 117–20
Hillman, Eugene, 131
Horton, Robin, 5, 14, 16, 108
Huddleston, Trevor, 163, 165

Huggins, Godfrey, 163
Hurley, Denis, 127, 136–7, 164, 167

Ibadan, 4
Idowu, Bolaji, 5, 27, 87, 90, 94, 126
Igbide, 42
Igbo, 45

Janssens, Governor, 157–8
Jesuits, 106, 108, 112, 156, 162
Jesus Christ, 55–6, 60–2, 64–5, 67, 115–16, 142, 145, 179, 183–4
John XXIII, 124, 126
John, Edmund, 152, 154
John Paul II, 188
Joinet, Bernard, 131

Kabuye, Rafaele, 9, 79–81
Kaggwa, Apolo, 8, 80
Kagubi, 57–9, 61
Kalemba, Mathias, 7
Kalilombe, Patrick, 19, 31, 92, 133
Kapuleya-Ndondolilwe, 40
Katigondo Seminary, 13, 19, 69, 71, 77, 123, 129, 133
Kato, Byang, 90
Kenya, 125–6, 133–4
Kevin, Mother, 51
Kibanyi, Lui, 8
Kimbangu, Simon, 59–61, 92, 140
King, Noel, 34
Kinshasa, 31
Kintu, Gabrieli, 8–9, 12, 69
Kipalapala Seminary, 13
Kiwanuka, Benedicto, 12
Kiwanuka, Joseph, 9, 12, 71, 81, 123
Knight-Bruce, Bishop, 161–2
Kolbe, Maximilian, 62
Kraemer, Hendrik, 93
Kumbirai, Joseph, 16–17
Küng, Hans, 28, 86
Kyagambiddwa, Joseph, 112

Lamont, Donal, 164
Lampe, Geoffrey, 61
Langalibalele, Chief, 159, 161
Lavigerie, Charles, 73
Lenshina, Alice, 49, 126
Lesotho, 187
Lewanika, King, 46–7
Lienhardt, Godfrey, 63–4
Livingstone, David, 42

Index

Lobengula, King, 161
London Missionary Society, 157–8, 160, 162, 166
Lourdel (Mapera), Symeon, 18, 74, 111, 114, 119
Luganda, 105–7, 111–13, 115–21, 184
Lugard, Frederick, 12
Lugbara, 107
Lugira, Aloys, 112
Lumku Pastoral Institute, 129
Lusaka, 45, 138–9, 155
Lwanga, Charles, 6–7, 18

Makerere University, 31
Malan, Dr, 168
Malawi, 113, 133–4
Mandela, Nelson, 62
Mariannhill Fathers, 48
Marx, Karl, and Marxism, 23, 54, 91–2, 167, 171, 176–7
Masaka, 5, 9, 69–71, 73, 77, 121, 123
Matabele, 161–2
Mayidi, 13
Mbele, Ma, 49
Mbiti, John, 5, 16, 27, 31, 87, 90, 94–5, 126
Mengistu, 178
Milingo, Emmanuel, 19, 31, 133, 138–55
Mizeki, Bernard, 41, 58
Mkhatshwa, Patrick, 137, 182
Mobutu, President, 11, 30, 125
Moffat, Robert, 42, 158–9
Mokwae, Princess, 46–7
Moravians, 37, 40
Moshesh, King, 47
Mozambique, 30, 133, 164, 173
Mugabe, Robert, 11, 51, 66
Mugwanya, Stanislaus, 8, 12, 48
Mukasa, Clementi, 7, 70
Mukasa, Joseph Balikuddembe, 7, 18
Mukasa, Victor, 77
Mulenga, Peter, 151–2, 154
Munaku, 13–14, 47–8
Mutendi, Samuel, 152
Mutesa II, 12
Mveng, Englebert, 92
Mwaggali, Noe, 13, 17, 47
Mwanga, King, 4, 6, 8, 69

Nabbogo, Angela, 48
Nalumansi, Clara, Princess, 6, 14, 47

Nakima, Sara, 47
Naudé, Beyers, 183
Nehanda, 57–8
Ngindu, A. M., 93
Nguema, 170, 176, 178
Ngugi, J., 125
Nigeria, 30, 39, 45
Nku, Ma, 49
Nolan, Albert, 32, 137
Nsubuga, Cardinal, 12, 135
Nsukka, 31
Ntsikana, 58–9, 61–2, 67
Nubia, 19
Numidia, 1–2, 4, 7, 11
Nxele, 58–9, 61–2, 67
Nyabadza, Basil, 58, 62, 189
Nyabadza, Francis, 188
Nyabadza, Francis II, 189
Nyagumbo, Maurice, 51
Nyakyusa, 44, 108
Nyamiti, Charles, 16–17, 87
Nyerere, Julius, 11, 30, 109, 125
Nyirenda, Tomo, 149

Obote, Milton, 12
Ondeto, Symeon, 126
Onitsha, 40, 46
Otunga, Maurice, 128

Pachomius, St, 3, 18
Paris Mission Society, 46
Parrinder, Geoffrey, 27, 34
Paul VI, 20, 131
Paul, Mrs, 49
p'Bitek, Okot, 27, 106
Peires, J. B., 58, 67
Phelps-Stokes Report, 45
Philip, John, 156–62, 164, 166
Pius XII, 123, 168
Pobee, John, 31, 90–1, 94–5
Price, Elizabeth, 42
Propaganda Fide, 24–5

Ragot, Mariam, 49
Ranger, T. O. 57, 60–1
Read, James, 39
Reeves, Ambrose, 164
Rhodes, Cecil, 161–2, 168
Rhodesia, 48, 161–3, 166; *see also* Zimbabwe
Robben Island, 59, 62, 65
Romero, Oscar, 67, 182

Index

Rubaga Cathedral, 12, 71
Rungwe, 40
Rusape, 165

Sanneh, Lamin, 31
Sanon, Bishop, 92
Sawyerr, Harry, 31, 90, 126
Schillebeeckx, Edward, 82
Scilli, martyrs of, 2, 12
Scott, Michael, 163
Sebbowa, Alikisi , 8, 48, 72
Setiloane, Gabriel, 5, 27, 90–1
Shaw, William, 158
Shembe, Isaiah, 140
Shilluk, 63
Shona, 57–8, 106, 113, 161–2
Shorter, Aylward, 131, 139, 144, 150
Sierra Leone, 46
Sithole, Ndabaningi, 33
Skelton, Kenneth, 164
Slessor, Mary, 38, 41–3, 51
Smith, Edwin, 25, 27, 89
Smith, Mrs, 40
South Africa, 32, 39, 46, 49, 91, 132, 134, 136–7, 157, 163–4, 166, 168, 170–83
Soyinka, Wole, 125
Soweto, 4, 65, 173
Ssewajje, Yohana, 73, 80–1
Streicher (Stensera), Henri, 8, 18, 69–70, 76, 121
Sudan, 30
Sundkler, Bengt, 59
Swahili, 105–6, 108–10, 112, 115–20, 128, 185
Swanson, Karen, 143

Tanzania, 25, 30, 108, 125, 127, 134, 137
Taylor, John, 26–7, 34
Temple, William, 66–7, 168
Tonga, 105, 107–8, 110, 112, 115, 117–18, 120–1

Torres, Camilo, 67
Triashill, 48
Tshibangu, Tarcisse, 87, 94
Tutu, Desmond, 32, 91, 156, 164–5, 169, 179–80, 183

Uganda, 26, 30, 69, 105, 123–5, 129, 133–4, 137, 170, 185
Uppsala, 61

Van der Kemp, Johannes, 39, 156–8, 169
Van Sambeek, Bishop, 111
Vatican Council II, 10, 12, 19, 28, 31, 33, 73, 105, 122, 125–6, 128, 130, 137, 188, 190
Verwoerd, H., 173
Villa Maria, 69–73, 76–7, 79–80

Waldron, Elizabeth, 40
Walesa, Lech, 67
Waliggo, John, 4, 195, 200
Walser, F., 103, 118, 120
White Fathers, 7–8, 14, 41, 71–2, 79, 105–9, 111, 121, 123
White, John, 162–4
Winter, Colin, 164
World Council of Churches, 61
Wrigley, Mrs, 40

Xhosa, 50, 105, 157, 160, 171, 183

Zaire, 123, 129, 134, 137
Zambia, 41, 105, 120, 125–6, 132, 134, 138, 140, 148–9, 151
Zimbabwe, 17, 23, 27, 29–30, 33, 48–9, 52–3, 90, 106, 136–7, 151–3, 164, 173, 188–9; see also Rhodesia
Zoa, Archbishop, 127
Zulu, 105, 159–61, 171
Zumbo, 18